Civil War Survivor

Incredible True Story of a Union Private

Michael P. Clark

Civil War Survivor Publishing

First Edition [2024]

ISBN: 979-8-9906963-0-3

Contents

Dedication

As the oldest son of an oldest son — and a journalist — it has been my honor and my pleasure to embark on this project in retirement. This book is a labor of love, or more accurately, about family. Therefore, I dedicate this effort to my entire family. I apologize for not naming every cousin, nephew and niece here. But I was thinking of them all as an impetus to do my best work.

This U.S. Flag has 33 stars representing the states in 1860. By 1865, there were three more states: Kansas (1861), West Virginia (1863) and Nevada (1864). (Credit: Gwengoat, iStock.)

My wife and inspiration, Molly DuCharme, encouraged me to write this book and refused to leave the Chancellorsville Battlefield Park until we had visited all the relevant sites. My daughters, Claire and Bridget, read the manuscript and enthusiastically offered suggestions.

My parents, Stanley and Suzanne Clark, fostered a love of reading with all of their children. Dad saved the Edgar W. Clark letters and conducted genealogical research. My mother shared the background of her family's interesting roots and inspired me with her creative pursuits in retirement.

My siblings — Candace, Peter and Elizabeth — are each highly successful, a Clark tradition. Thomas, a brother who died from complications of diabetes, was a sweet soul and would have loved to have explored Gettysburg.

Dad's siblings — Kay, Richard and Carolyn — mean a lot to me. Uncle Dick and Aunt Carolyn were my godparents, and I think of their love often. Aunt Kay, as the youngest child in her family, is still with us at publication. She has an ease of communication with her nieces and nephews. I recall that she encouraged me to visit the Civil War sites where Edgar served. Her late husband, Jerry Miller, was everyone's friend and brightened every room.

Each of the progeny of Edgar and Catherine Clark have their own connections to their ancestors. The fact that Edgar W. Clark lived and produced two sons after the Civil War, is a source of constant amazement.

Michael P. Clark

Introduction

"History is about people, and they speak to us across the years." — David McCullough.

"How could I know who I was if I didn't have a clue as to where I'd personally and collectively come from? — Bruce Springsteen, *"Born to Run"* autobiography.

This is a love story — love of family and of country.

Edgar W. Clark loved his wife and two young daughters, ages 1 and 3. That is clear in the 181 letters he sent to his wife, Catherine, during the Civil War. But he also loved his country enough to risk his life in order to save the Union and end slavery.

This book documents Edgar's story, which describes his view of the Civil War as one of 2 million Union members of the military, most of whom volunteered to save the Union and end slavery. Indirectly, it describes the difficulty his wife was having without him in Lansing, Mich.

Edgar was far from home. Between the boredom of army life, he was in the middle of many important battles. In total, he took part in 40 days of death-defying combat, 13 battles in all for the Army of the Potomac. He survived intense rifle and artillery fire, he persisted through months of illness, he was nearly captured by the Confederates, he was shot in the left knee and he overcame amputation and gangrene.

The Michigan flag includes a man with a raised hand that symbolizes peace, also holding a gun representing the fight for the state and nation. The elk and moose represent Michigan animals and the bald eagle represents the United States. There are three Latin mottos: E Pluribus Unum ("Out of many, one"), Tuebor ("I will defend") and Si Quaeris Peninsulam Amoenam Circumspice ("If you see a pleasant peninsula look about you" — the official state motto). (Credit: Gwengoat, iStock.)

In between the battles, he coped with damp cold, bad food, stubborn diarrhea, and — most of all — loneliness for the simple pleasures that he left behind. Edgar was so homesick that he dreamed that his oldest daughter did not recognize him.

All of this happened while his wife, Catherine, was at home in Lansing, Mich., rearing two toddlers, managing a garden, dealing with mortgage details, running out of money and expecting her husband to return in a few months. Instead, Edgar's time away from home lasted nearly 2 1/2 years. Catherine did not want him to leave. His mother-in-law said he had abandoned the family.

As a private in the 3rd Michigan Infantry Regiment, Edgar was on the front lines of the Civil War. However, the term "front lines" does not do justice to his experience in four battles — Chancellorsville, Gettysburg, Spotsylvania and Petersburg. The 3rd Michigan was thrown into confusing combat where lines were constantly changing or were non-existent. At Fredericksburg in 1862, while protecting artillery, a shell bounded over his head. At Chancellorsville in May of 1863, Edgar was in the middle of a tragic night attack when Union soldiers fired on each other. At Gettysburg, he was sent to the front in the Peach Orchard, the key to the second day's battle during a furious artillery showdown. A month later, Edgar went to New York City and Troy, N.Y. to protect the draft following the riots. That turned into a vacation of sorts, where fellow soldiers found girlfriends and even wives. In 1864, Edgar fought in the Wilderness, a Union defeat in terms of casualties except that Gen. U.S. Grant refused to retreat and moved south. At Spotsylvania, Edgar was in the initial 4 a.m. attack at the Bloody Angle, which was marked by hand-to-hand fighting that lasted about 20 hours.

At another point in the summer of 1864, Edgar was nearly captured. He had to throw down his knapsack and hightail it back to Union lines. Finally, on the second day's assault at Petersburg, Edgar charged Confederate fortifications, where he was shot in the left knee and carried off the field by his brother,

William. At the time, his wife was having premonitions of his death.

Edgar was lucky. He admitted that bullets often flew around him. In March of 1863 — before Chancellorsville and Gettysburg — his company had been reduced from about 100 to 39. By 1864, there were just eight men left. Most of his company's soldiers were gone — killed, wounded or missing. Edgar was almost the last man standing in his company. Certainly, his wife was well aware of that.

Edgar remained a private, and showed little interest in promotion. He mused about joining the cavalry or the nursing corps, believing correctly that both were less dangerous than the infantry, but he never followed through. The life of an infantry soldier was marked by long periods of idleness punctuated by moments of terror. During the down times, he confessed to becoming lazy. Edgar told Catherine to save the letters. It is a shame we don't have Catherine's point of view — other than indirectly via Edgar's letters — because she was sacrificing for her country as well. To quote a letter from Abigail Adams to her husband, John Adams, regarding the Revolutionary War: "Future generations who will reap the blessings will scarcely know the hardships and sufferings we have endured on their behalf."

That wisdom resonates today. Jeff Tiegs, who retired as a lieutenant colonel after more than 25 years in Special Operations for the U.S. Army, said in a podcast about his wife, "I owe her everything. ... You can't have a courageous fighting force without the woman keeping the homefront."

The letters from Edgar reveal all-American values: Midwestern simplicity, quiet persistence, a willingness to die for his country and a deep love of wife and children. As much as he missed his wife and two toddlers, Edgar felt a higher calling. As he wrote to wife Catherine: "I would like to see you very much but I would rather see this rebellion closed."

At times, his straightforward writing style became flowery when it came to the love of his wife: "On wings of a dove I would fly to your sweet bower and find a resting place with you." And in another letter: "My absence has taught me that deprived of you the world would be a wilderness and life a blank. I have to meditate here in solitude the many joys you have brought me, strewing my pathway with happiness and exulting my soul to a just prescription of the good and beautiful in life.

Edgar's patriotism was just as personal. He wrote, "If I was a girl, I would never marry anybody but a soldier, one who thinks enough of this country to try to help save it from rebellious hands." And he noted there were many men older than him withstanding the hardships of Army life. "No one can tell what the fortunes of war may disclose but one thing is for certain — the rebellion must be put down. I hope we will be successful and that peace may be restored to this now agitated country." On another occasion, his wife asked what he was fighting for: "Tell Mrs. Damon that war is a cruel thing but those who persist in open rebellion and ask no odds of the North nor nobody else must be put down if it takes every man in the North."

Patriotism came at a cost. In just two months after leaving home, Edgar became homesick. After a year, he missed his family so much that he thought of deserting.

During his first winter in the Army, Edgar sounded depressed, was hospitalized with diarrhea, suffered from an earache and a toothache, and confessed to his wife Catherine that his pain was punishment for not following her wishes to stay at home.

Though he enjoyed the Virginia countryside and was impressed by the sight of thousands of soldiers doing drills, there were times when loneliness got the better of him. "I would rather hear the children cry than all the drums and bands in Christendom. I would rather be with you and be poor and work hard for a living than be here in the Army. If I was a young man, nothing would suit me better, but if a man is married this is no place for him. I wish I had thought of it when I enlisted."

During the terrible battles of the war, when Edgar was surrounded by the dead and wounded, he spared his wife from most of the brutal details, though he included just enough to make her worry.

It started on Aug. 11, 1862, when Edgar enlisted for three years in the 3rd Michigan Infantry Regiment in the Army of the Potomac. Michigan was an enthusiastic participant in the Union cause. As Jack Dempsey wrote in "Michigan and the Civil War: A Great and Bloody Sacrifice," the state provided "stalwart leadership, critical manpower, abundant political and material support for the Union cause, Michigan was a true blue state." While Michigan had enslaved people during French and British occupations, it entered the nation as a free state in the Northwest Territory and contained strong antislavery advocates. Michigan voted for Abraham Lincoln in the 1860 presidential election. When President Lincoln called for volunteers to put down the rebellion, Michigan responded quickly.

Edgar's unit, Company G, included many men from the Lansing area, though it had been organized out of Grand Rapids. A roster of Lansing men in the 3rd Michigan Infantry lists 40 of them. Since a regiment typically numbered about 100 men, Lansing would have been well represented in this unit but did not constitute a majority.

Who was Edgar W. Clark? The National Archives and the U.S. Census have information. Steve Soper authored an encyclopedic four-volume history of the members of the 3rd Michigan ("The Glorious Old 3rd: Biographical Sketches of the men who served in the 3rd Michigan Infantry Veteran Volunteers 1861-1864"). He tapped official records to provide valuable documentation. For the 3rd Michigan, most soldiers were from 20 to 29 years old but there were about 30 men under the age of 17 and three men were over 60 years old.

Edgar was born on March 9, 1833, in Lansing, making him 29 in 1862. The 1850 census, when he was 16, listed him as a farmer. The 1860 census listed him as a sawyer. His 1862 enrollment papers listed him as a mechanic. The 1870 census listed him as a clerk in a state government office. Later census records listed him as a carpenter till his death. Unfortunately, we don't have a photo of Edgar or his family. He stood 5-9 with hazel eyes, dark hair and dark complexion. The average man in the 1860s was 5-7. Edgar grew a beard in the military, with only his upper lip shaved, Abraham Lincoln style.

During a portion of his service, he actually gained weight, weighing 160 pounds, the heaviest of his life. During his first winter in the army, he lost 15 pounds while hospitalized with diarrhea. You get a sense of the size of the people of that time by visiting a house from that era with the actual tiny furniture. One wonders how Lincoln at 6-4 had fit in the furniture found in his Springfield home. Mary Todd Lincoln once chastised her husband because he spread his legs across a second chair while guests were visiting. But one look at those tiny chairs makes it more understandable.

Edgar's wife Catherine Cryts was born May 6, 1836, in Wayne County, Ohio, southwest of Akron. At age 10, her family moved to DeWitt, Mich., just north of Lansing in Clinton County. In 1858, she married Edgar. They had two daughters before Edgar enlisted: Mina (age 3 in 1862) and Carrie (age 1). Catherine was illiterate when Edgar enlisted. She had to have help reading Edgar's letters and writing her replies. Edgar encouraged her to learn to read so they could communicate more intimately. By the end of the war, Catherine was reading and writing well.

Though we don't have Catherine's letters, we do have the wife's view of a Union soldier. Melissa Wells, wife of Benjamin Wells of Fabius, Mich. (south of Kalamazoo, near the Indiana border) of the 11th Michigan Infantry, wrote of spending "many gloomy and unhappy hours since you have been in the South. ... Many times I have received a letter from you and would think that perhaps it was the last I would receive."

In 1860, the state capital of Lansing was a rural town of just 3,074 residents, according to the 1860 census. Grand Rapids had a population of 8,085 and Detroit had 45,619. Yet of the 3,074 Lansing residents, about 500 men from Lansing served in the armed services in the Civil War, reported Matthew VanAcker in his book, "Lansing and the Civil War." The U.S. Census revealed there were 1,504 men between the ages of 20 and 29 in Ingham County, so about one-third of them served in the military. And that means the women were doing double and triple duty at home.

Edgar wrote that a soldier's pay of $16 a month was more than he could earn in civilian life. However, pay was often delayed to the point that Catherine applied to the state of Michigan for public aid. My father and I found receipts of these payments at the State Library in Lansing.

Edgar served with his younger brother, William, who was born about seven years earlier and had enlisted in 1861, a year earlier than Edgar.

Like many on both sides, Edgar expected a brief war. In fact, some in North and South, thought that war was unlikely. In his memoir, Union Col. Regis DeTrobriand quoted a Southerner as saying, "War will touch them in the place they hold most dear, their purse. They will not fight." In contrast, a Northerner told DeTrobriand that the "fire-eaters" of the South make noise about secession "but they will not dare attempt it."

The New York Times editorialized that the war would last just 30 days. On Sept. 2, 1862, Edgar wrote: "It is the opinion of all here that the war will not last over nine months." On March 21, 1863, before the loss at Chancellorsville and the victory at Gettysburg, he wrote: "The war will not last six more months." On May 1, 1864, Edgar wrote: "I hope it will be ended by summer." It ended a year later.

In fairness, few people could envision the terrible carnage of America's most devastating war. The United States had not fought a war of consequence since the Revolutionary War about 80 years earlier. The War of 1812 was a limited conflict that occurred before Edgar was born. The war with Mexico from 1846 to 1848 was a walkover.

Gen. William Tecumseh Sherman knew both North and South. Born and raised in Ohio, he graduated from West Point and then served in Florida, Georgia and South Carolina. In 1859, he was superintendent of the school that became Louisiana State University. Here is what he said about the Civil War: "You people of the South don't know what you are doing. This country will be drenched in blood, and God only knows how it will end. It is all folly, madness, a crime against civilization! You people speak so lightly of war; you don't know what you're talking about. You are rushing into war with one of the most powerful, ingeniously mechanical and determined people on Earth — right at your doors. You are bound to fail. Only in your spirit and determination are you prepared for war. In all else, you are totally unprepared, with a bad cause to start with."

Sherman wrote that the war began in error, was perpetuated in pride, that the North did not want anything in the South except "just obedience to the laws of the United States." In contrast, Sherman wrote that he found no signs of preparation in the North, leading Southerners to assume that the Northerners were lazy and cowardly and would not oppose Southern independence if it came to war.

A partly accurate prediction came from Confederate President Jefferson Davis. In a speech on the Senate floor on Jan. 10, 1861, Davis predicted long years of battle and terrible devastation, though he also predicted a final peace between two nations.

Sam Houston was more prophetic about the outcome. Houston, the Texas governor, opposed secession. He knew the character of the North and he told his fellow Texans that Northerners were determined to preserve the Union. "They are not a fiery, impulsive people as you are, for they live in colder climates," Houston said. "But when they begin to move in a given direction ... they move with the steady momentum and perseverance of a mighty avalanche."

That determination can be found in Edgar's letters. Preserving the Union was worth the sacrifice, he wrote. When President Lincoln issued the Emancipation Proclamation and freed the enslaved people in Confederate territory, Edgar accepted it simply as a measure to shorten the war.

Once in the field, a soldier focused on the basics of life like food and shelter. Food was desperately important. Edgar wrote that the typical soldier's meal was worse than the worst meal at home on washing day. Dried fruit was important for health. Diarrhea caused many deaths. Edgar was sent to the hospital during his first winter in the service. Though the battles were dramatic, twice as many soldiers died from illness and disease than in combat.

At one point, Edgar craved tea and butter. He expected boxes of foodstuffs from home; some boxes weighed 60 pounds. The typical Union diet involved pork, beans, coffee and hardtack — hard crackers made of flour and water. Soldiers found creative ways to make their meals passable. One food was "ash cake," which sounds terrible. Cornmeal was mixed with water, grease and salt, the dough was wrapped in wet paper or a clean wet cloth, then put on a fire and covered with hot ashes and coals. The dough would be pulled from the fire, the ashes scraped off and then the baked dough would be eaten with bacon broiled on the coals. Salt pork was the main meat ration, boiled by cooks and fried by the soldiers. It could be eaten raw on the march between two pieces of hardtack, kind of like a cracker. Shelter was essential as well. During prolonged inactivity in winter, Edgar and his friends constructed wooden walls and roofs to shield themselves. Sleeping in a rain-drenched tent was unbearable during the damp Virginia winters.

Apart from drilling and standing guard on picket duty, soldiers had extended periods of downtime. There was music, card games, reading and even a rudimentary form of baseball. Many regiments had musicians, often a fiddle player, a banjo player and a percussionist.

Edgar wrote that his backpack weighed 30 to 40 pounds, though the total could reach up to 50 pounds. Soldiers learned to shed weight on forced marches. During the rapid march north from Northern Virginia to Gettysburg, high temperatures led to some soldiers falling dead from the heat. It didn't bother Edgar much, though he commented that the woolen, blue uniforms were unsuitable in hot weather.

The typical weapon of a soldier was the musket. Loading it was laborious, involving about 17 separate steps, according to the Army drill manual. This justified the constant practice of loading a musket. Soldiers had to open a paper cartridge, pour gunpowder down the barrel, use a ramrod to push down a bullet, insert a firing cap above the trigger, cock the weapon, aim and fire. Fail at any of those steps and the musket would not fire. A well-trained soldier could fire about three times a minute. Under the heat of battle, though, harried soldiers sometimes stuffed several Minie balls in the barrel or wound up firing the ramrod instead.

A Minie ball, invented by Claude-Etienne Minie, was a hollow bullet invented for rifled muskets, allowing for more accuracy over long distances. When fired, the bullet expanded and then spiraled out the grooves of the rifle. This is one reason that soldiers in defensive positions were so effective when defending against assaults. Both sides had sharpshooters who could pick off a soldier at long distances.

Paddy Griffith, in the book "Battle Tactics of the Civil War," wrote that soldiers typically were organized two lines deep. The first line fired, then began to reload while the second line fired, and so on. In short order, there were flashes, clouds of smoke and explosions. Before long, the target would be obscured and directions from officers couldn't be heard. Given the time it took to load a musket, why weren't bayonet charges more effective? Griffith suggests that reluctance to charge was based on bluff. "It is unlikely that a regiment holding a line could literally shoot down a massed attack. In the time the attacker needed to cross the last 33 yards — a minute at the outside — a defender who had already fired a few shots would be incapable of bringing down enough accurate fire to hit more than a small proportion of the assailants."

That's presuming the defenders didn't have artillery pouring down on the attackers. And it's presuming the defenders didn't have the high ground and interior lines for quick reinforcements (Fredericksburg and Gettysburg) or a network of fortifications to protect them (Cold Harbor and Petersburg). Incredibly, Grant's soldiers achieved a massive victory by charging up Missionary Ridge at Chattanooga. As many as 24,000 Union soldiers led by Gen. George Thomas ("The Rock of Chickamauga") overran 9,000 Confederate soldiers — a Union advantage of nearly 3 to 1.

By the end of the war, repeating rifles were commonly used by the U.S. cavalry. Combined with new tactics by Gen. Philip Sheridan, the rifles helped to turn cavalry into an effective force that could end a battle, as at Appomattox. A Spencer repeating rifle could fire seven shots in 12 seconds. If the Union Army had produced a half-million breechloaders and a quarter-million repeating rifles by 1863, the war could have ended much earlier.

Once artillery pieces were placed on a hill, cannons could operate like large shotguns, firing canisters of iron balls that could tear through groups of soldiers. Therefore, when armies were placed on a hill, they had big advantages.

The importance of holding the high ground became crucial to Edgar's fate, because this was instrumental in the decisions of his general, the notorious Daniel Sickles, in the battles of Chancellorsville and Gettysburg. I will explore this in detail later.

In his book, "The Story of a Common Soldier," Leander Stilwell of Illinois described battle this way: "The incessant and terrible crash of musketry, the roar of the cannon, the continual zip, zip of the bullets as they hiss by him, interspersed with the agonizing screams of the wounded, or the death shrieks of comrades falling in dying convulsions right in the face of the living

— these things are not conducive to that serene and judicial mental equipoise which the historian enjoys in his closet."

Poet Walt Whitman saw death as he volunteered in Union hospitals. He described the case of Stewart Glover of the 5th Wisconsin, wounded in the Wilderness in 1864. About 20, he had served for three years and was nearing his discharge. He volunteered to bring in the wounded and was shot in the knee by a rebel sharpshooter. In his diary, he wrote, "Today the doctor says I must die — all is over with me. Ah, so young to die. " On another page, he wrote to his brother, Thomas, "I have been brave but wicked. Pray for me." Whitman concluded that the Union medical system was deficient for the wounded. When there were supplies, they weren't in the right places. "Of all harrowing experiences, none is greater than the days following a heavy battle. Scores, hundreds of the noblest men on earth, uncomplaining, lie helpless, mangled, faint, alone, and so bleed to death, or die from exhaustion, wither actually untouched at all ... when there ought to be means provided to save them."

In his reports to a local newspaper, Private Wilbur Fisk of the 2nd Vermont wrote muskets sounded like popping corn from afar. Up close, the sound was deafening.

Edgar doesn't describe many of the sounds of battle. We know that Union soldiers tended to shout "hurrah" while Confederate soldiers produced a series of high-pitched yips, the famed rebel yell. The sound of small-arms fire was described as a rattle. The sound of bullets was like a hum, whistle, whine or shriek. The sound of artillery firing was like a roar. Combining these sounds at the height of battle produced a sound like a tornado.

The story behind the letters

My family's introduction to Edgar W. Clark's letters came mysteriously. My father, Stanley J. Clark Jr., following his service in the South Pacific while in the U.S. Navy during World War II, was working in his father's dry cleaning store in Lansing.

Here is my father's description in his self-published memoir: "Someone came into my father's place of business one Saturday afternoon, spoke briefly with my father, introduced himself to me as a Clark and handed me a box of letters from the Civil War."

The box contained letters from Edgar. This Clark family member was a stranger. Why? Edgar's son Amos married an Irish-Catholic woman, converted to Catholicism and was cut off by the rest of the family. This was no big surprise to me. I was raised in the 1950s when Catholics were keenly aware they were a minority group. My father and I did some genealogical research. I hoped to find a photo of Edgar or his son, Amos. I tried to identify the relative who delivered the letters to my father and sought to contact one of the lost relatives but was unable to do so.

Amos and wife Agnes (maiden name McCourt) had one child, Stanley J. Clark Sr. He recalled seeing his grandfather, Edgar, on the streets of Lansing. Edgar was easily recognizable because he had one leg.

My father, Stanley Jr., was busy with a new family. Dad's parents died within a year of each other in the early 1950s, leaving Dad responsible for the dry cleaners, supporting his grandmother Agnes and serving as the patriarch for his brother and two sisters. Meanwhile, Mom and Dad were producing a Baby Boom family with four children in six years and eventually had five kids. The Civil War letters were stored in a closet and there they stayed. Then my father began to read them.

I was not always a Civil War buff. I recall the state capitol rotunda in Lansing — an easy walk from our Westside home — filled with Civil War memorabilia in the mid-1960s during the 100th anniversaries of the four-year war. My first newspaper reporting job from 1971 to 1973 was at The Illinois State Journal in Springfield. My wife and I visited Abraham and Mary Todd Lincoln's home and the historic structures in New Salem, Ill. as well as the old capitol building with its dirt floor and spittoons under the desks. Though surrounded by Lincoln's history in Springfield, I didn't spend much time on Civil War history in my early 20s.

Curiosity is the fuel of a journalist and author; it provides the stamina to persist in a project for years. The Edgar Clark story was more complicated than most. On the most basic level, Edgar has been accurately identified in official records as a member of both the 3rd and the 5th Michigan Infantry Regiment because he was a member of both. He entered as a member of the 3rd Michigan Infantry and was wounded just a few days after the 3rd Michigan Infantry Regiment was merged into the 5th Michigan Infantry Regiment. So he joined as a member of the 3rd, then was shot and was discharged as a member of the 5th. But 99 percent of his combat experience came in the 3rd Michigan Infantry Regiment.

Edgar's fate was tied to one of the most controversial figures in the Civil War, Gen. Daniel Sickles. In addition, Edgar was involved in three of the more confusing battles of the war: the nighttime attack at Hazel Grove in the Battle of Chancellorsville, the Peach Orchard salient at Gettysburg, Bloody Angle at Spotsylvania and one of the most ignored and important Civil War battles, the initial assaults at Petersburg. I never thought that Edgar's letters alone could justify a book, but once I filled in the gaps in his story and investigated other important issues of the Civil War, the book began to take shape. While the family story provides insights into daily life, the letters left many questions. What was happening during the battles? What were some of the political and military issues? Therefore, this book includes two stories: Edgar's letters to his wife and my journey to fill in those gaps in Edgar's letters with relevant historical details. In the process, I am sharing many facts about the Civil War that aren't widely known.

As a professional journalist, I wondered where Edgar was located during famous battles. So in my spare time, I read books about the Civil War and visited famous Civil War battlefields with my inspirational wife, Molly DuCharme. Thanks to a helpful ranger from the National Park Service at Fredericksburg, I was given battle maps that showed where Edgar's unit was located at Chancellorsville and Spotsylvania.

In researching this book, I learned that the Founders took many steps to prevent slavery, believing it would slowly die out; that most Southerners did not support secession; that opposition to the draft in the North involved thousands fleeing to Canada and many anti-draft riots; that the international slave trade was made a capital offense in the U.S. in 1820 but only one president allowed an offender to be executed; that the North's soldier advantage was due to 500,000 immigrants and 500,000 Black and White Southerners; that hundreds of Northern women disguised themselves as men in order to join the Union Army; that a great Union failure was not producing enough repeating rifles and machine guns due to bad management; that far from being a butcher, Gen. U.S. Grant paroled about 60,000 Confederate soldiers rather than send them to Union prisons; that a Southern general proposed enlisting enslaved people and freeing them a full 16 months before the war ended; that the South was two months away from winning its independence; that the 200,000 Black troops in the Union Army and Navy were increasingly important as the war ended and volunteering slowed in the North; that much of the most valuable property along the Southeast coast should have been settled by freed enslaved people; and that the true history of the Civil War has been smothered by the fictional Lost Cause mythology.

In the Lost Cause mythology, the losers of the Civil War persistently turned rationalizations and wishful thinking into history. Missing from the arguments of the apologists of slavery is one crucial factor — freedom. Southern defenders went to great lengths to justify slavery. Through the popular movie "Birth of a Nation" and the book and movie "Gone With the Wind," Americans were inundated with a romanticized and whitewashed version of American history. The mythology wiped out slavery as a cause of the war, imagined the South as a Shangri-La of brave knights and appreciative enslaved people and created phony issues like states' rights or tariffs as reasons to secede from the Union. The Lost Cause myth ignores the clear, bold and proud statements of the secessionists themselves.

The fiction imagines that the North only won through overwhelming resources against the romanticized South. This ignored the difficulty of conquering a large area. The Confederacy was larger than any European nation except Russia, equivalent to the size of France, Spain, Germany, Italy and Great Britain — combined.

The divisions in the North were swept under the rug. The North had organized opponents to the war — Copperheads who were willing to accept slavery in order to stop the bloodshed and many others who disagreed with Lincoln's Emancipation Proclamation. Also ignored by the slavery apologists was the fact that the South had a better chance of winning its independence than the American colonies did from Britain.

Bottom line: After the war, fiction won over truth — and in another rarity — the fiction is less interesting than the complicated truth, which is why the Civil War has been endlessly interesting to generations of historians and authors.

We have many memoirs of those who lived through the Civil War. Elizabeth Keckley, an ex-enslaved person, was the seamstress to Marina Howell Davis, the wife of Sen. Jefferson Davis before the war and of Mary Todd Lincoln during the war. In Keckley's memoir, "Behind the Scenes in The Lincoln White House," Marina Howell Davis told Keckley that secession was coming, invited Keckley to accompany the Davis family to the South and promised they would all return to the White House after the South won the war. "The South is impulsive, is in earnest, and the Southern soldiers will fight to conquer," Davis said. "The North will yield when it sees the South is in earnest rather than engage in a long and bloody war."

That certainly was not the "Lost Cause" theory but it took being defeated to motivate the South to create its elaborate rationalizations for losing the war. Keckley, by the way, described how she was whipped and raped while enslaved. When her owner died, a minister, she was sold and eventually earned her freedom. The boy she bore as a slave, who was three-quarters white, entered the Union Army as a White man in the 1st Missouri Volunteer Infantry and was killed in the Battle of Wilson's Creek in 1861 near Springfield, Mo.

Edgar Clark offered only a few comments on controversial topics like politics or religion in his letters but he was devoted to the Union cause and supported the Lincoln administration without exception. He wrote little about religion, though he did carry a Bible. He commented early that he joined the Union

Army with all sorts of people, including Blacks. As he wrote to his wife, "The Lord knows that I would like to see you before next winter, but we have got to free the Negroes before we come home and the whole race is worth all it costs. We need not be on the equity with them but this country cannot remain half-free and a part of the other half in the bonds of slavery. God forbid, let us do the best we can to make the whole country free from the curse of slavery and save the Union at all hazards."

Since people of that era recognized the importance of this historic series of events, many wrote letters that produced invaluable insights. Bell Irwin Wiley spent an academic career studying letters of Civil War soldiers and produced two famous books. He read about 10,000 letters from Confederates for the first book, "The Life of Johnny Reb" (1943). For "The Life of Billy Yank" (1952), Wiley read and organized over 20,000 letters.

Wiley noted that being far from home led many people to "write frequent and informative letters and to keep diaries." This revealed what life was like. Censorship was non-existent, which allowed comments to be shared in their raw, brutally honest form.

Though raised amid Confederate sympathizers in Tennessee, Wiley was concerned that his upbringing would bias his academic work when writing about Union soldiers, but he found that soldiers from both sides had much in common. Many were farmers or laborers. Common soldiers, Wiley wrote, had "pride in themselves and their families; a strong sense of duty; courage; a capacity for suffering; a will and strength to endure; and, for most, a devotion to country and cause which exceeded that of the folk at home."

Despite thousands of Civil War letters, few of them reflect the extent of front-line action that Edgar endured. How could anyone have survived all of those battles? If you could select a single unit to follow in the Civil War, the 3rd Michigan was among the best. It was involved in nearly every major battle of the Army of the Potomac. Edgar was there from Fredericksburg to Petersburg.

When Edgar W. Clark began writing these letters to his wife and daughters, he knew he was going to be involved in something historic. Little did he know that his letters would turn into a book written by his great-great-grandson. In that same spirit, I can imagine a future relative down the line reading this, as well.

The bloodiest war in American history helped to save the nation for, in Abraham Lincoln's words, "a new birth of freedom." Join me as I follow Edgar W. Clark's journey on the front lines of the Civil War.

— Michael P. Clark.

Author's notes

This book is best understood as a work of journalism. Edgar W. Clark's letters give the war a human dimension. To put it another way, I focus on stories, though I use a few interesting statistics. Though I started typing the letters several decades ago, I did not have the time to follow up with the research on the Civil War, especially the controversial battles where Edgar Clark participated. I have benefited greatly from recent scholarship on Hazel Grove at Chancellorsville, the Peach Orchard at Gettysburg, Bloody Angle at Spotsylvania and the initial attacks at Petersburg. The failures at Petersburg have been almost entirely ignored by Civil War books, and I would not have explored them had not Edgar Clark been shot there. Though I have long been a supporter of U.S. Grant as both general and president, his shocking lack of involvement in the initial attacks at Petersburg is difficult to comprehend.

I have used the Associated Press Stylebook rather than academic styles. I have never cared for putting footnotes in tiny type or making the reader go to the back of a book to read notes. If the notes are worth including, they ought to be placed in the logical location in body type. And the source of a quote or key fact ought to be included in the text. That has been my practice in 50 years of journalism and have never found this to be a problem for readers.

I also have produced photos, maps and illustrations in relatively large sizes. Too many Civil War books use photos that are too small to be appreciated. Also, I included copies of several actual letters so that the reader can view them. I touched them up for readability, such as adding periods that had disappeared.

I have not included every single letter from Edgar Clark. The main reason is that some of the letters are not legible. Some of the letters were written in pencil, which faded over the years. Some of the letters were redundant or simply boring. As a journalist, my first obligation is to the reader. I corrected some grammatical mistakes that would have distracted the reader and edited some phrases for clarity. However, I had no interest in substituting my style for his. I preserved enough of the archaic language such as "agoing" to make it clear these were Edgar's letters, not mine. Edgar's matter-of-fact style is preserved. He wrote as a pragmatic Midwesterner. But his style changed into flowery phrases when expressing love for his wife, Catherine. The original letters were donated to the Archives of Michigan, Michigan Historical Center, in Lansing.

The book is separated into two phases: Edgar's letters and my attempt to add military and political context to them, based on a bibliography of about 170 citations. Therefore, my commentary is clearly identified in italics. If you're not interested in battlefield tactics that surrounded Edgar's military service, you can easily skip to the next letter. The reason I included "survivor" in the title is due to Edgar's participation in some of the most brutal and controversial battles of the Civil War.

The total number of soldier deaths in the Civil War has been updated from about 620,000 to 750,000 thanks to research by J. David Hacker. He used census records. As James McPherson wrote in "The War That Forged a Nation: Why the Civil War Still Matters," the deaths of 2.4 percent of Americans in the Civil War equates to almost 7.5 million today.

Two spelling notes: The last name of Elizabeth Keckley, the seamstress to Mary Todd Lincoln has been spelled two ways. Her grave spells it as "Keckly." Her memoir spells it as "Keckley." In any case, her book offers wonderful, objective insights to Lincoln's wife. The name of the Washington, D.C. hospital where Edgar spent his initial rehabilitation has been spelled as Harwood and Harewood. It seems that Harewood is the most common spelling.

It is now more correct to use the phrase "enslaved person" rather than "slave," which I have used as a matter of respect.

Regarding capitalization, I follow The Washington Post guidelines that capitalize both Black and White as racial categories apart from direct quotes. Some respected news organizations have started capitalizing Black but not White. Regarding the capitalization of Black, it is simply a continuation of the style used for Negro and African American. It is true that race is an artificial and arbitrary concept but it also is true that it has been a painful reality in American history. You can't have a separate caste for Black Americans without having one for Whites. Refusing to accept the existence of a White race because it is the default is another example of White privilege. Another objection to using White is that it has been used by White supremacists. While I'm sensitive to that fact, supremacists also have used the Irish cross and the American flag and I am not going to give up either of them to bigots. That White Americans have received preferential treatment as a result of their race is undeniable. Author Tracie McMillan documents the financial preferences that she and four other White families received in her book, "The White Bonus." The preferences were so automatic that they often were received unconsciously. Therefore, I think it is appropriate to capitalize White unless there is a direct quote, though McMillan does not.

The podcast based on this book is not an audio book. It is an abbreviated version of this book in roughly 30-minute episodes on Edgar's letters with additional episodes on Civil War subjects. Civil War-era music is added to the podcast. A summary of the project can be found on the website, "Civil War Survivor."

Firing a Rifled Musket

A skilled soldier could fire a rifled musket in 20 seconds.

- STEP 01 Shoulder Arms
- STEP 02 Grab a Cartridge
- STEP 03 Tear Cartridge
- STEP 04 Empty Powder in the Barrel
- STEP 05 Disengage Ball From the Paper
- STEP 06 Insert Ball in the Bore
- STEP 07 Ram Cartridge
- STEP 08 Return Rammer
- STEP 09 Half Cock
- STEP 10 Remove Old Cap
- STEP 11 Place New Cap on Nipple
- STEP 12 Bring Rifle to Shoulder
- STEP 13 Raise Muzzle to Eye Level
- STEP 14 Cock With the Thumb
- STEP 15 Aim With Right Eye
- STEP 16 Press Forefinger Against Trigger
- STEP 17 Bring Down Rifle. Repeat

Source: "Manual of Arms: Drill, Tactics and Rifle Maintenance for Infantry Soldiers During the American Civil War" by W.J. Hardee, Springfield and Silas Casey" (1855, Jefferson Davis, Secretary of War). Photo credit: Library of Congress.

The rifled musket used in the Civil War could shoot a Minie ball accurately for hundreds of yards. But it took about 17 steps to load it. Miss any step and. the weapon would not fire. Though a soldier could fire three times in 60 seconds, it would take remarkable efficiency and coolness in the heat of battle. For instance, after the Battle of Gettysburg, 27,574 muskets were recovered, 12,000 were loaded twice, 6,000 were loaded between three and six times and one musket contained 23 bullets. (Jonathan James).

The statue of Michigan Gov. Austin Blair on the State Capitol grounds in Lansing shows his importance to the state and nation. Blair was a strong opponent of slavery and secession. He rallied support for volunteers to the Union cause, raising 85,000 volunteers of 90,000 Michiganders who served. He also supported the right to vote for women and opposed capital punishment. Michigan soldiers participated in nearly every major battle in the Civil War, including a cavalry unit that captured Jefferson Davis. (Michigan State Capitol Commission).

Camp Upson Hill Oct 1st 1862

Dear Wife

I hasten to write you again a few lines nearly two months has now passed since I took my departure from our much loved home and although I witness many strange sights and there is much in my business and daily transactions to engage my thoughts. Yet I assure you My Dear wife that I enjoy many fond reccollections of your affectionate kindness and love I am glad to inform you that all is well with me

Chapter One

Edgar leaves his wife, daughters

Edgar leaves his wife and family in Lansing, reflects on soldier pay, trains in Detroit and moves with his regiment near Washington, D.C. Extensive thoughts on slavery as the cause of the Civil War.

DETROIT — Aug. 17, 1862.

Dear Wife and Children: I write to inform you of my whereabouts. I am in Detroit yet. I expected to go with William but did not. I shall stay here a few days yet. I have not got my bounty money yet but probably will in a few days. Will started Friday night to his regiment. They will not let me go until the lieutenant comes to go with me. I would of written before but I expected to get my money the first day I came here but did not. I worked hard to get it but did not. You must try and get along as well as you can.

We drill two hours every day. I have not done but two hours of work this last week. We have very good times here. There are from 300 to 500 at every table and all eat with their hats or caps on. We have butter, bread, pork and beans for breakfast, sometimes cold and sometimes warm. Every meal is the same. We have fresh beef once or twice a week. We had a good time coming through to Detroit on Monday. I am somewhat lonesome today and wish I was home with you. We would have a time, I would bet you. But when I can see you, the Lord only knows but we must keep up good courage and all will come out well one of these days. You take good care of the children.

There is the 178th Regiment on one side and the 4th Cavalry on the other side, both within 40 rods in plain sight. *(A rod is 5.5 yards.)* They are both nearly full. I cannot think of much more to write until I get my money, then I will write again.

No more from your husband, Edgar W. Clark.

Historical context: Homesick already. The bounty Edgar mentioned was an enlistment bonus, a payment meant to encourage men to volunteer. Bounties were often paid by local citizens and local governments. This contributed to Edgar's financial incentive to join. As his service continued, and pay was delayed, financial pressures became more intense for his wife, Catherine.

DETROIT — Aug. 20, 1862.

Dear Wife and Children: I again take my pen to write you a few lines to let you know how I am getting along. My health is first-rate. I got $25 of my bounty today and there is $17 more I will get in a few days. You must pay up the lot with that and tell Henry he must let you have some money to live on. You must keep good courage and this will come out all right. A year will pass and then we will be together again never to part till death removes us. If you can, you must keep all of my letters till I come home. Get somebody to write for you Sunday if you can. I expect a letter from you or one of the folks every day.

From your husband, Edgar.

Notes: Catherine did keep all the letters, thus we are benefiting from them. In a continuing theme, this is Edgar's first reference to the fact that wife Catherine was illiterate and needed someone to read and write for her. This limited their ability to share intimate details. By the end of Edgar's service, Catherine learned to read and write. Edgar predicted they would be together in a year. Actually, Edgar was away from home for 2 ½ years.

DETROIT — Aug. 24, 1862.

My Dear Wife: I write to inform you of my health and other things pertaining to my welfare and happenings. My health is very good at present. I have been on guard for four hours today and calculate to be on guard for four hours tonight. This is the third letter that I have written to you. I sent you $20 last week. I don't know how long I shall stay in this place, perhaps not more than a day or two. I hear that we will go to the regiment tomorrow, but I don't know. We have so many stories and promises that we do not know what we will do the next minute.

Yesterday, I tried to get a pass to go downtown to see if I could get a furlough to come home for a few days but could not. I will try again tomorrow and if I can come home I will be at home Tuesday night and if I don't, I shan't be home at all. I would like to come home and see you again before I leave the state. Tonight was the first night that I tasted butter since I left home.

I could tell you a great many more things if you would read my writing, but seeing as it is, I must write so as not to offend anyone you may get to read my letters to you.

This from your husband, Edgar Clark, to his wife, Catherine.

Historical context: The 3rd Michigan Infantry Regiment was organized the previous year in 1861 out of Grand Rapids. So Edgar and his fellow soldiers would be supplementing a unit that had already seen battles. Of course, in 1861, Edgar had a newborn daughter at home.

DETROIT — Aug. 26, 1862.

Dear Wife Catherine: I hasten to answer your letter that I received yesterday. I have tried to get a furlough to come home but cannot. We will leave this place today or tomorrow. There are 100 new recruits leaving today. I was sorry to hear that Mina was sick. I hope she is better now.

It would certainly cost me $5 to come home and back. If it was saved and sent to you for your comfort and convenience it would be better for you than it would be for me to come home and only stay for a day or two and then have to leave for a long time. You would feel worse than you did when I left first. It was hard for me to part with you and my two little children who are dependent on me for their protection and support. I wish it were not so but this country must be saved and someone has to go. I see in this morning's newspaper that drafting is ordered immediately after the first of September. So it is a sure thing and I am glad that I am a volunteer and not a drafted man.

We have very poor fare. I thought I would have a change and bought two good mince pies and they were very good. There is everything to eat when men have the money to buy. Keep up good courage and I will write as often as I can. I wish I knew whether you received the money I sent.

From your husband.

Notes: Edgar made his first comment about why he joined the Army. There was a rebellion to put down. The Union government assigned a quota of soldiers to each state. So if a state had enough volunteers, then no men would need to be drafted. Edgar's poor opinion of draftees did not change, though Michigan had so many volunteers (85,000) that there were only 5,000 draftees. By the end of the war, few soldiers were reenlisting and volunteering was far less popular.

Historical context: On Aug. 26, 1862, the Confederacy won a second victory in Northern Virginia at Second Manassas or Bull Run. This was marked by the daring maneuvers of the new general in charge of the Army of Northern Virginia, Robert E. Lee, and his right-hand man, Gen. Stonewall Jackson. In a standard move, Lee split his forces and attacked the larger Union Army of the Potomac. He figured correctly that a vacillating Union general, John Pope, would allow the tactic to succeed. The two Union defeats at Bull Run against a poorly led Union Army began to develop a sense of Southern military dominance. A few such painful victories could lead to recognition by France or England and encourage the people of the North to agree to a peace that included an independent Confederate States of America. During the Revolutionary War, the French Navy helped George Washington win the battle of Yorktown.

DETROIT — Sept. 2, 1862.

My Dear Wife: I again write to inform you that I am well and hope these lines find you the same. I received a letter from Mrs. Damon this morning that stated that you had received the money that I sent you. I felt a little afraid that you did not get it. I feel more content about it. We will leave pretty soon and I thought I would write you a short letter before I go. You tell Henry he must let you have money enough to pay up the tax before the first day of October.

If I enjoy as good health while I am away from home, I shall feel glad. There are a good many going out with us, probably about 300. I would be glad to see you before I went out of the state, but it is impossible and we must make up our minds to put up with it.

It is the opinion here that the war will not last over nine months. I must tell you to take good care of the children. The horrors of war may find them fatherless and cast them upon the mercies and charities of friends and relatives but God forbid the thought. I still entertain the strong conviction that someday we will be together again in this world of sorrow and trouble. You must not feel melancholy. I thought I would fill up the sheet so you would not say I wrote short letters.

No more from your husband.

Historical context: Edgar expected the war would be finished shortly, a common sentiment in both North and South. Confederate President Jefferson Davis requested three-year enlistments but was granted just one-year enlistments. The Confederacy actually started a military draft about one year before the Union, despite its preference for states' rights.

It was rare for Edgar to refer to the horrors of war even after he had experienced them. He spared Catherine most of the bloody details. Regarding the reference to "filling up the sheet," the stationery was about 5 by 7 inches, folded into four pages.

Though there were photographs of the dead during the Civil War, firsthand descriptions are rare. In his book "Recollections of a Private Soldier in the Army of the Potomac," Frank Wilkeson, a journalist after the war, wrote this: "Wounded soldiers almost always tore their clothing away from their wounds, so as to see them and to judge their character. Many of them would smile and their faces would brighten as they realized that they were not hard hit, and that they could go home for a few months. Others would give a quick glance at their wounds and then shrink back as from a blow, and turn pale, as they realized the truth that they were mortally wounded. They knew when they were fatally wounded, and after the shock of discovery had passed, they generally braced themselves and died in a manly manner."

WASHINGTON — Sept. 7, 1862.

My Dear Wife and Children: I again write to inform you of my whereabouts and health. We arrived in this city about one hour ago after a long and tedious journey. We left Detroit Thursday night about 9 o'clock. We got to the train cars there and went to Toledo and got there about 1 o'clock. We laid over until 5 o'clock Friday morning, then we went to Cleveland and got there about 10 the same day. From there we went to Wheeling, W. Va. We calculated to go to Baltimore but the news came that the rebels had taken one town on that road and we could not get through. Then we were ordered to go by the Pittsburgh and Pennsylvania Railroad. We had to go 50 miles to get there, which meant about 100 miles of unnecessary travel.

I arrived at the regiment last night at about 10 o'clock. I found William well and all right. I am quite satisfied with the regiment. I shall make myself as contented as possible and write two or three times a week. I will send you some postage stamps. You must write as often as you can.

No more from your husband, Edgar W. Clark.

Historical context: Note the reference to West Virginia, which actually seceded from the Confederate state of Virginia and officially entered the Union in 1863. Confederate forces led by Robert E. Lee were defeated in West Virginia, battles that were marked by weaknesses that became a pattern for Lee: Lax control of his subordinates, occasional failure to take charge of the battlefield and overly complex orders. The mountainous areas of the Confederacy, places like East Tennessee and Northern Alabama, tended to be Union strongholds because their economies did not rely on slavery. For West Virginia, there were other factors involved in its move to the Union. Wheeling, W. Va. was just 60 miles from Pittsburgh but 390 miles from Richmond.

CAMP WILSON — Sept. 9, 1862.

My Dear Wife: I again take this opportunity to answer your letter that I received last night. I was very glad to hear from you, although I hardly expected it so soon after I got here. It done me a few dollars worth of good. I just went over to see Homer and his wife. They do not live as far from me as they do from you when they are to home. I made a mistake in the letter I sent you yesterday. I calculated to put in some postage stamps but I was in such a hurry I forgot it until it was too late. It is hard to get postage stamps here, so I bought $2 worth.

I was paid $13 just before I started from Detroit. If you do not need it, I will keep it, for I do not know how long it may be before something may happen that I will need it. I have not got all that was promised me. I shall get it all before long. Now I must stop for I am on duty today. Give my love to all.

From your loving husband.

CAMP IN AN ORCHARD — Sept. 11, 1862.

My Dear Wife: I hasten to write you a few lines informing you that I am well and in hope these few lines will find you the same. I went down to Alexandria yesterday and bought a few notions such as a shirt, a cup for boiling coffee, a plate and a spoon. We have moved 4 miles from where we were to a more secure position. How long we will stay in this position it is hard for me or anyone to tell. I got my likeness taken and will send it today. It is taken as well as I could have with the clothes that I had on. I hope you will be satisfied with it. If not, I will have it taken again when I get time.

I have not had time to write a very long letter because I have got to go on guard this morning. It's not hard work standing still for two hours and then off for four hours and so on for 24 hours. William is getting my breakfast.

No more from your husband, Edgar.

Historical context: Edgar makes only a few references to slavery in his letters but his views were clear. "We have got to free the Negroes before we come home and the whole race is worth all it costs. We need not be on the equity with them but this country cannot remain half-free and a part of the other half in the bonds of slavery. God forbid, let us do the best we can to make the whole country free from the curse of slavery and save the Union at all hazards." He notes that the original group of Michigan recruits included a variety of people, including African Americans, most of whom were cooks. He supported the Emancipation Proclamation. By the end of Edgar's service, he was sharing the battlefield at Petersburg with entire units of Black soldiers.

Edgar's brief mention of the rebels in Northern territory was a reference to Gen. Robert E. Lee's invasion of Maryland and the battle at Antietam. It was the first of Lee's major defeats once he left the friendly territory of Northern Virginia. He split his forces, a common tendency, sending one unit to attack the federal armory at Harpers Ferry. The discovery of Lee's battle plans, which were rolled around cigars, gave the Union forces advance information. The Battle of Antietam was incredibly bloody. Because Lee had to retreat, it was considered a Union victory; the army that controlled the battlefield was considered the victor. This was victory enough for President Abraham Lincoln to announce his plans to emancipate enslaved people in areas held by the Confederacy to take effect on Jan. 1, 1863. It was a war measure that would deny the South the labor of their enslaved people, produce manpower for the North and pressure England and France not to recognize the Confederacy. By 1862, every other major Western nation had abolished slavery. Even Russia began freeing their serfs.

The slavery issue was a simple matter of power. In the 1780s, there were 13 slave states. But as Northern states abolished slavery, Southern states were clinging to it. By 1850, there were 15 slave states and 15 free states. Therefore, proposals to ban slavery in new states in the territories threatened the dominance of the slave power in the federal government. By 1860, there were 18 free states (including California) and 15 slave states. Thus, the balance of power was shifting away from Southern dominance even before Abraham Lincoln was elected with his opposition to slavery in the territories.

That the South seceded over slavery is clear from primary sources — the Articles of Secession written by the Confederate states. Mississippi's Declaration of Secession was typical: "Our position is thoroughly identified with the institution of slavery — the greatest material interest in the world." In South Carolina's Articles of Secession, the North was accused of breaking the compact in the Constitution. How? Northern states denied the rights of treating people as "property" (enslaved people), denounced slavery as "sinful" and permitted the establishment of societies (abolitionists) to "disturb the peace" of their "property."

The influential Charleston Mercury newspaper, which had long supported secession, reacted to the election of Abraham Lincoln with a call for immediate secession by South Carolina. The Nov. 3, 1860 editorial began this way: "The issue before the country is the extinction of slavery."

In his final speech on the floor of the Senate, Sen. John C. Calhoun complained about a rising abolition movement in the North and the refusal of many in the North to comply with helping to capture fugitive enslaved people. The South would be forced to choose between abolition and slavery, he said.

In the Articles of Secession, you must look long and hard to find references to any causes for secession other than slavery. To contend that the war was not fought over slavery is to say that the founders of the Confederacy were lying or were massively misguided. In fact, they were proud of their peculiar institution.

Albert Brown, a U.S. senator from Mississippi, said that the secession crisis could only be resolved if "the Northern people would review and reverse their whole policy on the subject of slavery." In New England, abolitionists were strong, despite the existence of slavery there at one time. In the Midwest, slavery had been banned in the Northwest Territories, so there were hotbeds of antislavery culture there.

Henry Benning (the namesake of the former Fort Benning) encouraged Virginia to secede just like his native Georgia had seceded because "a separation from the North was the only thing that could prevent the abolition of her slavery." He warned that abolition would lead to having Blacks as governors, legislators and jurors (which he considered a bad thing). This actually happened during Reconstruction, but then voter suppression prevented the election of most Black elected officials in the South until the Civil Rights laws of the 1960s.

In a lengthy article in The Charleston Mercury in 1861, L.W. Spratt explained that conflict was inevitable between free states and slave states. In short, it was a conflict between a slave oligarchy and a democracy. "The principle that all men are equal and equally right would have been destructive of slavery in the South," Spratt wrote. How true.

John E. Cairnes, in his influential 1862 book, "The Slave Power," wrote that the South had two choices: Reform slavery as an *immoral institution or claim slavery as the cornerstone of a superior civilization. "The right of the white man to hold the Negro in permanent thraldom, to compel him to work for his profit, to keep him in enforced ignorance, to sell him, to flog him, and, if need be, to kill him, to separate him at pleasure from his wife and children, to transport him for no crime to a remote region where he is in a few years worked to death — this is now propounded as a grand discovery in ethical and political science, made for the first time by the enlightened leaders of the Southern Confederation, and recommended by that philanthropic body to all civilized nations for their adoption." Abolish slavery, Cairnes wrote, and the political power and social dominance of slave owners would be threatened, which is why they would never agree to eliminate slavery voluntarily.*

Slavery was the deciding motive for secession. In fact, when allowed to vote on secession, Southern counties with the lowest rates of slavery only gave 37 percent support to secession while counties with the highest rates gave 72 percent support. Secession had become "a slaveholders' movement," as David Potter wrote in "The Impending Crisis: 1848-1861." He studied the popular vote for state secession conventions and concluded, "At no time during the winter of 1860-1861 was secession desired by a majority of the people of the slave states." The Civil War was a war for the few rich planters who owned most of the enslaved people. For instance, two-thirds of Texas voters voted against secession, and Gov. Sam Houston refused to call a convention. So secessionists called one anyway. In Georgia, where just 33 percent of voters owned enslaved people, 87 percent of secession delegates were slave owners.

Sen. Alfred Iverson of Georgia said that the South would secede if a Republican were elected president and would never return to the Union without a full guarantee of the institution of slavery. "We are obliged to have African slavery to cultivate our cotton, our rice and our sugar fields," he said. "African slavery is essential not only to our prosperity but to our existence as a people." Iverson put this in exact order: Slavery was needed for the Southern economy and then slaveholders found reasons to justify it religiously, culturally and morally.

Enslaved people were the most valuable asset in the nation, worth $4 billion, more than the total investment in America's banks, railroads and factories. Slaves were incredibly valuable due to their flexibility as both people and property. As Edward Ayers wrote in "The Thin Light of Freedom," enslaved people could be lent or borrowed, rented by the task or the hour, or even held as collateral.

To claim that Southerners were not fighting for the value of their most important economic and social institution is delusional. As James McPherson wrote in "Battle Cry of Freedom," the Southern economy was described this way: "Sell cotton in order to buy Negroes to make more cotton to buy more Negroes." To put it another way, "enslaved people were both labor and capital," as McPherson wrote in "Ordeal of Fire: The Civil War and Reconstruction." They were treated as property or people depending on the whims of the slaveocracy. In fact, hiring slaves could produce a rate of return of 14 percent without the expenses, wrote Ruby West Jackson and Walter T. McDonald in "Finding Freedom."

In his address to the new Confederate Congress of April 29, 1861, Confederate President Jefferson Davis described a wonderful existence for enslaved people that would be hilarious if it wasn't so deceitful and tragic. "Under the supervision of a superior race," he said, the enslaved people had been transformed from "brutal savages" into "docile, intelligent and civilized agricultural laborers." Actually, the slaves had been cultivating rice and other crops in Africa for centuries. Davis wrote that enslaved people "carried the curse of Ham and so were enslaved by divine decree. How, then, could slavery be a sin? It was, he claimed, a moral, a political and a social blessing." It's a wonder that a Fugitive Slave Act of 1850 was even needed. Shouldn't Black people have been fleeing from the North to be enslaved in this Shangri-La in the South? Of course, the slavery apologists make no mention of freedom.

Losing enslaved people to escape was enough of a concern that the Missouri Legislature asked Congress in 1847 for effective legislation to stem "heavy losses."

In his book, "American Slavery As It Is: Testimony of a Thousand Witnesses," Theodore Dwight Weld wrote, "It is a marvel that slaveholders are always talking of their kind treatment of their enslaved people. The only marvel is that men of sense can be gulled by such professions. Despots always insist that they are merciful. ... We will prove that the enslaved people in the United States are treated with barbarous inhumanity; that they are overworked, underfed, wretchedly clad and lodged and have insufficient sleep; that they are often made to wear round their necks iron collars armed with prongs, to drag heavy chains and weights at their feet while working in the field ... " In any case, Southern leaders believed the full development of its cotton and tobacco industries required the "indispensable" labor of African enslaved people, as Davis wrote.

Though there were misgivings in the South regarding slavery, the sheer financial power of the institution was too strong. As William Seward said, "Did any property class ever reform itself? Not patricians in Rome, not landholders in Ireland and not aristocrats in England." And so money trumped morals. Slavery was the ultimate bad apple in a free economic system. Free people couldn't compete with slave owners. Southerners, defensive when accused of supporting an evil system, responded by claiming that slavery was good for both master and slave. But as Ralph Waldo

Emerson wrote in *The Atlantic* in 1862: "Well, now here comes this conspiracy of slavery — they call it an institution, I call it a destitution — this stealing of men and setting them to work — stealing their labor and the thief sitting idle himself." Emerson's bottom line: "Emancipation is the demand of civilization."

The tremendous conflict between morality and finances, won by greed in the South, is well illustrated by two American icons, Thomas Jefferson and Henry Clay. Jefferson wrote that "Slavery is a hideous evil, a foul blot on the country. It makes a mockery of our sacred creed, embodied in the Declaration of Independence." That's the importance of primary sources. People still debate if Jefferson included Black people in the Declaration. Jefferson wrote that he did: "I meant all men, not just white men."

Jefferson wrote that while working in Paris as the U.S. Minister to France, he had planned to free all of his 180 enslaved people. In an example of the self-delusions of slave owners, Jefferson wrote that slavery was "a perpetual exercise of the most boisterous passions, the most unremitting despotism." But after returning to Virginia, Jefferson discovered that he owed debts and needed a dowry for his daughter. So he remained a massive slave owner of 600 people, freeing just two people during his life and five others in his will. Jefferson was disturbed by the Missouri Compromise with the Mason-Dixon line separating slave states from free states. In a prophecy, Jefferson predicted increased national tensions that "one day will burst on us like a tornado." He wrote he would welcome death so he wouldn't have to see it.

Henry Clay, also born a Virginian, moved to Kentucky and made some abolitionist statements as a young man. He wrote that he soon discovered slavery was "a necessary evil. I need a large labor force to till my lands and the slave market is the only place I can get it. Goddam it, a man can't operate a plantation and *compete in Kentucky without slave labor." Clay freed only seven of the roughly 120 enslaved people he owned.*

Some Southerners rationalize that most Confederates did not own enslaved people and were not fighting for slavery but for their culture. But their culture was run by slave owners and no Yankees were going to tell them what to do. The people with the power and the money owned enslaved people. In short, money talks.

Jon Meacham wrote in "And There Was Light: Abraham Lincoln and the American Struggle" that slavery was essential to White Southern power in terms of creating wealth, maintaining White hegemony and holding sway in national politics." Limit slavery and you limit the reach of White Southerners; allow freedom to grow in the West and you put slavery in danger where it existed. When everything was at stake, nothing could be conceded."

Confederate President Jefferson Davis said, "Submitting to the Lincolnites, the Black Republicans and abolitionists who controlled the North would put our slave system at the mercy of an abolitionist majority. This we could not allow. Our cause, I told the Confederate Congress, was just and holy."

Confederate Vice President Alexander Stephens said that slavery was the cornerstone of the Confederacy, a positive good, not an evil to be gradually eliminated as the Founders said. The "Cornerstone Speech" infuriated Jefferson Davis. Though Stephens was right, Davis wrote, Confederate emissaries were trying to gain recognition from England and France. Therefore, in a precursor to the Lost Cause, Davis instructed them to play down the slavery issue. As Davis wrote, "We left the Union to free ourselves from the rule of the majority. Submitting to the Lincolnites, the Black Republicans and abolitionists who controlled the North would put our slavery system at the mercy of an abolitionist majority. This we could not allow."

The White men of the South were "a master race," pro-claimed Georgia Gov. George Fitzhugh in 1861. Poor Whites knew that they would never fall to the bottom rung of the economic ladder. In the book "How the South Won the Civil War," Heather Cox Richardson quoted South Carolina slave owner Henry Hammond. He said the Southern system was "the best in the world," and if the North tried to stop its spread, the South would win a Civil War. He also wrongly said the South could control any country on Earth by cutting off its supply of cotton.

But the conventional wisdom was wrong. Cotton was not king. The British stockpiled cotton and then found other sources in India and Egypt. The British diplomat in Charleston, Robert Bunch, saw through the duplicity of Southern diploma-cy. As described by Christopher Dickey in his book, "Our Man in Charleston," Bunch wrote to his superiors in Britain that there was no long-term benefit for Britain to support the Con-federacy. "This new Confederacy is based upon the preservation and extension of Negro slavery," Bunch wrote. He believed that the Confederates would be ostracized by world opinion.

After the Emancipation Proclamation, Robert E. Lee wrote that freeing the slaves was a "savage and brutal policy ... which leaves us no alternative but success or degradation worse than death if we would save the honor of our families from pollution, our social system from destruction." Then in an 1864 letter to Confederate President Jefferson Davis, Lee changed his mind: "As far as I have been able to judge, this war presents to the European world but two aspects. A contest in which one party is contending for abstract slavery and the other against it." Abstract! What is abstract about 4 million human beings or their $4 billion eco-nomic impact or the 750,000 people who died in the Civil War or the massive numbers of Americans whose lives were upended? But *that single word illustrates the depths of the South's rationalizations. Lee was forced to change his position.*

An important note on Lee. He stated, and it has been accepted as fact in the Lost Cause mythology, that Lee had no choice but to secede with his native state of Virginia. Not true, as written by Ty Seidule in his book "Robert E. Lee and Me: A Southerner's Reckoning with the Myth of the Lost Cause. Seidule, a native Virginian and retired as head of the History Department at West Point, noted that in 1861 there were eight colonels from Virginia in the United States Army. Lee was the only Virginia colonel who seceded. Seidule concluded that "Robert E. Lee committed treason to preserve slavery." In fact, after the war, Lee was charged with treason but he signed a loyalty oath and received a pardon.

In his memoirs, Midwesterner U.S. Grant (whose wife came from a slaveholding family), wrote: "The people of the South were dependent upon keeping control of the general government to secure the perpetuation of their favorite institution." Grant noted that the people of the North were "not willing to play the role of police for the South in the protection of this particular institution." In fact, the right to capture fugitive enslaved people was mentioned in the Constitution (Article 4, Section 2). The reference was not to property but to a "person held to service or labor in one state."

Northern cities and states passed laws in opposition to the Fugitive Slave Act or refused to enforce it. For instance, Michigan passed a Personal Liberty Act in 1855 that guaranteed liberty to all Michigan residents, regardless of race, a nullification of federal law. As reported in "Just Action" by Richard and Leah Rothstein, the Maine Legislature declared that any slave brought to the state would be free; the Connecticut Legislature confirmed the citizenship of all African Americans; and legislatures of Ohio,

Pennsylvania and New Hampshire refused to follow the Dred Scott decision.

The 1850 Fugitive Slave Act was even more extreme than the 1793 version that allowed slave owners to cross state lines to capture escaped enslaved people. The 1850 Fugitive Slave Act denied enslaved people a jury trial or the right to testify for themselves. The slave hunter was paid $10 if the captured ex-slave was enslaved and $5 if the ex-slave was freed. Slave hunters, often bounty hunters, could seize escaped enslaved people without due process and anyone aiding escaped enslaved people or obstructing their recovery was subject to heavy fines. In fact, three straight presidents — Millard Fillmore, Franklin Pierce and James Buchanan — called out the military to enforce the Fugitive Slave Act.

Under the Fugitive Slave Act of 1850, 332 escaped enslaved people were returned and only 11 were declared free, James McPherson wrote. So the South, which proclaimed states' rights, demanded strong federal action to maintain its slave empire. And when the election of Abraham Lincoln threatened its dominance, secession was the South's solution. While fugitive enslaved people received extraordinary attention, only a small proportion of enslaved people escaped. Estimates vary widely from about 40,000 to 100,000. The Canadian Broadcasting Corp. website refers to 30,000 enslaved people escaping to Canada.

But to the South, this was a matter of principle and honor. Slavery was more than an economic system, it was the central feature of the Southern economy and culture. U.S. Sen. John C. Calhoun of South Carolina said that "agitation on the subject of slavery" would end in disunion. The South feels bound by "every consideration of interest and safety" to defend the institution.

The Civil War occurred after decades of attempts to compromise over something that is a basic right — the essential humanity of Black people.

The Compromise of 1850 only delayed the inevitable. Among its key features were the admittance of California as a free state, no mention of slavery for the territories of New Mexico and Utah, abolishing the slave trade but not slavery in Washington, D.C. and a more powerful Fugitive Slave Act. The compromise, though ultimately a failure, had one great advantage: The delay allowed the nation to deal with the secession crisis with Abraham Lincoln as president rather than Millard Fillmore, a massive difference in presidential quality. During that 10-year delay, the North became more powerful economically and more able to wage a terrible war that settled the slavery issue once and for all.

Besides the Fugitive Slave Act, the 1850s were marked by other tensions: The Kansas-Nebraska Act, which annulled the Missouri Compromise and led to border state violence; the rampages of John Brown, which personified the fears in the South of a bloody slave revolt; and publication of "Uncle Tom's Cabin," which humanized the enslaved people and became a worldwide best-seller. In her equally impressive book, "A Key to Uncle Tom's Cabin," Harriet Beecher Stowe wrote at length about the truths behind her fictional characters. While living in Cincinnati, a major stop on the Underground Railroad, Stowe came in contact with many escaped enslaved people. She wrote that she understated the horrors of slavery in "Uncle Tom's Cabin" because she feared that real-life descriptions would make her book too difficult to read.

The decade of the 1850s ended with debates in Illinois between Abraham Lincoln and Stephen Douglas for the U.S. Senate seat in 1858. The Supreme Court's Dred Scott decision of 1857, which indicated Black people had no rights, made compromise impossible. As Lincoln predicted, the nation could not exist half-slave and half-free, it must become one or the other.

Once you accept that enslaved people are human beings, honesty compels only one conclusion: They deserve the protections of the

Declaration of Independence of life, liberty and the pursuit of happiness. As Stowe wrote with religious fervor, "What is peculiar to slavery, is evil, and only evil, and that continually." The difficulty of facing that evil is the motive behind the Lost Cause mythology.

As Stowe explained, slavery treated 4 million human beings as property. "They could not sue or be sued; they could not buy or sell; they could not own a foot of land; they could not form a legal marriage; they could not own or educate their own children; their family loves were all accidents of bargain or sale; they could not learn to read or write; they could not raise a hand against the will of any White person who might choose to insult or dishonor them or their wives or their children, on pain of death."

As Lincoln said, "The Negro is a man. ... There can be no moral right in connection with making a slave of another." As he said on another occasion, "If slavery is not wrong, nothing is wrong." Lincoln never claimed that Blacks were equal in every respect, but he was consistent in saying that they deserved enough equality to earn wages for their work.

Charles and Mary Beard, in "The Rise of American Civilization," noted the slaveholding class held the power in the Southern states and dominated the federal government; it practically chose 30 of the 62 members of the Senate, 90 of 233 members of the House and 105 of the 295 members of the Electoral College. As James McPherson wrote in "Why the Civil War Still Matters," between 1789 and 1861, two-thirds of the presidents had been Southern slaveholders and two-thirds of the Speakers of the House and Senate Presidents had been Southerners. Twenty of 35 Supreme Court justices had come from slave states and the slave powers always had a majority in the court. So it is no wonder that Southerners were shocked with the election of Lincoln, and believed that a contract in the Constitution to protect slavery was about to be broken. The three-fifths clause in the Constitution allowed slave states to count enslaved people as three-fifths of a person for purposes of unfairly large representation in Congress and unfairly large numbers of members of the Electoral College.

The Founding Fathers wrote into the Constitution that the international slave trade would be illegal in 20 years, in 1808. Then in 1820, the U.S. included slave traders in The Piracy Act, which called for the death penalty. As Carl Sandburg wrote in "Abraham Lincoln: The War Years," about 30,000 enslaved people were brought to Cuba in 1861. Corruption on a massive scale kept the international slave trade alive. For instance, one slave trader brought 1,300 Africans to Cuba, sold them at $1,000 a head, paid off Cuban authorities and made a $1 million profit.

As described in the book by John Harris, "The Last Slave Ships: New York and the End of the Middle Passage," the international slave trade continued with illegal Northern cooperation. U.S. slave traders were rarely arrested or convicted and, when they were convicted, received light sentences or pardons.

U.S. attempts to stop slave trading were comically ineffective, Harris wrote, using slow ships that were outrun by the slave cruisers, while U.S. Navy ships were based far from the slave-trading routes off the coast of Africa. New York City built a profitable business in slave-trading ships that offloaded their human cargo in Cuba, the Caribbean and South America.

Of more than 70 slave traders convicted under The Piracy Act, only one received death. That came on Feb. 21, 1862. As written by Harris, Nathaniel Gordon, a veteran slave trading captain, had completed at least four illegal voyages, reputedly earning him the nickname "Lucky Nat." In 1860, however, Gordon's luck ran out. A U.S. cruiser caught his ship after leaving the Congo River with almost 900 enslaved people. The enslaved people were returned and the Navy took Gordon to New York. After a mis-

trial, he was prosecuted, convicted and sentenced to death. Despite pleas for mercy from petitioners (including from Gordon's wife), President Abraham Lincoln declined to commute the sentence. Instead, Lincoln gave Gordon a reprieve of a few weeks. In his letter of Feb. 4, 1862, Lincoln wrote that the prisoner should "refer himself alone to the mercy of the common God and Father of all men."

Only one other slave trader had been sentenced to death but President James Buchanan — one of the worst presidents — granted a pardon in 1857. Buchanan, a Pennsylvanian, did not own enslaved people but he allowed Kansas to enter the Union as a slave state and supported the historically awful Dred Scott decision of the Supreme Court by lobbying Northern justices to support it.

The Confederate Constitution included a section that stated no law denying or impairing the right of property in enslaved people would ever be enacted. Yet the Confederacy wrote into its Constitution a ban on the international slave trade. How come? Because the United States developed a thriving domestic slave trade based on breeding enslaved people like cattle. Virginia, the most powerful slave state, did not want imported enslaved people reducing the value of its "property."

William C. Davis, in his book "The Cause Lost: Myths and Realities of the Confederacy," wrote that Southern leaders were "caught in a trap." With enslaved people representing one-third of the Southern population, freeing them suddenly could bankrupt the Southern economy. If slave workers were replaced with wage workers, it meant losing hard cash that was in short supply. President Lincoln was willing to discuss gradual abolition and compensation for slave owners. Also, the specter of 4 million former enslaved people let loose on the South was threatening to slavery proponents. Now we know that after the war there were few attacks by freed enslaved people; in fact, the opposite occurred, the Ku Klux Klan and others attacked ex-enslaved people. After the war, the South created a caste system of second-class citizenship for Blacks with sharecropping, tenant farming, prison work gangs and eliminating the right to vote. Thus, a second Reconstruction was needed in the 1960s. It can fairly be said that not until 1965 with the passage of the Voting Rights Act did America have equal voting rights for all adult citizens.

As Davis wrote, "The leaders of the South in 1860-1861 believed that their rights of property, self-government, the underpinnings of their culture and economy, all were mortally threatened by a Republican victory at the polls. ... In short, it is impossible to point to any other local issue than slavery and say that Southerners would have seceded and fought over it." Enslaved people were the most valuable asset in the Confederacy. And there was no compromising that fact. As the Richmond Examiner stated, "the war originated and is carried on in great part for the defense of the slaveholder in his property rights, and the perpetuation of the institution."

Lincoln said the South was willing to make war rather than let the nation survive while the North was willing to accept war rather than let the nation perish. Winston Churchill, who wrote about the American Civil War in his "A History of the English-Speaking Peoples," called it "the noblest and least avoidable of all the mass conflicts."

Frederick Douglass said that the rebellion of the South was unlike those in Europe that were intended to throw off the yoke of despotism. The Southern revolt was intended to maintain despotism. "It stands alone in its infamy."

As for the right to secede, some in the South said they never would have joined the Union if they knew they could never leave it. However, the transition from the state-oriented Articles of Confederation to the stronger federal government in the Constitution belies that argument. Under the Articles of Confederation, no change could be made without unanimous agreement by the states. During the Constitutional Convention, a New Jersey proposal to retain the nation as a league of sovereign states was defeated, reported Michael Waldman in "The Second Amendment: A Biography."

At any rate, the debate over secession was settled on the battlefield.

Chapter Two

Edgar quickly gets homesick

Edgar dreams of home and his young daughter doesn't recognize him. He comments on food and health while Catherine prepares for a Michigan winter. He notes the beautiful Virginia countryside. No battles for Edgar yet.

CAMP ON UPSON HILL — Oct. 9, 1862.

My Dear Wife: I again write to inform you that my health is improving. I do not feel as though I was agoing to write you a very long letter. I wrote a good long one to Henry yesterday. I must tell you that I put in a dollar and drew a prize worth $8 — a locket that I will send to you to put in the children's likenesses. William went and bought a pint of oysters but they are in a state of perplexity whether to stay up or go down. I think they will come up by my feelings. No more from your dear husband, Edgar.

Notes: Oysters are not readily found in mid-Michigan, so that delicacy would have been a stretch for Edgar's digestive system. And they can easily go bad.

EDWARDS FERRY — Oct. 12, 1862.

My Dear Wife: Today is Sunday and we have marched ever since yesterday morning at 4 o'clock. We started Saturday and marched until about 5 o'clock and you never saw such a set of men. There were seven regiments, probably about 5,000 men. We are within 10 miles of Harper's Ferry. We started agoing this morning at 6 and have traveled until about 11 o'clock today. We marched yesterday about 25 miles. We have stopped to rest. How long we will stay, I cannot tell, probably not more than an hour or two. I understand that we are agoing to march 8 miles more this afternoon. If we do, I will write a good deal more.

I received a letter this morning and was very glad to hear from you. I know you will get along first-rate, but I wish I was there to help. I am glad you have again drawn your portion from the county. I hope you will not neglect it every month. We cannot get any money until the last of the month. That will be the last of November. I feel very tired. We have carried about 25 pounds, besides our guns and ammunition. The rest of the boys say that yesterday was the hardest day's march that they ever had. I know it was hard enough for me. I never was tireder than I was last night.

I sent you a locket last week, Wednesday, for you to put in the children's likenesses. Sometime when you get good and ready, I will have mine taken again when my whiskers grow a little longer. I have only shaved on my upper lip for a long while.

We have six large cannon with us. We hear there were 1,000 rebel cavalry that crossed the Potomac River where we were last night. I expect them to cross back sometime today, but I expect no such good luck as to have them cross. We are within 30 rods of that river. Now you must keep good courage. There is hope as long as there is life. Our cause has been very successful of late. I think this will close before the first of January. I can see no hope for them now. They are out of provisions and everything else.

Your affectionate husband, Edgar W. Clark.

Notes: Edgar's reference to his beard with a shaved upper lip would have been similar to Lincoln's. His wife Catherine received payments from the county while Edgar was serving.

ONE MILE ABOVE EDWARDS FERRY — Oct. 13, 1862.

My Dear Wife: We moved yesterday afternoon about 10 miles to the above-named ferry and this morning were 1 mile above. We are camped and probably will stay awhile. My health is first-rate. William and I have just sent to get a good load of straw to make a bed. There are about 25,000 soldiers. I dreamed last night that I got home and Carrie was big enough to move around on the floor and Mina was a big girl and you went to work and made me a nice pie and we had a good time generally. I wish I was there this morning. Keep up good courage.

Your affectionate husband, Edgar W. Clark.

EDWARDS FERRY MARYLAND — Oct. 15, 1862.

My Dear Wife: As today is Wednesday and my writing day to you, I thought I would write you a few lines although I have not much to write, only to keep my promise.

My health continues to be as good as could be desired. We are still encamped where we were when I wrote to you before. William is making a pudding for supper. We put in a lot of those dried berries you let me have when I left home. I have half of them left. I wish I had a lot more of them. They are good when we get into winter quarters. We will have you send us about 100 pounds of things to live on this winter, such as pies and cakes, preserves or such stuff. This section of the country is as fine as I ever saw. Very rolling in some places. We can see the Blue Ridge Mountains to the north and west. We traveled over hill and mountains, which we could hardly see the top of when we were close to them. We went up a very steep hill about 1 mile long. I thought we would never get to the top, then we have to go down again. It commenced raining about sundown Sunday night after we had marched hard all day. Then we had to fix up our shelter tents the best we could. William and I and two others slept under cover that night and the rest laid on the wet ground with only a blanket under them and over them with the rain pouring down in torrents. Every little hole was full and some of the boys laid in water all night. William and I had it a little better. The rain did not fall on us but it filled a hole down to our feet, so every time we went to straighten our legs, we stuck them in a large hole of water. That is the first time in my life that I soaked my feet in water all night, but you are probably tired of my description of that march.

We have very good living. We draw good rations every other day. We have plenty of sugar and coffee, pork and hard bread. I dream about you every night, some good and some bad. I sometimes feel lonesome and sometimes satisfied, but I wish the war was closed so I could go home. If I ever get home I shall know how to appreciate a home more than I ever did before.

Your affectionate husband, Edgar W. Clark.

Historical context: The hard bread that Edgar referred to was a cracker called "hardtack." Soldiers struggled to stay dry in the Virginia rain. The key was to find a way to sleep above ground so soldiers would not get wet during a rain. One of the most popular tents was a kind of teepee.

EDWARDS FERRY — Oct. 19, 1862.

My Dear Wife and Children: This morning as usual finds me well and enjoying health and I hope you can say the same. We are still in camp near the above-named place. We have been on picket two days. We were near the Potomac about 3 miles from camp watching to see if any rebels crossed the river near us, though the river is so low that people can walk across it almost anywhere and not get over your shoes, so the river has to be watched the whole length. Our regiment extended 5 miles up the river from this ferry.

We have had men enough to stand on our post so one man has to stand only two hours and that was my luck to stand in daytime. It commenced raining about 8 o'clock in the evening and it rained very hard all night. We got wet, although we laid under a big apple tree with three blankets over us and we had our overcoats on and one blanket under us. So we did not get very wet although it did not become very pleasant to have the rain beating down on us all night. I did not sleep much, I can assure you. The place we had to guard was near the place where the battle of Ball's Bluff *(Loudoun County, Va.)* was fought about one year ago where Col. Baker lost his life. I think you will hear some stirring within the next two weeks. I do not know whether we will be engaged or not. Nothing but time will tell. The 20th Regiment was above us and they had marching orders with light loads. I think they are going into a fight.

You must not think that I am jealous because I write to you on this yellow paper for it is the only one that we have got and we cannot buy any today, so I had to write on this. I expect a letter from you tomorrow. The mail comes every third day. We are about 30 miles from Washington.

No more from your husband, Edgar W. Clark.

EDWARDS FERRY — Oct. 20, 1862.

My Dear Wife: I was sorry to hear the cattle had broken into the garden and destroyed some of the garden. You wrote that you wanted me to send you the money to fix the fence. I would if I could borrow it, but I cannot. If you can get someone to fix it until spring, so the cattle will not destroy the trees nor injure the neighbor's property with as little expense as possible, on my next payday I will send you the money to pay them. The pay will probably come in two or three weeks without fail. I am confident that this war will close by spring and then I will come home and the first thing I will build a new fence and paint the house, although if you could get $15 for the gun in cash you might get it painted once this fall so it would not take so much to paint it in the spring. I engaged with Henry to get you all the wood you want this winter for 25 cords and I guess that will last you that time.

I am well as usual and lonesome. I wish I was with you. I would have a good time. I sent you a locket a short time ago. I want you to write when you get it so I will not think it is lost. We are having easy times now and have plenty to eat and good water to drink and fine pleasant weather. Give my love to all inquiring friends.

No more from your husband, Edgar W. Clark, to his wife and family.

CAMP IN VIRGINIA — Oct. 20, 1862.

My Dear Wife and Children: I take my pen to write you a few lines on the sacred soil of Virginia. We started again yesterday and crossed the Potomac at White's Ford, or rather forded it. The water was up to our hips and cold enough to freeze snakes. You would have laughed to see 4,000 to 5,000 of us wading the river 80 rods wide and the current was very stiff.

I think we will see very active times before two weeks pass. I would not wonder if we see a battle before three days. We are waiting for some movement in front of us. The rebels are all around us and we do not know when we will feel their effects, but I apprehend no danger to myself. I think I will come out all right.

I will write as often as I can, knowing you will be anxious to hear from me, knowing that I am exposed to danger while you are taking comfort. Although you may see troubles, we do not know how long we may live nor where we will go nor when we may be engaged with the rebels. There are now about 100 who joined the regular cavalry from this regiment, 12 from this company.

I wish the war would close as soon as possible for I would like to come home and see you and the babies. I hope they are well and lively as ever. Tell them that their pa thinks of them all the time.

I would tell you who William's sweetheart is if I could write a letter to you or you could read my letters. I can say it is no one in our neighborhood. You can rest easy on that, although he may get letters from one in the neighborhood. You know he writes to everybody.

From your husband, Edgar W. Clark.

CAMP NEAR EDWARDS FERRY — Oct. 26, 1862.

My Dear Wife: I hasten to write you a few lines this Sunday morning to inform you that I am well and hope you can say the same. I wrote to you twice last Sunday and Monday. I expected a letter from you last night. Lieutenant Mason arrived in camp last Thursday. The talk is that he will be superseded by a captain from one of the other companies when it rightfully belongs to him. If they do, he will resign, and I would if I was in his place. I think we will go into winter quarters before long. I wish I was at home this morning to eat breakfast with you and have one clean and decent meal although we have plenty such as it is, but the coffee is not as good as you make, nor the beef, nor is anything as good as a woman can do, but we have to put up with it I suppose for a while yet, how long I cannot say.

I know you have a good home and nobody can take it away from you and I think you have enough wood and other things to keep you warm and comfortable this winter, although you will find someone on cold mornings to get help and build your fires. I guess I will not write any more this time.

From your husband, Edgar W. Clark.

Historical context: Edgar's poor opinion of his captain was typical of the democracy found in the Union Army. In some cases, soldiers voted for their leaders. In other cases, officers recruited men for their military units.

CAMP NEAR LEESBURG, VA. — Nov. 2, 1862.

My Dear Wife: I again take this opportunity to write you a letter. My health is good as could be expected. We again moved yesterday about 7 miles to this place. I think we are on a campaign. We can distinctly hear heavy cannon not far from here and you will hear of a large battle being fought on the first and second of November. I do not know whether we will be engaged or not.

We got here about dark last night. You ought to have seen between 2,000 and 3,000 soldiers run for rails to build a fire. It made one think of the Lincoln campaign when they used to carry rails. After the company got their guns stacked, William and I went and got a load of rails, then we went and got four big bundles of corn stalks. Some of the company went for chickens, some for the hind quarter of calves and some for ducks or turkeys and finally we made a good supper before 10 o'clock this morning.

My load consists of two pieces of shelter tents, one large blanket, one overcoat, two shirts, one pair of drawers, one knapsack haversack with three days' rations and a canteen full of water. Besides the clothes I have on and the other little notions, I also have my gun and 50 rounds of ammunition. It weighs 10 to 15 pounds. If I should ever enlist again, I should join the cavalry by all means. We can still hear heavy cannonading off about 15 or 20 miles. I should judge you will probably hear of this big battle. We are on the reserves now. I think if we live through this month, we will not be in any engagement this year. I hope that we will never see a battle but if I thought by going into a big battle, it would end the war, I would say go in by all means.

This is a beautiful country of land, as good as I ever saw in the world and some of the costliest residences I ever saw. We passed one yesterday that must have cost nearly $100,000. Please give my respects to all inquiring friends and save a double share for yourself.

No more from your husband, Edgar W. Clark.

Historical context: Edgar mentions he would rather join the cavalry because it involves carrying less weight. The cavalry had fewer casualties than the infantry. For most of the war, the cavalry was used for raids and reconnaissance, not for intense battle. Later in the war, Gen. Philip Sheridan began using cavalry with their breech-loading rifles as an adjunct to the infantry and cut off the escape attempt by Gen. Robert E. Lee at Appomattox.

CAMP — Nov. 7, 1862.

My Dear Wife: We marched Thursday, Nov. 6, until after dark. Snow has fallen about 2 inches deep, which makes it rather uncomfortable for us who have to lay outdoors all night. I have two bundles of wheat straw so I will stay comfortable tonight. I miss our bed these cold nights but we must put up with it. I am willing to do my share to have this war closed as soon as possible for I would like to be at home as soon as I can, certainly by this spring. I think we will be in camp for a day or two. We are now encamped about 6 miles from Warrenton, Va. That is probably our destination. We hear that the rebels are there.

You tell Mina her pa wishes he could see her very much. Tell her she must be a good girl and mind her ma and pa will fetch her a present. I dreamed about being at home last night. I thought I saw her standing in the door when I was getting over the fence between the house and where Whiting lives. I thought I came up to the door or I thought Carrie was running around on the floor but did not know me. She cried when I went up to her. She was afraid of me.

It is snowing very hard now and we have not seen a newspaper for a week so we do not know what the news is. We are quite a ways from any railroad station. We have made a long and heavy forced march. I hope it is for some good. This part of the country is very hilly and mountainous. The Blue Ridge Mountains are on one side of us. They look nice. I wish you were here to see them. We are now 60 miles from Washington by railroad. You must not be worried if you do not get a letter from me as often. If we get to a place where we can send letters, I will do so. Write as often as once a week whether you hear from me or not.

No more from your husband, Edgar W. Clark.

Notes: The nightmare probably indicates that Edgar is sensing danger. He had not experienced battle yet. Warrenton, Va. is about 33 miles from Fredericksburg, Va.

Chapter Three

Marching to Fredericksburg

Edgar supports total war. He starts "cramping," taking food from the Virginia countryside. He is on the way to Fredericksburg. Also, a survey of Lincoln's views on slavery.

CAMP NEAR WARRENTON, VA. — Nov. 10, 1862.
My Dear Wife: This fine and beautiful morning finds me well and enjoying good health. We are now waiting for provisions and I thought I would write you a few lines. We heard today that our provision train was cut off. If so, we will have to wait a day or two here. We are now living on borrowed rations. The quartermaster borrowed enough yesterday to last one day. We can cramp enough chickens and fresh meat but we can't cramp our bread. We strip the country of everything that we come across. We take fence rails to keep us warm. The weather is quite cold for this climate and it takes a good many rails.

William and I sleep warm and have enough to eat and plenty of water. I mean there is nothing else in the Army. I will be glad when this campaign is over but I don't think it will be over very soon. We have had no newspaper here in quite a while. We do not know what is going on. I would be glad to think we will be in battle very soon but we cannot tell. The rebels are all around us. Every house is searched. We take everything that we can find and it is right. If I had my way, I would burn every house. I would make them feel the effects of their rebellion and I believe they do wish they had not rebelled.

You must not get discouraged. I have it a good deal harder than you do and I have got to put up with my lot. I will give you a ride in the cart when I come home. I am sure I will in a year-and-a-half anyhow, but I hope sooner. I would not want to come home and come back here again. You must give my best respects to all of my friends. Kiss the children for me.

Also yours in true love, Edgar W. Clark.

Historical context: The word "cramping" refers to stealing items from the local populace, and stripping the country of everything that troops come across, taking food and stripping rails from fences for shelters and fuel. As Gen. James Rusling wrote in "Men and Things I Saw in Civil War Times," an army is like "a city on legs." Imagine 100,000 men taking everything with them — clothing, food, medicine, ammunition. It takes skillful organization to keep an army ready for battle. Edgar clearly believed in the total war principles of Gen. William Tecumseh Sherman. It had been only three months since he had left home. Let them stop the rebellion, Edgar wrote, and then he and others would return home.

WARRENTON, VA. — Nov. 10, 1862.

My Dear Wife: This morning as usual finds me well and I hope you can say the same. I got a letter from mother yesterday saying that you are well, for which I am glad. You probably are glad to hear often from me. I would write most every day if I had postage stamps and paper. We may not get any money until we get back.

We expected a battle Wednesday. We started from camp last Tuesday at sundown and marched about 5 miles toward Culpeper and the next morning we marched back again to this place. I don't know when we will be in a fight but not before long and I hope before the wet weather sets in. I hope we will end this war for I am anxious to see you and the children. It has been a little over three months since I left home.

I wish I was to home to take breakfast with you this morning. All I had for breakfast was six hard crackers soaked in cold water until they were soft *(hardtack)* and then fry some meat, take out the meat and put it into the grease, sprinkle some salt on the hard crackers and then eat them with some water. We have coffee when we are a mind to make it but I can hardly bear to drink it.

I will send some money to pay some of my bills and to buy you some things just as soon as I can. It may be possible that we will not draw any until sometime in January. Do not worry about me. I am well enough off. I have good clothing and enough of it to keep me warm and when we are in camp a few days at a time we have a bed good enough but when we march late nights we have to lay the best we can on the cold ground or anywhere we can catch it.

No more from your husband, Edgar W. Clark to his wife and children.

CAMP ON ROAD TO FREDERICKSBURG — Nov. 21, 1862.

My Dear Wife: I again write you a few lines concerning my health this morning, which is good, and hope you can say the same. It has rained every day since last Sunday and we have marched every day until yesterday. We are now within 7 miles of Fredericksburg. We will stay here until the road gets settled a little, then we will go to Fredericksburg. How long we will stay there, it is impossible to say. Our destination will be Richmond. If the weather is favorable, it will be before the first of January. There is no doubt that when the rebel capital is taken, peace will be declared. We have the report from good authority that there are no less than 250,000 men marching on that place from different directions. We are the reserve. When we do fight we will give a good account of ourselves.

We commenced marching last Sunday and have marched about 10 miles every day until Wednesday. The rain will hinder our progress some but our marching is certain until this rebellion is put down. There are no winter quarters for us. We will have some tough times but I guess we will stand it. I am willing to undergo most anything to hurry up the rebellion or cause them to give up.

I wish I could see you and the children today but it is impossible. I will have to wait until this war is closed, then if the Lord is willing, we will never part again until death.

This is a good country. We see nobody in the houses but a few Negroes and then a poor class at that. Our armies make a good sweep when they are passing through this country. All the fences where we stay all night go like the snow before the sun.

Our living is good. We have the best kind of pork and hard crackers, good fresh beef twice a week. I wish my health would always stay as good as it is now. I ate up the last of the dried fruit I took from home yesterday morning. I wish I had more of it. I will let you know when you can send us something. Butter is out of the question with us. It is worth 50 cents a pound. You must try and do the best you can and it will come out for the best. Write as often as you can.

No more from Edgar W. Clark to his wife and children.

Historical context: Edgar and the huge Union Army are located just across the Rappahannock River from the Confederate Army. Though the distance was short, moving thousands of troops across the river became a chore that delayed the Union's advance and allowed the Confederates to prepare for the attack at Fredericksburg. Edgar was incredibly specific about the battle plans, realizing that his wife would not receive the letter until the battle was finished. And his hopes were dashed by a foolish series of assaults up fortified hills at Fredericksburg.

CAMP NEAR FALMOUTH — Nov. 28, 1862.

My Dear Wife: This morning finds me well and earnestly I wish you can say the same. I got your letter which Caroline wrote a day or two ago and was very much pleased with it. I wish I could be to home with you this morning. We would have a good time telling our trials and troubles since we parted nearly four months ago. It seems a short time.

We have marched about 10 miles. We are now near Fredericksburg about 3 miles from the last place. I would not wonder if we have a fight with them soon, for they are determined not to surrender the place until forced to do so. They have removed all the children, old and infirm. We have over 100 large cannon commanding the town and as soon as the railroad trains arrive we can get our provisions without any trouble before making the advance.

We have lots of men here ready to fight and willing to crush the rebellion in the shortest time possible. All of the Michigan regiments lay not more than 2 miles from us. We have a large Army here ready to fight of nearly 100,000 strong and if they will not do something to crush this rebellion, I will wonder.

My postage stamps are getting low and they are hard to get until we get our pay. There are none in the company that I can borrow. We see some very cold nights and tough weather. We have nothing but shelter tents. They keep off the rain, but that is all. I have suffered as much by the cold in Virginia as I ever did in Michigan. You must not get discouraged for it is always darkest just before day. I feel content knowing that you are well off as most families in the country. You must get along the best you can and it will come out right one of these days.

No more from your husband, Edgar W. Clark.

Notes: Despite the more temperate latitude, that damp cold in Virginia caused suffering. Being in a shelter tent implied that Edgar had to sleep on the cold ground.

CAMP NEAR FALMOUTH — Dec. 3, 1862.

My Dear Wife: I hasten to answer two letters that I received from you today. One was from you and Mina and the other from you and *(sister-in-law)* Lydia. You cannot imagine what a kind and welcome stopping place they found with me. I had to laugh like fury when I saw Mina writing. It done me a good deal of good. I can realize what she would say and though I could not read it, there was a good deal of meaning.

We have now been in camp about 10 days, the longest since we left Upson Hill and in that time we have marched over 200 miles. We expect to march every day and then it will be to fight, but I do not know whether they will give us battle near Fredericksburg or not. If they do, I think they will see warm times. I think we have got the advantage of them at all points and they begin to see it. I read the president's proclamation today and he lays down a policy, and if the rebels will take it, I think we may see peace soon. If they do not submit, we will have to subdue them by force of arms.

You cannot imagine how glad I would be to see you today and the children, too. I would tell you some long stories about the war and some short love stories, too. I sometimes thought we had it hard to get along but if I was home now I would be perfectly content to stay there and try to get along the best I could. I hope someday to realize the blessings of home.

I have plenty to eat but only one kind of bread and that is hard crackers. We have pork and beef aplenty. We have quite comfortable quarters. The weather is warm and pleasant, the roads are very dusty and it looks as though we are agoing to have rain soon. I dread wet weather. You must get along the best you can and keep an eye peeled for number one and wait for better times, which will surely come.

Edgar W. Clark.

Historical context: Lincoln offered to end the war if the states in rebellion agreed to an immediate or gradual emancipation of the enslaved people. This included financial aid to rebellious states. Lincoln had long proposed reimbursing slave masters as part of his moderate emancipation proposals, and such a proposal was enacted in Washington, D.C. in 1862. Slave owners were compensated $300 for every freed enslaved person. No compensation to the enslaved. Freedom was granted to almost 3,000 people. The colonization of African Americans would continue with *their consent. If the states in rebellion did not agree to Lincoln's proposal, then on Jan. 1, 1863, all enslaved people in rebellious areas would be declared free. The Emancipation Proclamation specifically identified those areas. Also, any enslaved people who have escaped, deserted or had been captured by the Union would be declared "forever free" — which included the slave states in the Union. Further, no slave who escaped into Union territory would be returned, thus nullifying the Fugitive Slave Act. In one historic stroke as a war measure, the Emancipation Proclamation converted the most valuable asset of the South, enslaved men, into able-bodied Union recruits.*

CAMP NEAR FALMOUTH — Dec. 3, 1862.

My Dear Lydia and others with interest in my welfare: Your kind and affectionate letter found a welcome stopping place with me today. You cannot tell how much good a letter from home and kind friends does a soldier. You wrote about apples being so cheap. Here they would be 1 shilling apiece. I wish I had one good one out of your cellar today.

I think the prospects about the war look brighter than some time ago. I hope it will continue to grow brighter until it is closed. We have to drill twice a day, which makes our victuals first-rate. Yesterday there were 4,000 soldiers all drilling at once. Our whole brigade was on drill. It looked nice to see so many soldiers all with guns drilling. They make a string four deep about 1 mile long. I wish you could see some of the world and its inhabitants. There are nearly 100,000 soldiers around here. I hope we stay here for some time because we have comfortable quarters. We are in a nice land. I have not seen a marsh or a bridge since I have been in Virginia over three months and traveled over 20 miles, so the country is different than it is in Michigan in that respect. We have cold nights but when the sun shines it is quite warm. I think we will see cold weather soon, probably not as cold as you see in DeWitt this time of year. I would send this letter separately if I had the postage stamps. They are all played out. You must answer immediately.

Yours, Edgar W. Clark to Lydia Cryts.

Notes: Lydia was the sister of Edgar's wife, Catherine. She lived in DeWitt, Mich., which is just north of Lansing. Presumably, Lydia was reading and writing for Catherine.

Historical context: President Abraham Lincoln's views on slavery have been exhaustively examined by historians. He was consistent in saying that enslaved people deserved to be paid for their labor and that he found slavery to be personally offensive. He probably was influenced by his own father, who loaned out young Abe for work and took the proceeds. But Lincoln was on record as supporting the voluntary removal of enslaved people to Africa and said that White people would be reluctant to grant them equal rights. But his genius was his empathy and ability to grow. By the end of the war, Lincoln supported the vote for Black veterans. In fact, he mentioned this in a speech, which spurred John Wilkes Booth to take up his assassination plans.

As Lincoln said in the Lincoln-Douglas debates, the Founding Fathers believed slavery was on the road to ultimate extinction. Prohibiting its spread to new territory presumably would do the trick. In his Peoria speech of 1854, Lincoln itemized the ways that the Founders intended to slowly extinguish slavery.

The law establishing the Northwest Territories in 1787 banned slavery in the future states of Ohio, Indiana, Illinois, Michigan, Wisconsin and part of Minnesota. In 1802, during a territorial Constitutional Convention in Ohio, the delegates voted down a resolution to allow slavery by just one vote, wrote David McCullough in "The Pioneers." The Founders in 1794 prohibited selling enslaved people from the U.S. elsewhere. In 1798 they prohibited bringing enslaved people from Africa into the Mississippi territory, the future states of Mississippi and Alabama. In 1800, they prohibited American citizens from trading enslaved people with foreign countries. In 1803, Congress passed a law helping states to restrain the internal slave trade. In 1807, they passed a law banning the African slave trade about a year before it could take effect due to the 1808 date listed in the Constitution. The Piracy Act of 1820 called for the death penalty for international slave trading.

On the other hand, slavery was approved for the new state of Kentucky, which was carved out of Virginia, as well as territories carved out of Georgia, North Carolina and Mississippi.

In his 1854 speech at Peoria, Lincoln said, "The plain unmistakable spirit of that age toward slavery was hostility to the principle, and toleration only by necessity. But now it is to be transformed into a sacred right."

The cotton gin (invented in 1793) changed everything. It allowed the rapid removal of seeds from cotton fibers. Production of cotton became so profitable that unpaid labor through slavery became an indispensable part of the Southern economy. So defenders of slavery adjusted their principles. Alexander Stephens, the vice president of the Confederacy, said in his Cornerstone speech of March 21, 1861, that the prevailing ideas of the Founders thought slavery was wrong and would pass. "Those ideas, however, were fundamentally wrong. They rested upon the assumption of the equality of races. This was an error. ... Our new government is founded upon the opposite idea. Its foundations are laid, its cornerstone rests, upon the great truth that the Negro is not equal to the White man, that slavery subordination to the superior race is his natural and normal condition."

Fredericksburg. Crossing the Rappahannock River was the "easy" part of the battle for Union forces. Confederates waited behind entrenchments outside the city for the fatal charges of the federals. (Chronicle / Alamy Stock Photo).

Camp near Falmouth Vir Dec 17th 62

My Dear
Wife and Children
I now hasten to write you
a few lines to inform you
that I am Still in the land of
the living tough and hearty
but have seen tough and trying
times since I wrote to you before

Chapter Four

Spared at Fredericksburg

Edgar sees battle. He chats with Confederates afterward. He supports freeing the enslaved people as the implementation of the Emancipation Proclamation nears. He spends Christmas with the Army of the Potomac. He sees the importance of good generalship and battlefield tactics.

CAMP NEAR FALMOUTH, VA. — Dec. 8, 1862.

My Dear Wife: I received your letter this morning with papers, postage stamps and envelopes and was glad to hear from you. I have plenty now and will write twice a week.

We still remain where we have for the last two weeks. The rumor is that we will move into better quarters in a day or two. We have had two days of very rough weather. The snow fell about 4 inches deep last Friday, Saturday and yesterday. We're very, very cold. A man who enlisted about the same time as I did died in the regimental hospital last Saturday and was buried about 4 o'clock that same day. He left a wife and one or two children. He died after a relapse of typhoid fever. He was sick just a few hours after the second attack. Yes, I wish I was to home to see you today. We would have a jolly time, I assure you.

You think the prices are high in Lansing but if you were here you would think they were low. Eggs are worth 6 cents each or 72 cents a dozen. You must do as well as you can if the prices are high. You must try and make yourself comfortable through the winter. Get good clothes for yourself and the children. We will send you $20 or $30 or as much as you want. I want you to be saving it if I come home in the spring or next summer. I want to fix up the house and fence and it will take some money to do it with but there are some debts that must be paid without fail.

It is now about sundown and the snow has almost gone. We would like 15 or 20 pounds of good butter; it is worth 50 or 60 cents a pound here. I have not tasted a bit of it in two months. It is hard to find for love or money. It would not be worthwhile to send me many apples because they weigh heavy and do not amount to much. Answer this as soon as you get it and let me know what you think of it.

Yours, Edgar W. Clark.

Historical context: Edgar made several references to thousands of troops on the move. Edgar has referred to a possible battle at Fredericksburg since Nov. 21. President Abraham Lincoln replaced Gen. George McClellan with Gen. Ambrose Burnside. Rather than be too timid, Burnside was too bold, attacking a heavily fortified position over and over again.

Plans to attack at Fredericksburg, a key railroad junction, were stalled on Nov. 15 because pontoon bridges needed to cross the Rappahannock River were delayed. That cost Burnside the surprise factor. Otherwise, he could have captured Fredericksburg practically unopposed. While Burnside waited, Gen. Robert E. Lee built fortifications on the hills behind the city of Fredericks-

burg. The Confederate position was so strong that Lee supposedly thought the Union attack was a diversion. Union soldiers fought in house-to-house combat through the city, a precursor to Gettysburg. Like Gettysburg, one side maintained control of high ground outside a city. Burnside attacked anyway on Dec. 13.

The resulting battle underscored a few military constants of the Civil War. Having control of the high ground gave the defense a huge advantage, especially when artillery could fire on advancing troops. Attacking the flank would reduce the casualties of the attackers, but it wasn't always possible. Nevertheless, a frontal assault up a hill was bound to produce a defeat unless the attackers had about three times as many troops. Canister turned the cannon into a giant shotgun, sending golf ball-sized lead into the enemy. And the rifled musket, with its effective range of several hundred yards, was deadly. Union attacks at Marye's Heights across about a half-mile of unprotected, open ground provided a shooting gallery for the Confederates. Repeated assaults cost the Union 12,500 casualties to the Confederacy's 5,300. Pickett's Charge at Gettysburg had a similar result but different victors. The firing was so furious at Fredericksburg that one tree in the line of fire had 250 bullets in it, Carl Sandburg wrote. At one point, Union soldiers piled their dead, dug a trench, threw dirt on top and created a human earthworks.

Col. Regis DeTrobriand wrote in his memoirs that the Union defeat at Fredericksburg was entirely due to poor generalship. He wrote that if the Union forces had crossed the river above Fredericksburg, it would have forced the Confederates to leave their fortifications. A visit to Fredericksburg, like a visit to Gettysburg, makes people shake their heads when they see those slopes. How could anyone send troops up that hill to be slaughtered?

Still, there was one Union opportunity, which was stifled by poor generalship. Gen. George Meade led a flanking maneuver on the Confederate right through an undefended marshy area, a surprise. When he asked for help, Gen. David Birney refused, noting that Meade did not outrank him. Meade, who later led the Union victory at Gettysburg, was furious but to no avail. Union forces had to retreat. Edgar was lucky because his 3rd Michigan Infantry was guarding Union artillery rather than making suicidal assaults. Letters from Homer Thayer, also of the 3rd Michigan Infantry, quoted in Steve Soper's book, indicated that "it was pretty warm work for a time as the rebel batteries were shelling us from the edge of the woods about 1,000 yards away, but the field was soon clear of the enemies' infantry, and comparative quiet restored until toward dark." Thayer wrote that only five men from the 3rd Michigan Infantry were wounded, none seriously. "The Pennsylvania reserves had fought off this ground just as our brigade came up, and their wounded still lay in the field beyond our picket line and could be heard asking piteously for water and to be brought off the field but it was not in our power to assist them."

The Confederate victory at Fredericksburg (Dec. 11 through Dec. 15, 1862) brings up another continuing theme of the Civil War — the inability of both sides to follow up victories in battle and destroy opposing armies. In the book "Battle Tactics of the Civil War," Paddy Griffith describes the four battle tactics needed to destroy an enemy army: Fast mobility on horseback, willingness to fight on foot when the enemy is close, repeating rifles to enhance firepower and a mounted reserve ready to make a saber charge. The cavalry used in this way made a "magnificent multiplier" force of the infantry, Griffith wrote.

The Union later found a solution that involved the use of Gen. Philip Sheridan's Union cavalry, armed with repeating rifles, which managed to intercept Gen. Robert E. Lee's supplies and force a surrender at Appomattox.

In the Appomattox campaign, Sheridan's troops captured 6,000 Confederates in one attack and then 10,000 in another led by Gen. George Armstrong Custer.

The rifled musket could be amazingly accurate in skilled hands, as described by Joseph T. Glatthaar in "Writing the Civil War: The Quest to Understand." At 100 yards, 10 shots could be grouped in a 10-inch diameter. From 400 yards, a soldier could hit a 6-foot square target regularly. But most often, amid the smoke and confusion of battle, it took many shots to actually hit a soldier. Griffith quotes a statistic that after the Battle of Gettysburg, 27,574 muskets were recovered; 24,000 were loaded; 12,000 were loaded twice; 6,000 were loaded between three and six times; and one musket contained 23 charges. Also, it was common for a soldier to fire the ramrod instead of the Minie ball.

The importance of the repeating rifle cannot be overstated. The Spencer repeating rifle required only four steps to fire one round compared to 17 steps for a percussion-rifled musket, according to the Army drill manual. The Spencer could fire seven shots in 10 seconds compared to a musket firing three shots in 60 seconds. But repeating rifles weren't provided in quantity till the end of the war because Union ordnance officials worried they would waste ammunition.

The Union's head of ordnance, Gen. James Ripley, was so hidebound that President Lincoln forced his retirement in 1863. Lincoln made him purchase the Spencer repeating rifles. By 1864, Union cavalry had shifted to the Spencer rifle for cavalry, which meant that, with additional magazines, a soldier could fire 70 rounds in five minutes, according to Robert Bruce in "Lincoln and the Tools of War." By the end of the war, 85,000 Union soldiers carried Spencers," wrote James McPherson in "Tried by War." But that was still too little and far too late.

The Henry repeating rifle was so popular that the Ordnance Department bought 1,731 of them while state and private purchasers bought 8,372 — still too few to have a major impact, according to Webb Garrison's book, "Brady's Civil War." Bruce and Fred Albert Shannon in "The Organization and Administration of the Union Army 1861-1865" stated that the Union could have won the Civil War in 1862 with the widespread use of repeating rifles. Given all the extraordinary steps that President Lincoln took to win this war, the failure to force the mass production of the latest weapon technology cost the nation hundreds of thousands of lives.

Similar bureaucratic bungling prevented the Union from using new machine guns. Burke Davis, in his book "The Civil War: Strange & Fascinating Facts," wrote that President Lincoln was given a demonstration of a machine gun in June 1861. Dr. Richard Gatling, a North Carolina family doctor, patented his six-barrel machine gun in 1862. Each of the six barrels could fire 100 rounds per minute. But the Gatling gun was used spottily, such as protecting The New York Times building from draft rioters in 1863. Gen. Benjamin Butler bought 12 of them. However, the War Department was skeptical, thus wasting a huge opportunity to dominate the battlefield. It wasn't until after the war, 1866, that the U.S. Army formally adopted the Gatling gun. When author Shelby Foote spoke of the Union fighting with one arm behind its back in the Ken Burns documentary on the Civil War, I suspect he was referring to the Union's manpower advantages, but the failure to mass produce repeating rifles and Gatling guns is a better example of the Union wasting its advantages.

CAMP NEAR FALMOUTH — Dec. 17, 1862.

My Dear Wife and Children: I now hasten to write you a few lines to inform you that I am still in the land of the living, tough and hearty, but have seen tough and trying times since I wrote to you before. I thought I would write sooner than this but I will try to explain.

We had the order to march for battle Thursday morning at 6 o'clock. We accordingly started and went about 3 miles when we stopped about sundown. Then we started and marched about 1 mile further and then stopped for the night. We stayed in that place until Friday about 4 o'clock, when we again started about 8 o'clock and stopped again for the night. And Saturday morning we started about 5 o'clock and marched about 2 miles and we heard musketry and we kept on marching and crossed the river about 2 miles below Fredericksburg and all this while we were going into a big fight. We marched up in front of the enemy where their cannon balls were flying over our heads. We laid down on the ground after we had the order to load our guns and a big cannonball from one of the enemy guns struck the ground 2 rods *(11 yards)* ahead of the regiment and bounded over and struck the ground about some distance behind. That made us look out for sharpshooters and in a few minutes we had the order to march and we went up in the rear of one of our batteries and laid down while they were sending their cannon balls at us and we were doing the same at them at the rate of 100 a minute from about 50 guns.

You had better believe we had lively times from 1 o'clock until after dark supporting that battery with the rebels in front. They tried once to capture us but could not do it. Musket balls flew in every direction but fortunately, few in the regiment were hit. The 5th Michigan Infantry was to the right of us and they lost 10 killed and 83 wounded including their lieutenant colonel who commanded the regiment. After dark Saturday night, we were ordered to go on picket and we went to within about 15 rods *(78 yards)* of their pickets and laid there all night watching them. The night was a long one but morning finally came around. We thought we would have a big battle Sunday but had none.

We stayed on picket all day Sunday and were relieved after dark. Then we marched back a few rods and tried to go to sleep but the regiment that relieved us kept firing at the rebels all night. In the morning, we marched up and supported the battery again all day Monday. But there was no cannon fired by us nor them with both sides in plain sight. About 4 o'clock, a flag of truce was accepted and our side and their side went to take care of the wounded. This was Monday night and the wounded lay on the field from Saturday afternoon to Monday night. We could hear them groan for help but we could not get to them because they were inside of their picket lines. Our dead they stripped of all their clothing and shoes. Our flag of truce was granted for only one hour. The men that were detailed fetched over 100 dead and wounded before the hour was up. They got all the wounded they could find but did not get 11 of the dead. We left Monday night about 8 o'clock and recrossed the river and marched about 2 miles and camped all night Tuesday. We marched back to our old camping ground, glad we had come off as we did.

I wrote to you about sending us some stuff but it is so uncertain about us getting it that you better wait. We would be very glad for something good but we will have to wait until we can get it. I wish I could see you and the children today and would be more glad if I could come a week from tomorrow on Christmas and have a good supper with you. You must try and get along as well as you can. Give my love to all and a double share for yourself.

No more from your husband, Edgar W. Clark.

Historical context: The terrible Union generalship of Ambrose Burnside cannot be exaggerated. Union forces made 14 useless assaults at Marye's Heights at a cost of 14,000 men. No wonder Gen. Robert E. Lee said, "It is well that war is so terrible, we should grow too fond of it." Right, especially when you can arrange for awful Union generals to wage useless assaults against an impregnable position. Yet, Lee made the same mistake at Gettysburg.

CAMP PITCHER — Dec. 25, 1862.

My Dear Wife: This fine Christmas I wish you may have a merry day. Things move along with us as usual. I am better than I was and not able to do duty yet. My cough troubles me nights although it is a good deal better than it was. I would like to know what old Santa Claus put in the children's stockings last night for their goodies. I am almost certain that if he had been at home there would of been something nice. I hope Santa Claus has done something for them. I hope before another Christmas will pass I will be at home. You wrote you would send me some money if I wanted it. I would like to buy some things that would taste good but I probably will draw my money before you could send it, so I will not put you to the trouble of sending it. I would send you all the money I do not actually need when I draw my pay. I am owing Amos Turner $4 or $5 and some to Mosely. Next payday I will pay others and so on until all are paid. The prospect of peace looks gloomy enough but it may look fairer in a few days.

In this last battle, the rebels have gained courage and we have been defeated although we are not discouraged. We think the cause will ultimately triumph. I think it will be hard for us to try to march much more this winter.

The nights are cold and the weather is uncertain. About the woolen shirts, you said you would send them if we needed them. I can say we do not need them because I have four good woolen shirts, two that I drew from the government are good and the other two I bought in Detroit before I left the state. It is impossible for us to get an express box here because it is all that the government can do to furnish rations for the Army here. It is now 12 o'clock. Time passes like the wind. I never saw time pass so fast as it does now. We have nothing to do but to take things as the boys say, easy.

Holmes is in the regimental hospital as a nurse. He gets $21 a month. I don't see how he got it, being a new recruit, but he was sick in the hospital here and visited the sick and that is the way he got in. He makes a good nurse. There are a good many in the company that would like this position for the extra pay, myself for one, though it is a good deal harder than to be a soldier. I must hurry and write. My letter is most full. I wish you a happy Christmas and a Happy New Year. I will write again on New Year's Day.

No more from your husband, Edgar W. Clark.

Notes: Edgar says that being a nurse is harder than being a soldier. It was unusual for women to be army nurses. At this point, he had spent a lot of downtime and had been in just one battle with a few casualties in his unit. It's interesting that Edgar referred to Santa Claus. According to history.com, the legend became popular in the late 1700s, then it was popularized by the stories of Washington Irving in 1809. Stores began to advertise Christmas shopping in about 1820 and newspapers began offering special sections in the 1840s.

CAMP PITCHER — Jan. 1, 1863.

My Dear Wife: I wish you a Happy New Year. This morning I wish I could be with you today. We would enjoy it first-rate. I guess the first day of January finds me about the same, although I am not able to do much duty, but my health is improving fast. We have had a little better living within the last week. We have only drawn for our rations pork and hard crackers, coffee and sugar with beef once or twice a week. In addition this time we drew our rations of flour, potatoes, onions and beans, which made a good change for us. I never had potatoes taste so sweet and good as they did yesterday.

I ought to have received a letter from you today. I have received one every Thursday for a long while. I guess it will be along in a day or two. I wonder what you are doing today. Christmas night we had 3 quarts of molasses and a lot of molasses candy and we had a good time. There were about a dozen of us to eat it. Today some of the boys got some whiskey and are having a good time. I bought today a can of condensed milk to put in my coffee. One teaspoonful will make a quart of coffee look white. I also bought 15 cookies and we got along first-rate. We have not drawn our pay yet.

There is a rumor in the camp that we are soon agoing to move and the rumor says back toward Washington. There is no news of much importance here to write. We see papers once in a while. The nights are quite cold but days are warm and pleasant and every day is alike. I expect to see worse weather in a few days. The folks say through this section of the country that this is the finest weather they ever saw in these parts. I presume that you have good sleighing in Lansing now and quite cold weather. I think of you getting up and building your fires. I wish I was there to do it for you and to live in peace and comfort around the family fireside. I will know now how to appreciate the blessings of home and to enjoy them. Give my love to the folks. Write often and you will much oblige your husband.

Edgar W. Clark.

CAMP PITCHER — Jan. 2, 1863.

My Dear Wife: I know it's hard for you to live alone. I am in hopes this will not always last. My health is not very good today. I have taken a bad cold caused by sleeping on the ground and being exposed to the cold nights without any shelter, only our blankets over our heads, and we have few enough of them. I have put in a requisition for one more blanket. We have our tent fixed by now so I guess it will be a little more comfortable if we can stay here to enjoy it. We have built a log body up about three deep and put our tents on top of that. We have built a good fireplace in it and put our beds up from the ground and cut some pine boughs and can sleep a good deal that way. We tried it two nights and it goes better but it's not like home.

We suffered a sad defeat a week ago in the Fredericksburg battle although we could of defeated the entire Confederate Army. Our armies were about three-quarters of a mile from them. They were in the woods and we were in an open field and between us there was a ditch where they fired on our men as fast as they came up to it. There were other ditches between us and them where their sharpshooters picked off our men as fast as they came up.

There was a flag of truce on Monday and the pickets on both sides met and shook hands and had quite a chat for about an hour. Their pickets said they were tired of the war and would be glad when it was ended, and we told them the same. You said the first ball that came should hit me. I am sure that a great many balls flew all around but never hit me although I expected every moment that one would hit me. We had good luck. It may be that I will be lucky next time.

From your husband, Edgar W. Clark, to his wife.

Historical context: In a devastating battle, a unit might lose one-third to one-half of its soldiers. Over time, if a soldier is constantly in battle, it stands to reason that luck might run out. Next year, Edgar's Company G was reduced to just eight men and the 3rd Michigan Infantry Regiment lost so many men that it was merged into the 5th Michigan Infantry Regiment.

CAMP PITCHER — Jan. 5, 1863.

My Dear Wife and Children: Never was a person more tickled to receive a letter from home than I was this afternoon. I am not very well. I took a heavy cold the night we recrossed the river. I had a bad spell but not so bad as the one I had at home last spring but I think I will be longer getting over it because I do not have as good nursing as I did at home. I thought I would take a walk today and as I went over to the railroad about a half-mile from camp, I thought I would never get back, but I did and found your letter. I think we could get an express box from you now if you could send it to us. We wrote for you to send butter and that is what we need most. Send dried fruit, as much as you can, and not any bread because it would mold before we could get it. A tent mate received a box today of 60 pounds. The cake and two loaves of bread spoiled but the cookies kept good. They put in a lot of grapes and they were smashed up. The best way is to put them in cans and seal them tight. If you send us about 60 pounds, that is all we can ask.

If we stay longer than this winter, prospects look rather dark. We may ask for more next winter but I hope before another winter comes the soldiers will be home. The Lord knows that I would like to see you before next winter, but we have got to free the Negroes before we come home and the whole race is worth all it costs. We need not be on the equity with them but this country cannot remain half-free and a part of the other half in the bonds of slavery. God forbid, let us do the best we can to make the whole country free from the curse of slavery and save the Union at all hazards. I must bid you goodbye again. Tell Mina her pa will make her a table when he comes home.

No more from Edgar.

Historical context: Though few battles occurred during the wet weather of winter in Northern Virginia, Edgar was in more danger of dying from disease than combat. In fact, of the 750,000 deaths in the Civil War (James McPherson writes in "The War That Forged a Nation" that 750,000 is the best estimate based on recent research), two-thirds came from disease, reported Dr. Stanley Burns, the medical historian of the "Mercy Street" series on pbs.org. Diarrhea and dysentery claimed the most lives. Pneumonia, tuberculosis and malaria followed as causes of death. Water sources were often too near latrines. Diarrhea was so common it was called "The Virginia Quickstep." Treatment for diarrhea often consisted of something as common as castor oil, whiskey or other liquids that would be considered poisonous today, such as strychnine, turpentine, camphor, laudanum and blue pills of mercury and chalk.

Chapter Five

Lingering illness, hospitalization

Edgar is seriously ill with diarrhea. Opium is the cure. He walks with a limp due to rheumatism. He sees soldiers die while being neglected in the hospital. Pleasant weather arrives. Edgar is released and hopes for a box of food from home.

CAMP PITCHER — Jan. 11, 1863.

My Dear Wife: I hasten to write you some lines this morning telling you of my prospects. My health is not good. It has been over a month since I have done my duty. I am not sick but this diarrhea I have had for the last three months seems to wear on you. The doctors check it with opium but the opium is gone and I hope that with a stay in the regimental hospital and a change in diet I will get well in a few days. You must not worry about what I have written because there is nothing dangerous — weakness and a kind of chill fever. And the victuals we get from the government are not like the victuals at home. I hope you will send us something that will taste good. I would rather be home with you and the loving children but hope before another Christmas or New Year passes.

Edgar.

CAMP DIVISION HOSPITAL NEAR FALMOUTH — Jan. 16, 1863.

My Dear Wife: I write to inform you of my health at the present time. I think it is improving. I feel better today though the rheumatism is not much better. I do not care nor think much about that because it will lay me up for a spell and if it continues I will not be able to do much more service for the United States. We had an order yesterday that all who are not able to walk 10 miles would have to go to the division hospital. We have very good quarters but not so good as we had in the regimental hospital.

I think this Army is going to make another big strike soon and probably before you read this letter. I will be out of it this time. There will be a big battle not far from up the river.

I want you not to feel worried on my account for I know how to take care of myself. I do not worry about you and you need not worry about me as long as I can write once or twice a week. You may consider that I am able to be up and around. I am able to sit up all day. My rheumatism does not pain me so much when I sit up as it does when I lay down nights on the hard ground and that makes it worse. I have blankets and two big overcoats. We went and got some Virginia feathers last night *(pine boughs)* and laid them on the ground and we had a good bed for a soldier. Our doctor was up from the regiment and said they were agoing to build some hospital accommodations and we would go there in a day or two. We are now about 2 miles from the regiment. I feel lonesome today. The days are long and the nights are longer. Time passes wearily and slow. The nights come too often to suit my rheumatism but I guess I can stand it. You must try to get along as well as you can and it will all work for the best. I will write again in a few days. So keep a stiff upper lip. Kiss the children for me and tell them that their pa thinks of them every day and longs for the time to come when I can come home and see them.

Goodbye for this time from your husband, Edgar W. Clark.

DIVISION HOSPITAL — Jan. 22, 1863.

My Dear Wife: I write to inform you that I am a little on the gain. I feel better than I did a week ago today, although my rheumatism does not get much better and it will not as long as we are so poorly fed, but we will live through it. We are having the worst weather since we have been on the march. Mud — no bottom to it.

The regiment is about 10 miles from here. I would not be surprised to hear any minute that they were back on their old camping ground. It is now impossible for me to get any mail from you at present or until we get to some hospital where they have mail communications. What letters you write will go to the regiment and William will get them out to me. I do not care so much about hearing from you as I do to have you hear from me because I am in the hospital and it is quite important that you hear from me as often as you can.

I hope the regiment will come back today and if they do we will get our pay in a short time. I know you need it but when it will come, I cannot tell. This hospital contains about 300 sick and the deaths average about three per day. One died in a tent about 4 feet from me yesterday. I saw him die. Another will die in a day or two with the brain fever. The poor fellows have no care. Nine out of 10 died from sheer neglect. If they are taken with any disease and their constitution is stronger than the disease, they will get well and outlive the disease. You must not trouble yourself about me. If I could tell you a little secret and no one but you knows it, you would feel content and not worry about me. You must do the best you can and all will come out right one of these days. You must give my love to all of my good friends and poor enemies. Kiss the children for me. I look at your likeness every day and it does me a good deal of good.

No more from your ever true husband, Edgar W. Clark to his wife.

Historical context: Edgar saw death in the hospital. Poet Walt Whitman, who volunteered in hospitals during the war wrote: "Some of the poor young chaps, away from home for the first time in their lives, hunger and thirst for affection; this is sometimes the only thing that will reach their condition." Neglect and poor care in the division hospital were upsetting Edgar. After all, the war had been under way for nearly two years. It's no wonder that twice as many soldiers died from illness than in battle. And one wonders what wife Catherine thought of her husband being neglected.

CAMP IN HOSPITAL — Jan. 28, 1863.

My Dear Wife: This evening I will write to inform you that I am about the same that I was when I wrote to you before. I do not seem to gain any strength. My rheumatism does not get any better. It is a curious disease. There are very painful nights and when I walk it makes me limp considerable. I went over to see William last Saturday. The regiment is about a mile from the hospital and I got your letter, which done me a good deal of good. The news was quite interesting to me.

The Army of the Potomac made an advance and a heavy rainstorm set in that frustrated the whole design of the generals and they had to return to their old campground. It is now likely that they will remain in the present position for some time, probably until about the middle of March. I am halting between two opinions. I will tell you what they are, but I do not think it will do any good, if my rheumatism does not get any better soon, it is liable to keep me in the hospital for a long time and not be of any good to my country. I think I will get my discharge sometime in March.

If I cannot get any better, maybe I can get a furlough to come for a month or two. It will cost me $50 to come home and back. I think we will be sent to some general hospital in a few days. I hope so, for we will be better provided for. I know that it is the general impression among us that when a person is sent to the general hospital, it is certain death, which is a wrong idea. There are about 15 of us in this tent and we all can wait on ourselves but we have a good nurse, a man from Michigan who waits on us first-rate.

I expect the regiment got their pay today. It has been so stormy that we have not heard from the regiment whether they got their pay or not. I heard that we will get but two months' pay and then I cannot send you as much as I would wish. I have told you the truth and you must believe that I am safe and right with the exception of my back and left hip. I would write oftener if I had stamps. We can get enough after we get our pay and then I will get back to my old principles of writing twice a week.

No more from yours, Edgar W. Clark.

Notes: Six days after writing about terrible neglect in the division hospital, a good male nurse showed up, though Edgar was still referring to the patients depending on themselves.

DIVISION HOSPITAL — Jan. 31, 1863.

My Dear Wife: I write to inform you that I am doing well at present. I received your kind and affectionate letter today. I was very glad to hear from you. I will be glad when that box comes. I wish Homer would have brought it. We would have got it sooner. You probably sent considerable. We have been very much disappointed in getting paid. The paymaster was at the regiment and paid two months' pay when he ought to have paid four months' pay.

You must try to get along the best you can. I will do the best I can to get the money. I do not worry about you. I know you are provided well enough with friends who would not see you suffer. I have as much on my mind to occupy my thoughts and to get along as well as I can. There are no prospects of moving from this place very soon. We are well enough off here. We have to get in the hospital two months before we can apply for a discharge and then if there is no prospect of our getting better for some time they are obliged to discharge us. I have been in the hospital since Jan. 12.

Edgar W. Clark.

DIVISION HOSPITAL — Feb. 3, 1863.

My Dear Wife: I hasten to answer your letter. You wanted me to send you that article of agreement between me and Homer. I saw Homer yesterday. I told him there was never any article between us. I told him I trusted to his word. William is here with me now. He will take that letter back and let Homer see it and Homer will manage it all satisfactorily, I guess.

I wrote to you last Saturday night the full particulars of my disease. It will not be necessary to say anything about it now. I am better as long as my appetite is good and my hand does not tremble. I will keep you informed of my health, so you need not worry. We received the receipt for the box of things you sent. I will not write as much as I have before. You must try and get along as well as you can and I will send you what money you want when we draw our pay.

No more from your husband, Edgar W. Clark.

DIVISION HOSPITAL — Feb. 3, 1863.

My Dear Wife and Children: I think I can do better and make better wages to be a company nurse. There are three or four needed now in this hospital but I do not calculate to do that until I get better than I am now. I cannot draw a bucket of water nor cut wood enough to supply a tent and we have good times here. We have a man to bring our water and the cooks bring us all of our victuals so we do not have to go out of our tent until we have a mind to and that is not very often. I am blessed with a toothache.

You must try to get along with what I sent. I am very glad you got a deed for the lot. I consider it safe now. I have worried some about it but I am glad it is safe. I did not know that Homer had gone to Michigan until we got letters. I am glad he made you a visit. I wish I had been there to visit with him. I think we could of enjoyed ourselves first-rate.

Any health since I wrote to you has been middling good although my rheumatism is no better. The doctor does nothing for that so I guess it will not get well very fast. He is doctoring me for the diarrhea. This disease is the most curious thing you ever saw. I have to take opium all the time to keep it checked. My appetite is good and as long as I can eat, you need not worry about me. In my last letter, I wrote to you about getting a furlough. I have made up my mind to wait and see if I don't get any better. There are two other reasons I want to stay. I think the war will be closed in May and if it is, it will be better for me.

Another reason is I want to stay to see the spring they have here in Virginia. I don't think I will ever go back into the company if I get better. I am tired of carrying a gun and knapsack weighing 30 or 40 pounds.

No more from Edgar W. Clark.

Notes: Edgar's poor predictions continued. He didn't become a nurse. He didn't get a furlough. But he did recover enough to return to his unit. May would bring a Union loss at Chancellorsville. The war would not end soon.

DIVISION HOSPITAL — Feb. 9, 1863.

My Dear Wife: I again will try to inform you of my health. I feel about as I have for the last three weeks but still grow weaker every day. My hand trembles and I can hardly write this afternoon. My rheumatism does not trouble me as much as it did although I feel it almost every day and more. As I told you in my last letter, a person has to be in the hospital two months before he could have an examination. Then a person has to be examined by a medical board of doctors of three or more. Then if they think your case is such that you will not be able for duty within a year or so or will not be fit for duty at all, they will give you a discharge. As you see, a person has to be very sick or very nearly used up before he can get his discharge. I am agoing to make a try on the first of next month. Anyhow, my constitution is not strong enough to be a soldier in the Army.

You never saw pleasanter weather in your life. It makes me think of May in Michigan although we have sudden changes here as well. Your box has not come yet. We look for it every minute. It has been on the road for two weeks today by your letter. I hope it will come soon for I want to once more taste some of your fruits and cookies. I am almost afraid you and your friends have robbed yourselves for our comfort but I hope not. You will be repaid one of these days, if ever.

Butter is worth 60 cents a pound and other things in proportion. There was quite a number of pounds sold in this tent today for that price. I wish I could see you today. I know that I would get better soon. It is hard to live away from home and friends. The days pass by very slow and the nights slower. It will be six months today since I bid you goodbye and it seems almost like six years. You must try and get along as well as you can. I will send you 20 cents, all the money I have. You may send me three or four postage stamps. We hope to get our pay soon if I get all that is due me it will be nearly $65. I will send you half of it, although if there is any probability of my getting discharged I will not draw any until I come home. I feel better today. You must not worry.

Yours, Edgar W. Clark.

Historical context: After six months, Edgar only saw limited action at Fredericksburg and then suffered from serious illness in camp. As he explained, it was nearly impossible to be relieved of duty due to illness. February in mid-Michigan can be brutal, so it had to be a pleasant shock to see mild weather in Virginia. Before July 1, 1863, postage rates differed by distance traveled. Under 300 miles, rates were 5 cents per half-ounce. If sent over 300 miles, letters cost 10 cents per half-ounce. Later the cost of a postage stamp was 3 cents per a half-ounce.

REGIMENTAL HOSPITAL — Feb. 15, 1863.

My Dear Wife: Through the mercies of a kind providence, I am writing to you again. My health is about the same as it has been for the last three months. I am very weak and that is the most that ails me with the exception of this chronic diarrhea, which troubles me considerable. I have to keep drugged with opium to keep my bowels within bounds. My appetite is good or I would not stand it as well as I do. I have not received a letter from you since the third of this month. I am waiting anxiously to hear that you are well. William says you are soured on me. I tell him that I will risk it. In my last letter, I wrote that I would send you 20 cents for you to send me some postage stamps and I was in such a hurry to send it off that I forgot to put the money in the letter.

I have changed my place from the Division Hospital back again to this hospital. There were 11 of us there and we all came back. I am glad of the change because William and I are nearer together than we were when I was up there. We have better care here. We have watchers all night long. We have grand medical attendance and good provisions to eat. We have not got the box yet but probably we will get it soon. You cannot realize the amount of express that is sent to this Army and the railroad is hardly enough to bring the supplies for the Army and to bring the express.

I have got a good deal to write but dare not do it for reasons that I will tell you when I come home. Our paymaster will be here again this week, then I will send you some money. I will send all I can spare. You must use it prudently for you cannot tell what may happen within the next two years. I wish I could see you today. You must try and get along as well as you can. Give my love to all friends and save a double portion for yourself.

No more from Edgar W. Clark.

REGIMENTAL HOSPITAL — Feb. 22, 1863.

My Dear Wife and Children: I again am permitted to write you a few lines to inform you of my health and circumstances. Today is the stormiest of the season. It makes me think of a Northeaster in Michigan. Tomorrow the sun may shine as pleasant as a June day.

My health does not improve very fast. I have lost 15 pounds since I have been sick. Today we had a national salute from every cannon in the Army of the Potomac. It sounded grand. Today is a sad and lonesome day to me. You may rest assured that if I were home it would not be lonesome. We would spend a time in visiting and talking over old times and our prospects and have a good time generally. I got a letter from you last Thursday and was glad to hear from you. You must not be discouraged or downhearted for I will come home someday to make you and home happy and comfortable if it is in my power. If I were home, I never would enlist and never leave home to engage in such a war again. I do not think it will be everlasting. It will come to an end one of these days.

My tooth stopped aching after I wrote. My ear aches today. I do not know how to manage that unless I come home and let you pull it for my not minding you to stay home last summer. I have got to be punished some way and I guess I can stand it if it comes no harder than that while I am in the Army.

Our box has not come yet. It has now been one month on the road and we must get it in a few days. We have as good quarters as anybody in the Army. We have a large wall tent with a big parlor stove in the middle and beds fixed up on crutches and slats made of pine with those Virginia feathers *(pine straw)* that I told you about. You can be assured that I will come home as soon as I can and will not let a day pass without being on my way if I can help it. I will write as often as I can.

No more from your husband, Edgar W. Clark.

Chapter Six

Fruit is like the best medicine

Edgar returns to camp. A box from home arrives with precious dried fruit. He comments on delayed pay, promotions, camp entertainment and Copperheads. No more Lansing friends in his unit. The role of women is examined.

REGIMENTAL HOSPITAL — Feb. 23, 1863.

My Dear Wife and Friends: I received your letters this morning and was very glad to hear from you. I wrote you yesterday and saw that I got some letters from you and Lydia. I am very glad that I got them for I feel downhearted and lonesome this morning, but when I got your letters, it revived me. I would like to have you enjoy yourself as much as you can. I know you and the children must be lonesome at home without me. I wish I was with you. I don't think you would be so lonesome. It may be I will be there one of these days to make life joyous and happy.

The sun shined warmly today as I predicted yesterday. The snow fell about 8 inches deep yesterday. It is so warm and pleasant that I will venture out and take the fresh air today. I will go over and see William in his tent. He is well and as tough as can be. I guess my appetite is middling good so I am not dangerously sick as long as I can eat, although my victuals do me no good. You must take good care of the children and kiss them for me. I will write a few words to Lydia in this.

No more at present from your husband.

Lydia, I will answer those few lines that you wrote. I got those stamps. I seem to think you will get your pay back some day. My hand trembles so that I can hardly write this morning but I am almost through so I will stop writing and say goodbye for this time. Write as often as you can for you do not know how much good a letter does a soldier.

Yours, Edgar.

CAMP PITCHER — March 1, 1863.

My Dear Wife: I am writing to you again under favorable circumstances. I am again in the company doing duty. I wish we had our box now. I would gain strength very fast. We are afraid we will never get it. This is the lonesomest day that I have seen yet. Nothing agoing on in camp worthy of note. The weather is warm and pleasant. It rained all night.

I wish I could write once a day. It is as much as I can do to write once a week what with guard duty and other work. In the morning we get up at roll call and then get our breakfast — fry some meat and then make some flour gravy to eat with our bread. Sometimes we have pancakes.

It will be seven months on the 11th of this month since we parted. I hope this war will be closed so that seven months will not pass again before I will be permitted to see you. If it is, I will be homesick, sure. I believe this war would of been closed long ago if it was not for Northern traitors. The South looks to them for support and they get a good deal of it. It is they who are to blame for this war and keeping the men from their homes and families. I hope something will befall them so they will be obliged to help us put them down. And the conscription bill now being passed in Congress will make them sweat worse than ever.

It seems curious that we do not get paid. I have got $78 owed me and the government owes me about $16 more; this last cannot be received until the close of the war, but if I could get $75 to send to you and some for me to use it would help me and you a good deal. Everybody seems to think we will get all of it about the middle of the month. I hope we will. I would like to send you $40 or $50 and what you did not use you could put in the bank so there would be no danger of having it stolen or taken away. You must try to get along as well as you can. You must write whether you draw your proportion from the county. I wish I could see you but we must wait until circumstances bring us together. Be kind and good to the children.

No more this time from your soldier husband, Edgar W. Clark.

Historical context: Since Jan. 12, Edgar had been writing from hospitals. Now, almost two months later, he was writing from camp. Edgar disliked Copperheads, mostly Democrats in the North, who were willing to sue for peace and allow the Confederacy their independence. Edgar was willing to take any action to put down the rebellion.

There were Union sympathizers in the South, mostly in the highlands far from the cotton-based economies, but the Copperheads in the North were an entirely different matter. Lincoln was one of the most vilified presidents in American history. Editorial cartoons were brutal.

REGIMENTAL HOSPITAL — March 8, 1863.

My Dear Wife: I take my pen again to write a few lines to inform you how I am getting along at this time. I wrote you last Sunday that I was back to the company. I stayed four days and I was taken worse and had to come back to the hospital again. I am better this morning. It is this chronic diarrhea that ails me. When I take opium and live on beef tea and bread, I get along first-rate, but as soon as I eat pork and beans, it makes me worse.

I was very glad to hear from you. I am afraid you will not see me this month. I am able to be up. I took the currant wine and fetched it over to the hospital and gave some to one or two of the sickies and they thought it was the best they ever tasted. Those pickled peaches were excellent. I can assure you I fetched them over to the hospital with me.

I asked the doctor if the wine and dried berries would hurt me and he said they would not if I did not eat too much at a time. My health is no worse than it was for the past week. I wrote you a good long letter yesterday but I thought I would write you again tonight to let you know that I got the box. I like to write to you to pass the time and you may rest assured that my thoughts are with you night and day, thinking over the good times that we have had together and sometimes wonder if we will ever have as many more. I looked for a letter from you this morning.

I expect our money soon and hope we will not be disappointed. My health is the same this morning. If nothing should happen that I am worse, I or William will write every day. You need not worry on my account. Keep a stiff upper lip and all will end well one of these days. Give my love to all inquiring friends and save a share for yourself.

No more from your husband, Edgar W. Clark.

GOVERNMENTAL HOSPITAL — March 15, 1863.

My Dear Catherine: I again write to inform you how I am getting along. My health is improving but very slowly. I have not heard from you in two weeks, the longest that I have been without a letter since I left home. I hardly know what to think, but I guess you are all well. I had some curious dreams for the last three or four nights, which makes me think more about it.

I have not done my duty in three months but if I don't have any pullback I shall go again into the company in a few days. I wish I could come home and stay two months and fix up the house but I think this war will not last all summer. I think with our armies we ought to whip them in a short time. There is no news in camp, only we will soon move on the enemy from this place. I wish this war would be settled without any more fighting.

We have had so many promises about our pay that I am almost discouraged. I do not know how bad you want money but I think you wanted some long before this time. You must write about all your affairs, write about everything that you know will interest me. We are feasting on those good things you sent us. I wish I could send you something to repay you. I sold some of the butter for 60 cents per pound. I will get my likeness taken before I leave this place to send to you. It costs $1 to get it taken and when we do get our pay I want to send you money and have yours and the children's taken and sent to me.

We are having a thundershower today. There are 12 now in the hospital, none very sick. Only one died in this hospital this winter. We have good doctors and good nursing, all by men. My diarrhea is not much better. The doctors think I will do as well in the company as here in the hospital. I think so, too. I am sure of one thing. If the doctor can't cure me in the hospital, he can't cure me in the company. You must take good care of the children and yourself. Think of me often. I will try to take care of myself to come home happy after this war. Give my love to all inquiring friends and save a share for yourself.

No more from your husband, Edgar W. Clark, to his wife, Catherine, and children.

Historical context: Doctors thought Edgar would do just as well in the company as in the hospital, which explains the difficulty of getting a discharge due to illness. It's a Catch-22, which refers to being trapped by two contradictory conditions, such as trying to get out of the dangers of combat by claiming to be insane, which means you're not insane. For Edgar, being well enough to make a 1,300-mile trip home to Lansing, Mich. from Northern Virginia meant he was well enough to return to his infantry company. Twice as many soldiers died from illness as in combat. Common diseases in camp were typhoid, malaria, smallpox, measles, mumps, scurvy and tuberculosis. Dysentery and diarrhea were common. Note that his nurses were men. Women were breaking into nursing roles during the war and provided invaluable treatment and support.

CAMP PITCHER — March 21, 1863.

My Dear Catherine: As I have written a few lines to mother and Henry, I must not forget one that is nearer to me than the others. For a wife is nearer than anybody else. I got a good letter from you last Monday. The news that you wrote is good, especially those that relate to your neighbor.

My health is rapidly recovering. I am glad of it. I thought one time that I would be disabled entirely. I would rather have my health and stay my three years and then come home tough and well and be of some use after this war is over in trying to support my family than to be discharged and not be fit for anything at home or anywhere else. I got my likeness taken last Monday. I hope you will see how I look and think of me. I wish I could see you. I could talk over a good many tough stories and true. I don't think we will move from this place. The country is such that a little rain makes it awful muddy. I think this war will not last six months longer. I am anxious to see you and the children. I hope you will get along as well as you can.

Mother wrote that Peter paid $5 for 10 yards of sheeting. That is awful. I never expected to see such times. You must try to get along as well as you can. I am due almost seven months' pay. Three men got their discharge from the company. They were wounded in the battle last August near Bull Run. I must stop and bid goodbye this time and hope these few lines will find you well. You must not worry on my account.

From your husband, Edgar W. Clark.

Notes: Without seven months of back pay, Catherine had to be hurting.

CAMP PITCHER — March 25, 1863.

My Dear Wife: I received your kind and welcome letter Monday and was very grateful to hear from you. Although I am sorry you placed so much confidence in my coming home; you thought that I was worse than I was. I had no idea that I was sick enough to get a discharge. It is true what Lydia said, that a man had to be so sick that he could not help himself before he could get his discharge. I have not been so sick as that yet and hope I will not be. I would rather stay in the Army my three years and then come home sound than to get my discharge and be of no more service to myself nor to anybody else. The Lord knows that I would like to see you and the children ever so much today.

I am quite sure my health is rapidly improving. Today is the first duty that I have done in three months. I have gained so much by being sick although the duty that we do here in camp is not very hard but it is sometimes very cold and tedious and stormy. I have got to stand guard tonight. That is from 11 to 12. I shall not go to bed until after that time. I have to walk backward and forward in one place about 10 rods *(55 yards)* long with a gun on my shoulder and 60 rounds of balls, powder and caps. The place is before the colonel and officers' tents to see that no one disturbs them in the peaceful slumbers and silent repose. We have good times here. There were about 400 men that we mingle with every day and when not on duty we are playing ball or pitching, running, jumping and many other games too numerous to mention. In my tent, while I am writing to you, two are playing checkers and two are looking on and some are trying to get some sleep.

I cannot tell you much news about the war for I know but little. A soldier is not supposed to know anything about Army movements or anything of the kind. All he has to do is obey orders from his superior officers. We can see tents that accommodate 100,000 men. We are going to have a corps review tomorrow of probably 30,000 men. It is quite a sight to see so many men. Every regiment has from two to three large flags and from four to five drums and fifes. I must tell you something about our company. It now numbers about 43 that draw rations every day. When I shall get a promotion I cannot tell. I am not very desirous of a promotion. You may think this strange but it is so. All the men that you are acquainted with and those who left Lansing have been killed or discharged or are now off sick in the hospital.

The country is very beautiful. No swamps nor marshes as we generally find in Michigan. The country is very hilly. The streams rise and fall quick. I have calculated to write a good long letter so I have to write something to fill up the sheet.

I am glad you got the deed to the house and lot. You ought to have had it long ago but if you have got a good deed, I shall be satisfied by waiting. I hardly know what to tell you about the fence. Would it not be better for you to buy some more boards and hire a man to nail them on enough to make it safe? If you want a nice picket fence around it this spring, I will try to send you all the money I can. I will send you $30 anyway if I can find some secure way to send it. We could not get a check without going to Washington and that would be impossible. I think there would be no doubt that if I should send you so much it will come out safe. I will answer you some other time. You find out how much it costs to winter the cow and you can judge how long the wood will last. You must try to get along without any hard feelings if you can among your friends.

No more this time from me, Edgar W. Clark.

Notes: It is interesting that in just six months in the Army, Edgar is about the only one of his Lansing friends still in service, and he barely survived illness. It is entirely possible that Edgar's reference to "playing ball" was a crude form of baseball that was played under various rules on both sides of the Mason-Dixon line. One of the forms of baseball involved throwing the ball at the runner to make an out.

CAMP PITCHER — March 30, 1863.

My Dear Wife: I am glad of another opportunity to write you a few lines in answer to the one I received from Henry and Caroline on the 28th. I was on picket and very glad to hear from you all. I was about 5 miles from the camp. Our regiment was on the banks of the Rappahannock in sight of the rebels. They were about 20 rods *(100 yards)* from us all the time. We had very good times on the picket. It rained one day but we did not get very wet. I had to stand guard four hours out of 24. We came in camp today. I am somewhat tired but feel well. I can eat all I can get ahold of.

I hope you will get Mr. Jones or somebody to build a nice picket fence like the one that Mrs. Turner has in front of her house. I will send you the money in a few days to get it done. You must write to me who will do it and get it done as soon as you can and cheap. Catherine, I am going to send my Bible to you. It is unhandy to carry around. The agent from the American Tract Society gave me a nice small one that will be easy to carry.

No more from Edgar W. Clark.

Notes: Edgar makes few references to his faith except for this comment on carrying a Bible. Sending his Bible home was smart since on a long march soldiers often jettisoned much of their material. It is likely that he was a Protestant.

CAMP NEAR POTOMAC CREEK — April 5, 1863.

My Dear Wife: I embrace this opportunity to write you a few lines to inform you of my health this morning. William told me that it was Easter so I went out and bought a dozen eggs so I could have some to eat. We left our winter quarters Thursday and moved east from the winter quarters toward the Potomac about 4 miles. The object was to get nearer wood. The wood that we used there had to be towed about 4 miles and it was hard work to get all that we wanted to use. I think we will stay here some time. We were told to build up good quarters.

No more from your husband, Edgar W. Clark.

CAMP NEAR POTOMAC CREEK — April 9, 1863.

My Dear Wife: I will try this afternoon to answer your letter that I received a day or two ago. We had so much to do on duty and when not on duty fixing our quarters. We have got a nice little house where four of us stay together. We cook and eat together and have good times generally. Time passes fast. It is now about noon.

We have had brigade inspection by our commander and division commander Gen. David Birney and staff yesterday. We were on a grand review by the president of the United States and Major Gen. Joseph Hooker. There were three corps, probably 90,000 men. It was a grand sight to see so many soldiers, all with guns and bayonets gleaming in the air. For the first time, I saw the president. He is a young and better-looking man than what I had thought. His bodyguard was about 500 men on horseback with the staff of Hooker. He passed close by where I was, so I had a full view of him and then the soldiers all passed by him. We had to go about 4 miles from our camp to the review ground. We were tired when we got back to camp from the review ground.

This morning finds me well although somewhat stiff and sore from my tramp yesterday. My health is good again, as good as it was when I left home. The dried fruit and those things you and your folks sent I believe was the only thing that done me good. I cook some once in a while for a change. They taste good. I have got half of what you sent me. William and I divided them. He took half and I took the other half. I will write to Lydia in a day or two and tell her what was spoiled and what was not. We expect to be paid any day. I will send you $35 or $40 for you to use as you please. You can do as you think best with the cow. I think if you let someone take her all summer and give you some share of the butter it will be better than for you to keep her down home or in Lansing. You must take good care of the children. I am sorry they have been sick. I hope they are better now. Give my love to all and save a share for yourself.

From your husband, Edgar W. Clark.

Historical context: Edgar's letters constantly referred to the challenges faced by his wife to raise two toddlers and handle all the household chores by herself. Women played a vital role in the Civil War both in the armed forces and at home. Too often, their role has been ignored, wrote Catherine Clinton, the author of multiple books on the subject. Ken Burns, in his famous documentary on the Civil War, ought to be "consumed by guilt over his de-gendered re-rendering of the war," Clinton wrote. The material was available, but Burns, like so many others, did not consider women's roles essential enough for more than token content. Edgar mentions women during his time in hospitals. They truly were angels in helping wounded men to heal.

But some women could be found on the front lines. Women near the front often carried water or ammunition, reported Michael J. Varhola in the book "Everyday Life During the Civil War." About 250 to 400 women disguised themselves as men and fought alongside them in combat. The enlistment physicals were cursory, to say the least. As Elizabeth D. Leonard wrote in "The Civil War Soldier: A Civil War Reader," the exam might consist of holding out hands to display a working trigger finger and teeth strong enough to rip open a papered Minie ball cartridge. Also, there were many teenage or even boy soldiers, so women could easily pass. About 100,000 Union soldiers were 15 or under. A determined woman, refused entry at one location, could find a more welcoming opportunity elsewhere. One woman gained fame during her time with the 3rd Michigan Infantry. Anna Etheridge, wrote Steve Soper, served in various roles with the Army of the

Potomac as a nurse, laundress, cook, and hospital transport aide and then accompanied them to the front. She first joined with her husband, but when he deserted, she stayed. At Chancellorsville, she was on the front lines and rallied the troops while bullets whizzed by her. In effect, she was a medic. According to Bruce Catton in the book "Glory Road," Etheridge at Chancellorsville under heavy Confederate bombardment encouraged a Union battery not to abandon their pieces. Many soldiers described her in letters, wrote Bonnie Tsiu in "She Went to the Field: Women Soldiers of the Civil War." Etheridge was described as "unflinching in the face of danger — even amid exploded shells that shredded her clothing as she dressed the wounds of the injured." For her bravery at Chancellorsville, she was awarded the Kearny Cross. After the war, she married a one-armed veteran, received a pension and at a reunion was called "The Florence Nightingale" of the 3rd Michigan. Another woman who was so active in battle that legends grew around her was Bridget Divers (or Deavers), an Irish immigrant nicknamed "Irish Biddy" or "Michigan Bridget." She was attached to the First Michigan Cavalry.

An excellent book on the subject is "They Fought Like Demons: Women Soldiers in the American Civil War." Co-authors DeAnne Blanton and Lauren M. Cook offer fascinating accounts of these women. The stories were widely reported in newspapers at the time, Blanton said in an interview with the author. In some cases, reporters were so eager for these stories that they made them up. Blanton, who worked for the National Archives, could only document 250 women who dressed as men in combat and found no proof for the 400 number. Since these women were disguising themselves, it is logical to assume that many cases were never publicly revealed. One woman worked as a prostitute in Nashville, left the profession to join a Michigan regiment as a man; then after the war, moved to Au Sable, Mich. Blanton and Cook note that women pretending to be men gained male advantages, including the right to vote. They could also drink, smoke, curse and gamble, which helped their disguises.

Women often came from farms where physical labor was common. As one woman said, carrying a backpack is no more trouble than carrying a 30-pound child. Often, their true identities were discovered when they were wounded. Occasionally, they were found out in humorous ways. Imagine the surprise when an apparently male soldier delivered a child! As Blanton and Cook summarized it, "Relying on cleverness, hard work and a little luck, women soldiers not only performed their assumed duty to their country to the best of their ability, but they also found a level of personal freedom and self-determination unavailable to them in their true identities as women."

Most women were joining husbands, fathers, brothers or fiances, wrote Marissa Ross in "A Soldier's Secret: The Incredible True Story of Sarah Edmonds, a Civil War Hero." However, Edmonds was alone, escaping an abusive father and a forced marriage. Edmonds joined the 2nd Michigan Infantry as a male field nurse named Franklin Thompson. She was a Canadian. She moved to Flint, Mich. in search of education. She claimed to have infiltrated the South as a spy, using aliases and disguises, though there is no official record of it, reported The National Park Service. After contracting malaria, she had to give up her male alter ego and became a female nurse in a hospital for soldiers in Washington, D.C. She enjoyed the privations of military service, perhaps out of the spirit of adventure: "Patriotism was the great secret of my success." She received an honorable discharge, a pension and was the only female member of the Grand Army of the Republic. The malaria she contracted in Virginia led to her death in 1898 at the age of 56.

Chapter Seven

No action, daughter is ill

Camp duty is light. Edgar appreciates receiving a box with dried fruit from Catherine. A Lansing doctor makes house calls on daughter Carrie. The stage is set for the Battle of Chancellorsville.

CAMP NEAR POTOMAC CREEK — April 12, 1863.
My Dear Sister-in-law Lydia: I received your kind letter last Tuesday and was very glad to hear from you. We have been very busy building little log houses big enough to accommodate four persons. I am on guard. I stand from 11 till 1. My turn comes to go on guard once every eight to 10 days. So you see that is not hard work. If you could only look at our city of tents here it would be the largest city you ever saw. We have to go on inspection almost every day. Our guns have to be kept perfectly clean and dry. We are not allowed to go dirty. Everything has to be kept perfectly nice. Military law is very strict in this respect.

That wine that your kind mother sent did more to restore my good health than all of the medicine I took all winter. I drank that all myself, only I let two in the hospital have a taste. Those dried blackberries were good, too. I keep it for special purposes or when I am sick and for visitors. There was nothing spoiled but the chicken and the eggs and bread and pies. The cookies and crackers were mostly good.

I am sorry the children are sick. I hope they will get well and not trouble you more than necessary. I wish I could be there to help take care of them but that is impossible until this war is closed or until my time is out, which will be in two years and four months. It is eight months yesterday since I left home. Time has passed very fast.

It takes everything to make an Army, all sorts of men from the lowest to the highest, from the Black Negro to the White man. The law says that there shall be one chief cook and two Negro helpers for every 30 men. Our company numbers 44 men. There is a man coming to Lansing from our company. We will send some money by him. He will probably leave this week.

No more from your brother, Edgar W. Clark.

Historical context: Edgar refers to "Negro helpers." Before long, Black soldiers would be needed for combat duty and would do well.

CAMP SICKLES — April 15, 1863.

My Dear Wife: I hasten this morning to write you a few lines to let you know that I am well. My health is good and I hope you can say the same. I heard in one of William's letters that Carrie was very sick and the doctor came three times a day to see her. I hope she is better now. There has been a good deal of excitement fixing to move the past two or three days. We had orders yesterday to pack all of our baggage and send it to the rear. I think we were going in a reconnaissance for six to eight days but it rained torrents since last night. I calculate we will start again as soon as the weather allows. You must not worry.

We had good luck today to draw our pay and I will send you $40. You must pay Turner $5 and use the money to the best of your judgment. You must write as soon as you get this, for I want to hear about this money that I sent you. You must try to get along as well as you can and I will try to do the same. Give my love to all our friends and save a double share for yourself. This is the first letter that I have not filled up since I have been to the war.

No more from your most affectionate husband, Edgar W. Clark.

CAMP SICKLES — April 19, 1863.

My Dear Wife: Your kind and welcome letter found me about an hour ago. I was very glad to hear from you. I heard last Sunday a week ago today that Carrie was very sick and the doctor came three times a day to see her and they thought she would not live three days. So you will see how anxious I was to hear from you. William and I got a letter from Henry last night that stated that Carrie was nearly well. I had all sorts of dreams but it all turned out well.

My health is very good, probably as good as it ever was. The boys say I am getting fat. All I want to have done with the side fence is to be made perfectly secure from anything outside so nothing will be destroyed in your garden. I have carried about two dozen watermelon seeds in my pocketbook ever since last fall. I took them out of a big red core melon that I calculate to send in my next letter. Then you will get them soon enough to plant. There have been some promotions tonight in the company and they have to shell out cigars, apples and other things the boys want. I just got a big apple and a big lump of sugar. They are rare. We can buy oranges and lemons cheaper than we can buy apples. We had marching orders last Wednesday but when the time came to move, it rained and we were delayed.

I think you will hear some stirring times before long from this Army. I do not care how soon. I feel anxious to put down the war as soon as we can and then we can come home. The drums are beating for us to go to bed. I can hear no less than 20 agoing at once and the same number of fifes. I am sick of such music. I would rather hear the children cry than all the drums and bands in Christendom. I would rather be with you and be poor and work hard for a living than to be here in the Army. If I was a young man, nothing would suit me better but if a man is married this is no place for him. I wish I had thought of it when I enlisted. You may think I am homesick, we will let that pass. I will come home one of these days and then we will live over our time so fast that we will hardly know that a vacancy existed in our lives. You must try to do the best that you can. I know you do.

You must write as often as you can and I will do the same. When on a march the facilities for writing may not be as convenient as it is now. Give my best wishes to your folks. Write how the boys are getting along. Write all the news that you can think of at home or in Lansing. I cannot think of much now to write tonight. We were reviewed today by Gen. Hooker and his staff. We have good excitement but not enough to keep me from thinking of you and the children. Try and do the best you can and I will be satisfied.

Please accept my best love, Edgar W. Clark.

Notes: The Lansing doctor made three house calls in one day!

CAMP SICKLES — April 21, 1863.

My Dear Wife: I will write you a few lines today to inform you that I am well and hoping you and the children can say the same. It rained again yesterday. We are still waiting for the roads to become good to make a move. We have packed up for the last week and we have not seen a pleasant day since. I understand that a part of the Army is in motion and we will start in a few days.

You must not borrow my troubles for me. I will try to take care of myself and you must do the same. I know the children are a worry but they have been sick and you must humor them some. I wish I could be there today to see them with you included. It would be all that I would want. I will send you those watermelon seeds. You must plant them in some good spot in the garden. I will try and get a furlough this fall and come home to help you eat them. I know they will be food for the melon they came from was the largest and best melon that I ever saw and ate. You will have to hire somebody to help fix up the garden and plant it and be careful not to lose any of the money. Make every dollar count.

No more this time from your husband, Edgar W. Clark.

CAMP SICKLES — April 22, 1863.

My Dear Wife: William and I took it into our heads to go and get our pictures taken this morning. So we started about 8 o'clock and went about a mile-and-a-half further and got some writing paper and envelopes and returned to camp about noon. We are only allowed to be gone until 2 o'clock. We had a brigade drill in the afternoon where about 3,000 soldiers were on drill. You can hardly think how nice it looks to see so many soldiers obeying the commands of one or two men and everything working like clockwork.

My health is very good. My appetite is first-rate. It has to be to eat the rations that we eat here in the Army. Think of the poorest dinner that you could think of for two or three men on washing days when you wanted to hurry and get through as soon as you could and it is better than we live on for months at a time. If we want anything extra, we go to the sutlers to get it. For instance, William went yesterday and got about a dozen small onions and a couple of small codfish weighing 4 pounds. We had to give 2 shillings for the onions and 15 cents a pound for the codfish. The fish made us four or five good meals tonight. I boiled about 2 pounds of smoked bacon and 2 pounds of pork together that will last us three or four days with our hard bread and coffee.

I like to write to you. And it is right that I think that for there is no one that I like so well as I do you. I declare, if I am not careful I will write a love letter before I know it. I have seen some big love letters lately and maybe I have learned some of the expressions. You may guess who I mean.

We are to be ready to move in the morning at 5 o'clock. Something has got to be done in these parts and I do not care how soon this comes to an end. You are right when you say that I would not stay in the Army 24 hours if I was not obliged to. I think too much of you and the children to be away any longer than I can help. You tell Mrs. Thayer that Mr. Turner has got those deeds. You will have to get them and get them on record. Have the fence put on the line in front. You had better not get it painted until we draw some more pay in July. Then I will send you $30.

No more from your husband, Edgar W. Clark.

Historical context: Camp Sickles is a reference to Gen. Daniel Sickles, one of the most controversial generals in the war. Sickles as a general is best known for his aggressive tactics in contrast to the passive field operations of Gen. George McClellan and Gen. Joseph Hooker. The tactics of Sickles have been widely criticized as reckless though his supporters contend that they were effective. He conducted two of the most daring and criticized maneuvers in the war at Chancellorsville and Gettysburg. Sickles led the 3rd Corps.

He was a congressman, a prosperous lawyer, a militia officer and a student of the military arts. He was best known for fatally shooting his wife's lover in broad daylight in Washington, D.C. (Philip Barton Key, son of Francis Scott Key) and then getting acquitted on the basis of his wife's adultery and his temporary insanity. He had a dream team of lawyers that included future Secretary of War Edwin Stanton.

Sickles had served in the New York State Assembly and had been corporation counsel in Manhattan where he helped create the boundaries of Central Park. After the war started, he resigned from Congress and raised troops in New York. Because he was a Democrat, he gained the favor of President Lincoln and became the highest-ranked, non-West Point officer in the war. He also ingratiated himself with Mary Todd Lincoln. After the war, the one-legged Sickles became the lover of Queen Isabella II of Spain. Thanks to all of this sensational baggage, both before and after the war, combined with his aggressive tactics at Gettysburg, Sickles has been endlessly fascinating to historians. One of the biographies of Sickles was titled "The Man Who Got Away with Everything."

Chancellorsville. The importance of holding the high ground is illustrated at Hazel Grove with the Chancellor House in the far background. Union Gen. Daniel Sickles occupied it on the second day's battle and wanted to use it for a counterattack. Instead, after a disastrous night attack, Sickles was ordered to retreat. Once Confederates gained this high ground, their artillery struck Union forces, including the Chancellor House were Union Gen. Joseph Hooker was shaken up. (Michael P. Clark)

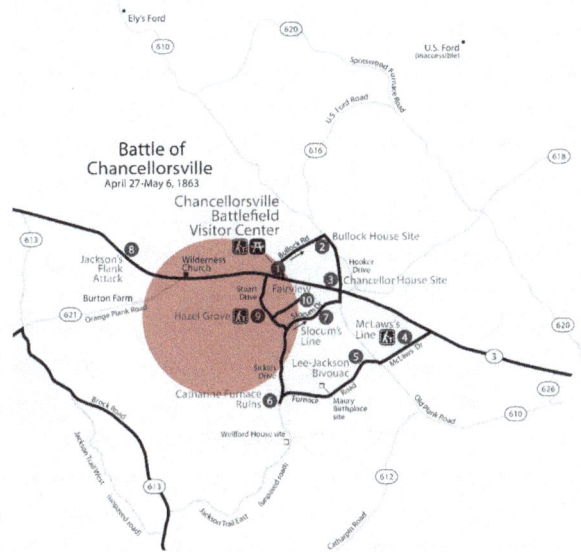

Hazel Grove was the centerpiece of the Battle of Chancellorsville. While it stuck out from the lines as a salient, its elevation made it an excellent platform for artillery. Confederates were able to combine their forces there. (Jonathan James).

Chapter Eight

Friendly fire, night attack

Edgar's unit sees tough action in the Battle of Chancellorsville. Union soldiers fire on each other at night in the woods. He describes the terrible sights of wounded soldiers and scenes of death. He dreams of home and dreads battle. Edgar backs President Abraham Lincoln. The Michigan governor visits the troops. As the weather warms, the stage is set for Gettysburg.

CAMP IN BATTLEFIELD — May 5, 1863.

My Dear Wife: I hasten to inform you that I am alive and have seen some very close times since the last day of April. For five days, the battle has raged *(at Chancellorsville)* and how it has gone I cannot tell. We have held our ground. Sunday *(May 3)* our regiment suffered very bad. We lost five killed and 46 wounded in our company. We lost our captain, Joseph Mason. A piece of solid shot struck him in the breast and killed him instantly. Orville Ingersall was wounded in the leg above the ankle and Nelson Shattuck had his finger shot off. William and I feel confident that we will come out safe. Yet we are now laying in rifle pits waiting for the enemy to pounce on us. Our pickets are now constantly firing to draw them in and if they make a strike upon us they will get very badly whipped.

You must not worry about me. I will try to take care of myself. I have only time to write a little. We have not got any mail since the 27th. How soon we will get some, we cannot tell. I will write as often as I can. I do not know when you will get this; I hope soon after the battle is over. I will write you some of the incidents and particulars of the battle. You must keep good courage. Tell my friends not to worry on my account. We are safe up to 5 o'clock of this day. Give my love to all and save a double share for yourself.

From your husband, Edgar W. Clark.

Historical context: At the Battle of Chancellorsville (April 30 through May 6), Gen. Joseph Hooker had a daring plan that could have worked if he had the will to carry it out. Chancellorsville and the Battle of the Wilderness the next year were fought in the same area, marked by thick stands of scrub brush and second-growth timber. Hooker sent one corps as a diversionary attack at Fredericksburg while another corps crossed the Rappahannock River and its tributary, the Rapidan River, to attack on the Confederate left flank. Hooker hoped to drive Gen. Robert E. Lee away from the river, and force Lee to retreat to protect Richmond to the south. Lee had already sent south about one-quarter of his infantry led by Gen. James Longstreet. Hooker's maneuver worked at first. He moved 70,000 men to the left of Lee's Army. He set up his headquarters at a large house owned by the Chancellor family.

Lee was severely outnumbered almost 3 to 1 — 45,000 Confederates vs. 125,000 Union troops. But Lee didn't retreat. Lee, rightly sensing Hooker's lack of will, split his outnumbered troops again. He left a small force at Fredericksburg under Gen. Jubal

Early and sent Gen. Stonewall Jackson around the Union right flank with two-thirds of Lee's remaining forces. They had maps of roads through the woods that kept them screened from the Union.

On May 2, Jackson's rebels moved in a column about 12 miles long, including the support vehicles. Scouts for Gen. Daniel Sickles saw the movement. It was first thought that Lee's soldiers were retreating. Sickles attacked and captured about 500 Confederates but it turned out he had only struck the tail end of the Confederate advance.

About 5 p.m. on May 2, Jackson's 27,000 Confederates attacked from the west, crushing the Union's right flank. Union soldiers in the 11th Corps were surprised, some were cooking dinner.

The Confederates were behind the 3rd Corps of Sickles, so he moved his troops to face the Confederate attack and rallied at a high point about a mile from Chancellorsville called Hazel Grove. While it was a salient, jutting out from the lines like a sore thumb, it was elevated and allowed a good view of the entire field, a perfect place for artillery Confederates attacked but Sickles along with Pleasanton's cavalry and artillery retained the position. As night fell, Gen. Stonewall Jackson was shot by his own troops while scouting for new routes of attack.

Hazel Grove became the centerpiece, the key location in the battle. It could prevent the two groups of Confederate soldiers from uniting and could be the centerpiece of a Union counterattack. As night fell and the noise of battle dimmed, Sickles decided it would be a perfect time to attack. Night attacks were rare in the Civil War, especially in wooded areas where visibility was poor. Edgar's unit, the 3rd Michigan, was there along with the 1st New York and the 37th New York.

Before midnight, May 2, Sickles conducted one of the most daring, reckless and disastrous attacks of the war. As Stephen Sears wrote in "Chancellorsville," Sickles failed to send scouts or skirmishers to assess the Confederate strength. As described in the book, "Sickles at Gettysburg" by James Hessler, the idea was to crash into the Confederates with a bayonet assault. But in the dark woods, the attack soon became chaotic. Artillery was fired in the woods along with about 15,000 muskets. Sickles failed to notify Gen. Henry Slocum of the 12th Corps. "So confused was the affair that the 3rd Michigan (Edgar's unit) boldly captured a 12th Corps battery," Hessler wrote. The terrible attack was a footnote in a long war, but it was tragic for men like Edgar who were in the middle of it. And it became part of the Sickles legend. A total of 196 Union casualties were reported, undoubtedly some by friendly fire.

Col. Regis DeTrobriand in his memoirs described the scene in detail. Union troops were told to silently advance about 200 yards toward the Confederate lines in the woods. It was eerily quiet. There were no rebels stationed at the entrance to the woods. Then a voice called out, "Halt! Who goes there?" Immediately, the place lit up with gunfire. Union companies lost direction in the dark woods. Soldiers were fired on from all sides at one point — like a circular firing squad. The sounds were "an infernal concert ... The groans of the wounded, the orders of officers, the oaths of the soldiers, the whistling of the balls, the roaring of the conical projectiles, the cracking of the branches, the rolling of the fusillade, the thunder of the artillery."

What happened was later described by Gen. Alpheus Williams, a lawyer, judge and journalist: "A tremendous roll of infantry fire, mingled with yelling and shooting almost diabolical and infernal, opened the conflict as Sickles' divisions went into the attack. ... I could distinctly hear the oaths of the rebel officers, evidently having hard work to keep their men from stampeding."

Williams: "Human language can give no idea of such a scene — such an infernal and sublime contemplation of sound and flame and smoke and dreadful yells of rage, of pain, of triumph or of defiance. Suddenly, almost on the instant, the tumult is hushed, hardly a voice can be heard."

Observers wondered how anyone survived the conflagration. One of the defenders of Sickles, Edgcumb Pinchon, author of "Dan Sickles: Hero of Gettysburg and 'Yankee King of Spain,'" wrote that Sickles had seized the initiative at Chancellorsville and improvised effectively. Pinchon notes that in one day, Sickles had fought three different types of battles: a pursuit, a check and a counterattack — all improvised, each one successful and two of them executed amid pandemonium.

Pinchon quoted J.H. Stine, in his "History of the Army of the Potomac," that by striking Jackson's right and rear, Sickles prevented a disaster. "His subsequent night attack against Jackson was one of the most brilliant actions in military history." In contrast to Pinchon, Hessler wrote that the night attack was "a chaotic mess." Hessler described the action of Sickles at Chancellorsville as aggressive "but lacking in military judgment." Edgar would agree.

Hooker ordered Sickles to abandon Hazel Grove, which allowed the Confederates to command the heights with artillery and unite the Confederate forces. "Hazel Grove," Pinchon wrote, "the strategic key to the whole field of battle, held at terrible blood cost, still could have been used to mount a counterattack in overwhelming force ... To hand it over to the enemy was a gift that was, for Sickles, the bitterest experience of his military career." Remember this when Sickles is at Gettysburg two months later.

Hazel Grove, a gift to the Confederates, allowed them to dump artillery fire on the Union, including Hooker's headquarters at the Chancellor House. Even today, the view from Hazel Grove, looking down, provides an instant appreciation for the advantage of the high ground. Hooker was shaken up by an artillery strike, which left him dazed and even more hesitant.

On May 3, the two sides engaged in a series of battles, mostly conducted in the forest of the Wilderness, an advantage for the outnumbered Confederates. The woods made artillery and cavalry almost useless.

With J.E.B. Stuart replacing Stonewall Jackson, the rebel forces pushed the Union back. Hooker, already weakened by indecision, ordered a retreat, leaving the field to Lee and the Confederates. Near the end of the battle, Gen. George Meade asked for permission to attack the Confederate left flank. He would have had the same flanking advantage that Stonewall Jackson had. Hooker denied it.

Bottom line: Lee, severely outnumbered, took the offensive and won. Hooker, with the advantage of surprise and superior numbers, lost his nerve and the respect of his troops and his president. Lee's brilliant maneuver only worked with the aid of a scared opponent who planned well and executed poorly.

As with too many previous battles, the Union forces retreated while many soldiers were held in reserve. Hooker, like other Union generals before him, wasted a good plan and numerical superiority. Pinchon describes the initial attack as "a brilliant surprise" that ended in a "grotesque defeat."

If ever a battle appeared to justify faith in Lee and the inadequacy of Union generals, it was Chancellorsville. And perhaps this led Lee to be overconfident at Gettysburg. DeTrobriand wrote that Hooker lost the battle by giving up the advantages he had earned in the offensive and became hesitant — badly so. "So we were completely beaten — beaten on account of the general-in-chief, who, after having prepared his army for the best opportunity of being victorious that it ever had, threw to the winds all of his advantage."

Hooker was replaced by George Meade, a feisty general who hailed from Pennsylvania and was uniquely suited to deal with the Confederate invasion on his home ground in a little over a month.

Beyond the Confederate victory and Lee's daring tactics, Chancellorsville is best known for Gen. Stonewall Jackson's death after having been shot by his own men. As for Private Edgar Clark, he was able to survive a tragic mixup of friendly fire among Union troops.

By the end of the battle, neither side had gained any advantage. Both returned to their previous lines. Though Lee won the battle, he couldn't afford to lose about 11,000 casualties to about 17,000 for the Union. Beyond the loss of Jackson, the rebels lost 64 of 130 regimental commanders. So the loss of Jackson, the subject of innumerable "What if Jackson had been at Gettysburg theories," obscures the larger Confederate losses at Chancellorsville, a victory that played a key role in the Confederate defeat at Gettysburg. The 17,000 Union casualties were higher in number, but on a per capita basis were lower. As Gen. James Longstreet insisted, the rebels generally did their best on the strategic offensive and the tactical defensive (inviting a Union attack on favorable ground for Confederates), as at Fredericksburg. In fact, losing so many soldiers eventually forced Lee into an entirely defensive approach at the end of the war.

Author Edward Bonekemper III has written in "How Robert E. Lee Lost the Civil War" that Lee's offensive-minded tactics were fatal. Like George Washington in the Revolutionary War, all the South had to do was maintain a deadlock and wear down the other side.

"Northerners violently disagreed on slavery, the draft and the war itself," Bonekemper wrote. "The South was outnumbered by a

ratio of 4-to-1 in terms of White men of fighting age and could not afford to squander its resources by engaging in a war of attrition."

Yet, the South nearly did succeed when it appeared President Abraham Lincoln would not win reelection in 1864. More on that later.

Bonekemper calls Chancellorsville *"the victory that wasn't"* due to Lee's massive casualties. Lee had costly losses with aggressive attacks at Malvern Hill, Antietam and Gettysburg. And he had costly victories at Second Bull Run and Chancellorsville.

Bonekemper notes that Lee had 121,000 men killed or wounded during the war — 27,000 more than any Union or Confederate general including Gen. U.S. Grant, though Grant gained the reputation as a *"butcher"* due to his costly frontal attacks in the Overland campaign of 1864. Grant has been rediscovered in recent years as his victories in the West have been recognized. His victory at Vicksburg involved brilliant maneuvers while his victory at Chattanooga involved a successful attack up the side of a mountain.

Grant gained the surrender of three entire Confederate armies at Fort Donelson, Vicksburg and Appomattox. For the last two, he actually paroled the Confederates rather than send them to prison. That's right, *"the butcher"* let the rebel soldiers go at Vicksburg and Appomattox after surrendering their muskets with only the promise not to take up arms against the Union.

By the way, the hero-worship of Confederate Gen. Nathan Bedford Forrest ignores the fact that he fled from both Fort Donelson and Chattanooga when confronted by Grant. He also was a non-factor during the Confederate defeat at Nashville. The best description I read of Forrest is that he played a major role in minor battles and a minor role in major battles. He was no more than a nuisance to Gen. William Tecumseh Sherman's march to the sea. In his memoirs, Sherman wrote that when Forrest *broke up railroads in Tennessee, "he did his work so hastily and carelessly that our engineers soon repaired the damage."*

In fact, the most daring and effective raid of cavalry during the Civil War was conducted by Union Col. Benjamin Grierson through the heart of Mississippi — a key part of Grant's victory at Vicksburg. Grierson was a musician and band leader from Jacksonville, Ill., west of Springfield. He disliked horses because he was kicked in the head as a youth, yet the Army put him in charge of cavalry. He was so good at it that Grant sent him to lead the diversion from Vicksburg. It worked. Grierson tore up railroad tracks, burned Confederate munitions, avoided Confederate pursuers and escaped south to Baton Rouge. The movie "The Horse Soldiers" by John Ford was loosely based on Grierson's raid but its fictionalized scenes couldn't match the true story. Since nobody would believe a band leader could outfight the South through Mississippi, John Wayne as Grierson was presented as a railroad engineer in the movie.

CAMP SICKLES — May 8, 1863.

My Dear Wife: I again am permitted through the mercy of a kind providence to write to you from our old camp, which we arrived at the day before yesterday. We have seen some very tough times since the 28th of April. We were in the middle of fighting for six days and some of the time were under the worst fighting the regiment ever saw.

I wrote to you on the 5th and told you some of the particulars. I sent the letter by a man who was agoing to New York. He said he would put it in the post office in New York. Our mail has been stopped. Today is the first day that we have got any mail for the last nine days. I certainly expected to get a letter from you and I felt disappointed. I have not got a letter from you in over two weeks but I think one will come soon. What our next move will be I cannot tell. We are under marching orders. How soon we may go it is impossible to tell.

I hope we will not try to cross the river again in this place. We have tried three times and I think that is enough. The last time we lost five killed and 46 wounded. We lost our captain and two are missing. The shell that killed our captain and wounded many others exploded over our heads. We fought *(May 2)* until midnight. We fought and drove a division of our own men thinking that they were the enemy. We killed quite a number. So much for poor generalship. It was a bad thing, I tell you.

From your husband, Edgar W. Clark.

CAMP SICKLES — May 11, 1863.

My Dear Wife: Your welcome letter found me well. I was very glad to hear from you and to get those pictures. I think they look natural. You make me think back to when you were a girl or before we were married. There is only one fault and that is nothing. I would very much like to see the original and be with it this morning but that is impossible. We are many hundred miles apart but I am confident that the time will come when we will meet again, although it may be a long while to wait. It is just nine months today since I left you and the time has passed quite fast part of the time and other times it has passed slow.

We had a very hard time in battle but William and I got through it without a scratch. We may not be so lucky again but I think we will pass through this rebellion safe and if I do I will not begrudge the time that I have spent in the service. I will now try to answer your letter. You say that you are well. I am very glad of it for nothing can be more desirable than good health. I know that you would write oftener if you could but as it is we have got to be content with it. You must not worry about me.

As soon as you hear that a battle has been fought, it takes a week to find out and you will hear from me by way of a letter.

Our division has received a good deal of praise for our gallantry and good conduct in battle. Our division was engaged the most where we were. It was nothing to see men killed or wounded. I saw one man who was blown into a dozen pieces and other men without arms or legs. One rebel was wounded and had a leg shot off close to the hip. We took him prisoner. He said he fought us at Fair Oaks last summer and was wounded and then fought us at Fredericksburg last winter but did not get hurt. This time he got his leg shot off and I guess he will not fight us anymore. There were a good many prisoners taken by us. Most of them are fighting under a delusion or what their officers tell them, and there is not a word of truth in what they say.

I am glad that you got that dollar that I sent to Lydia. I am glad that Mina goes to Sunday School. I hope she will be a good girl and learn all she can and mind her teachers and she will get some good books and papers. Tell her that her pa thinks of her every day and hopes to see her one of these days. Tell her I kissed her likeness a dozen times and only wish that it was reality. Tell her I say she must mind her ma. Kiss Carrie for me. No one can tell how well I would like to see her. I am glad to hear she is mischievous. I thought you would have weaned her long before this time but you thought best and I am perfectly satisfied. I am glad that you have the side fence built. I hope it is safe from cattle and hogs.

I think you had better pay the debts with as much as you can spare after getting the fence built. We will draw $52 more in the middle of July and then I will send you $30 or $40 more to pay for the fence. It will cost you from $12 to $15 to get the fence built.

I would like to hear all of the news from you and my folks every day. I hope I may live to see them all when the rebellion has ceased and peace and happiness is again restored to this destroyed country. Tell Mrs. Damon that war is a cruel thing but those who persist in open rebellion and ask no odds of the North nor nobody else must be put down if it takes every man in the North. I must stop writing and again bid you goodbye, hoping to see you someday when we will not have to again part. Keep a stiff upper lip and be a good girl and a true and faithful wife. Give my love to all.

From your husband, Edgar W. Clark.

CAMP SICKLES — May 15, 1863.

My Dear Affectionate Wife: This fine and beautiful morning I cannot find anything to busy myself with, only in writing a few lines to you about my health and prospects. I am well as usual although since our last battle I have taken quite a cold and am not as well as I was before the battle. However, I am able to do duty in the company, which is not very hard. I have been on duty this morning cleaning up in front of our tent, sweeping the streets. We have to be as particular every morning as a woman does about her house. Our orderly tells us who is to clean up and we have to keep our tents as nice as we can. We have to keep our shoes blacked or greased all the time. Our clothes have to be kept clean and nice. We have to put on our best dress uniform on parade every night. Our duty will be more now for we have to drill four hours every day but Saturday and Sunday, which is a good sign that we will not move very soon. We will move when the time comes.

This Army is very quiet now. There is nothing agoing on to amount to much. I hope we will not move very soon but if I thought it would do any good, I would not care. I want this rebellion to be put down and the quicker the better for I would like to be at home with you. I dreamed I was at home last night on a furlough. I dreamed I had a good time generally with you and friends. I wish I could realize such a thing. I would like it and I guess you would, too.

The woods begin to look very green and nice. How swiftly time passes by. It will not be a great while until fall and then winter. The regiment has not quite a year to stay yet. They will come home next spring. It will not be a great while if we only make good use of time. It will fly by and we will not know that we have been separated. You must keep a stiff upper lip and do the best you can.

Our company is in command by Jerome TenEyck, and a good officer he is and a brave and gallant soldier. I cannot speak too highly of his goodness as an officer and a gentleman. You must write as soon as you can. Kiss the babies for me. Give my love to all inquiring friends and save a double share for yourself.

No more from your devoted husband, Edgar W. Clark.

CAMP SICKLES — May 19, 1863.

My Dear Wife: I write to inform you that I am well and enjoying myself as well as I can under the circumstances. I have not received a letter from you yet this week. I hope to in a day or two. Everything is quiet here. We drill four hours a day except for Saturday and Sunday when we have general inspection on the Sabbath. It takes about as long as it does to attend a sermon in Lansing and the drums commence beating about the time the bells commence tolling for meeting.

I wish you could see the tents displayed by us soldiers. We get cedar boughs and make all sorts of things. We have a row of shade trees, cedar trees. They keep green a long time. I wish I could see you today as plain as I saw you in my dreams last night. I dream about you and the children almost every night.

I think the rebellion is on its last legs. I sent you a newspaper with the Battle of Chancellorsville on the day we were engaged. It may look bad to you but it is a very true picture.

We are having very fine and pleasant weather. The weather is warming and everything looks like summer. The woods are very green. My stories have about played out. You must write as often as you can.

No more from your devoted husband, Edgar W. Clark.

Historical context: Though Edgar thought the war was almost over, there was little evidence of it. Gen. U.S. Grant achieved the surrender of two armies in the West at Fort Donelson and Vicksburg, in the East but it would take almost two more years to achieve a surrender at Appomattox.

CAMP SICKLES — May 20, 1863.

My Dear Wife: This fine and beautiful morning finds me well. I take this opportunity of answering your letter that I received yesterday. It had been in camp for two days before I got it. We went on picket last Sunday morning and were gone for three days. We came into camp yesterday. We had to go 8 miles in front of the whole Army on picket. We had to go on division review and there were 20 regiments there. It was a sight like any Fourth of July you ever saw.

My health is better now than it has been since I have been in the Army. I am very glad to hear that you are well. I am glad that the fruit trees are doing well. I am sorry that one of the cherry trees died. I hope that you have a good nice bed of strawberries and it will do you some good, if not this summer then in the future time. I wish I could have some of the milk the cow gives. I have not had much milk since I have been here. On picket, a few of us put in some money and went to a farmhouse and bought a quart of milk to put in our coffee. We paid 25 cents for the quart.

Yes, Catherine, if I do not know how thankful you are that you have got kind friends. I can realize how thankful you ought to be. You are not more thankful than I am for if there is ever a need for friends, it is in such cases. I very highly appreciate their kindness and hope some day to repay them if possible. You may be sure that it will be something other than war that divides us. Yes, there is nothing so nearly attractive here in the Army as home.

We are so used to the war that we dread it. I suppose that we will be reviewed today by Gov. Blair. You cannot realize the slaughter that was done when we crossed the river *(at Chancellorsville)*. I have no doubt but that many of our men are now rotting on top of the ground. In 10 minutes, we were driven about 2 miles from where Mason died and none of us know what became of his body, where it is buried or not. Some of our wounded were not fetched from the field in eight or 10 days. That is the worst feature of war, the suffering from wounds on the battlefield. I must close this letter by saying take good care of yourself.

Edgar W. Clark.

Historical context: Michigan Gov. Austin Blair was known as the "Civil War Governor." So many Michigan men volunteered that some men joined regiments from other states, reported Ira Brown for the Bentley Historical Library, University of Michigan. There were 30 infantry regiments, 11 cavalry regiments and one regiment each of engineers, artillery and sharpshooters. *In a message to the Michigan Legislature in 1864, Blair wrote: "All*

the blood and carnage of this terrible war, all the heart-rending
casualties of battle and the sad bereavements occasioned by them,
have the same cause — slavery — the greatest, vilest criminal of
the world. It must perish." He supported a war loan of $1 million
and the Soldiers Relief Act, which required Michigan counties to
provide relief to families of soldiers. Edgar's wife Catherine bene-
fited from that relief. Blair also raised the 102nd U.S. Colored
Troops, which included two sons of Sojourner Truth. Michigan
raised over 90,000 soldiers, about 75 percent of the eligible men
ages 20 to 40. Michigan soldiers participated in over 800 bat-
tles, and the 4th Michigan Cavalry Regiment captured Jefferson
Davis in May of 1865. Blair supported the vote for women and
Blacks and opposed capital punishment. In fact, Michigan was
one of the first states to ban capital punishment. Only one execu-
tion has been carried out in Michigan since it gained statehood.
Michigan became the first English-speaking territory in the world
to ban capital punishment in 1847, with the exception of treason.

CAMP SICKLES — June 1, 1863.

My Dear Wife: You do not know how glad I am to hear from
you. I am glad you are agoing to have a good garden. I really wish
I could be there to help you take care of it. Yes, I hope before
another spring I will be with you. All we can do is hope and
wish. I know it must be very lonesome to you. It is the same
with me but I have to stand it. You say you have your garden all
planted. You must not work it too hard so as to make yourself
sick. You must hire it hoed. I wish I could buy some of your
butter. We have to pay 60 cents a pound for it here and 50 cents
for a dozen eggs. We do not buy much. If we did, we would not
save a cent.

You say that I read more lies than you do in the Republican.
I must say that I read the first number in the Journal and I fail

to discover which can tell the biggest lies. You asked a question that is very hard for me to answer, what I am fighting for. I think in the president's proclamation last September, he told them what they might depend upon and in his annual message in December he gave them another offer and they have discarded them all and I hope this war will continue until they will be glad to come back into the Union. I am for total annihilation of the whole territory of the Confederacy as they do not ask for any odds from the North. They say if they can get the North divided and bring about some doctrine that will divide the North, they will be sure to gain their independence, which they will never do. I am for sending Copperheads South and join their Army than bring on civil war in the North.

Gov. Blair made us a fine speech last Thursday. He said we had the finest camp he had seen in Virginia. He told us that he was going home and fill up the Michigan regiments to their full quota, which I hope he will. Give my love to all inquiring friends and save a share for yourself.

No more your husband, Edgar W. Clark.

Historical context: This is a rare letter that touched on politics. Edgar totally supported President Abraham Lincoln and the Emancipation Proclamation. Once Lincoln issued it, he turned the conflict into a war against slavery as well as a war to restore the Union. When Lincoln received peace feelers from the South, he always included the requirement that slavery be ended. The irony is that by seceding, slavery ended much sooner than under the official Republican stance of limiting it where it existed.

CAMP SICKLES — June 7, 1863.

My Dear Affectionate Wife: I hasten to answer your letter that I received tonight. I was very glad to hear of your continued good health. Mine continues to be good. I sat at *(a religious)* meeting today for the first time since we left the fortifications around Washington. It was a noble sermon. I have not put on a shirt that has been ironed since I left home. If I can get these woolen shirts washed, I will be glad. I have not worn a cotton shirt since I left home. We wear drawers with big heavy woolen pants. The sky blue color makes it warm for this weather. I will be glad when the war is over so I can come home and tend to my own affairs and I think it will come to an end by fall if not sooner. How long we will stay in this place, I cannot tell. We are under marching orders with three days of cooked rations in our haversacks. Our extra blankets and overcoats and the sick in the hospital have been sent to the rear. I was on guard again yesterday. I slept on the ground with only one blanket — half under and half over — with my cartridge box for a pillow and did not sleep very well but I think I will make it up tonight. I certainly would if I was at home in a good feather bed with you. We are watching the enemy's movements all the time. There are two balloons that look over the rebels all the time, so we are very well posted on their affairs. Hoping that we may soon meet again.

I remain your husband, Edgar W. Clark. Kiss the children for me.

Historical context: There were so many spies in this war and the armies were so large, it is amazing that either Army could move by surprise. Edgar refers to hot air balloons being used by the Union to watch Confederate movements. Yet Gen. Robert E. Lee was able to shift his Army north through the Shenandoah Valley and Union troops had to hustle to stay between the rebels and Washington. Lee intended to take the pressure off the rebels in

Virginia and resupply on Northern soil. Edgar noted that rebels had stripped shoes off the Union dead at Fredericksburg.

If Lee moved North, he could choose land favorable for defense and the Union would feel obligated to attack. That was the understanding of Gen. James Longstreet, who had seen what an army behind a hilly, fortified position at Fredericksburg could do to an attacking force. Edgar reported preparations to move from camp on June 7, but by June 13 the Union Army started a fast march north. Some of the infantry died from sunstroke and were left on the road. During the march, they crossed the Bull Run battlefields about 30 miles west of Washington, where skeletons remained on the ground.

The rebels spent about two weeks moving through Pennsylvania while panic spread. They nearly reached the Pennsylvania state capital of Harrisburg. Lee made a serious mistake by allowing J.E.B. Stuart to make a raid to the east around the Union forces, which separated Stuart from providing important reconnaissance for Lee's forces. Stuart had recently been embarrassed in a battle and apparently was trying to repeat a successful raid he conducted early in the war. In the process, however, he lost touch with Lee. This is one of Lee's continuing issues, giving his subordinate generals too much latitude. Grant, in contrast, generally wrote clear, curt orders.

The Union lines looked like a fishhook with the curved portion up top near the city of Gettysburg while the lower line was marked by the hills of Big Round Top and Little Round Top. Gettysburg had strategic value due to a series of roads meeting there.

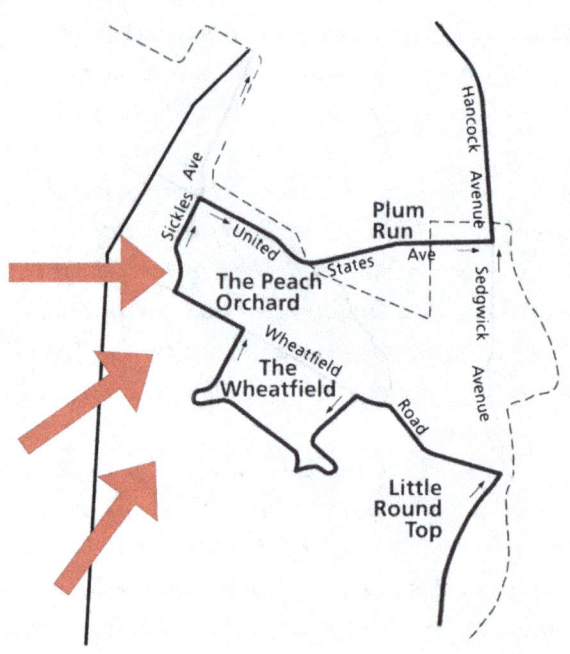

Gettysburg. Gen. Robert E. Lee thought the Peach Orchard would be unoccupied on the left of the Union lines. Instead, it was filled with Union forces, including Edgar Clark's 3rd Michigan Infantry Regiment. A furious battle ensued that forced the 3rd Michigan to retreat and give up its position. The Wheatfield, where the 5th Michigan was stationed, was called "a whirlpool of death." (Jonathan James).

The height of the Peach Orchard on the second day at Gettysburg beckoned to Union Gen. Daniel Sickles like a mistress. Sickles must have recalled Hazel Grove just a month earlier. Gen. Robert E. Lee had planned to capture the Peach Orchard and use it to smash the flank of the Union forces. Once Sickles occupied it, Lee's plans were interrupted. The Peach Orchard jutted out from the Union lines, exposed to rebel attacks from several directions. (Darryl Wheeler).

Chapter Nine

Out front at Gettysburg

Edgar marches from Northern Virginia to Pennsylvania as the Army of the Potomac chases the Confederate Army led by Gen. Robert E. Lee. Union soldiers drop from the heat. The Battle of Gettysburg ensues. The 3rd Michigan is in the front lines protecting artillery in the Peach Orchard. After the battle, Edgar provides water to the wounded, including rebels, then marches in pursuit of the rebels. Edgar is in good spirits after the victory.

NEAR BLACKBURN'S FORD, VA. — June 16, 1863.

My Dear Wife: I take this first opportunity to write you a few lines, not knowing when or where I can put this in the post office. I left Camp Sickles on June 7 and marched 10 miles and stopped for the night. The next day we marched to Bealeton Station on the Grand and Alexandria Railroad. We stopped there for two days and then marched to Manassas Junction. Now we are on picket about 5 miles away. I cannot tell you our destination. My health is good.

We had some hard marching the last few days. Yesterday was the worst. Our corps lost nearly 100 from sunstroke. They would be marching along and fall down dead. I stood it first-rate. I keep up with the company all day, when nearly one-half fell out from sore feet and sickness, but they have all come up this morning, mostly well but tired and sore.

I wish you could see us now. You would think we were the dirtiest set you ever saw. We have not had rain since the 6th of May. We marched through woods, fields, crops, roads and every way that can be thought of to keep out of the dust. We have nothing to hinder us, no fences nor rivers but what is easily forded. We get along first-rate but the sun is awful hot in the daytime.

I think our destination is the fortifications around Washington. How long we will stay there is impossible to say. I hope long enough to get washed up and rested a little. We are now waiting to get started on a day's march.

You must not feel worried about me. I will take care of myself as well as I can and you must do the same. All I have had for breakfast is some hard crackers and some sweetened water and all that we have had on the march is coffee and crackers and pork. The pork we do not have time to fry, so we boil it on the coals on a stick, whittled sharp. We have it pretty hard on a forced march but it is all for one's country. We have to put up with it for this rebellion has got to be put down, let the consequences be what they may. I must stop writing now till some future time. I will probably get a letter from you when we get our mail. We have not had our mail since the morning of the 12th.

Goodbye. Edgar.

Historical context: Col. Regis DeTrobriand wrote that there were so many Union soldiers collapsing in the heat that there weren't enough ambulances for them. During a forced march, soldiers often disposed of items to lessen their weight. Leander Stilwell in "The Story of a Common Soldier" wrote that Army knapsacks were "awkward, cumbersome" — the straps and buckles chafed the back and shoulders. Instead, soldiers would fold blankets, tying the two ends together. Inside, they would stuff an extra shirt and a few light articles.

NEAR EWEN SPRINGS, VA. — June 21, 1863.

My Dear Wife: I am permitted again to write you a few lines although we have not had any mail in nearly two weeks. When I wrote you last we were in Centerville. We are now about 10 miles from them toward Leesburg. We have been all packed up for three hours ready to start for someplace near Leesburg. We can hear heavy cannonading in that direction but probably will be too late to see any of the battle today.

It is now nearly 1 o'clock. My health is good as I could wish. We have had a very hard time marching lately. I think we will stop soon where we can get some mail. I have not much news this time. I am very anxious to hear from you. I will not finish this till tomorrow morning. We are having considerable rain, which makes it pleasant marching to what it was when the dust was 2 inches deep. This is the pleasantest part of Virginia that I ever was in but the land is very poor from too much war. I would like to live in this place first-rate. There is quite a village here, a schoolhouse, church and blacksmith shop and there was a considerable business done here before the war, I presume.

I wish I could see you on the 4th. You must do the best you can and be a good girl. Take good care of the children and when I come home we will have a good time generally. All is well, plenty to eat, good spirits full of fun and enjoying myself as well as I can and I hope you can say the same. I do not think we will have a battle in some time yet unless the rebels attack us on this side of the mountains, which they did to the 5th Corps yesterday and were driven back. We are in the 3rd Corps, so when you hear of that corps engaged you may think that we have a hand in it.

No more from your devoted husband, Edgar W. Clark.

CAMP NEAR MIDDLETON, MD. — June 28, 1863.

My Dear Wife: The regiment has not had any mail in three weeks. I have not had much time to write you; we march about 10 miles every day. We left Virginia on the 25th. We are within 10 or 15 miles from where the Battle of Antietam was fought last fall. We hear all sorts of rumors about the whereabouts of the rebels. I presume we will find them before long. Keep up good courage. I am confident of that so put your trust in our confidence to put down the rebellion and all will come out well.

Edgar W. Clark.

NEAR HONEYTOWN, MD. — June 29, 1863.

My Dear Wife: We are continuing on the march. We are now about 6 miles from the state line of Pennsylvania. We march every day from 15 to 20 miles.

Edgar W. Clark.

NEAR TANEYTOWN, MD. — June 30, 1863.

My Dear Wife: We left our camp on the 11th of June and marched until midnight and we have marched from 15 to 20 miles every day since. The people are a different sort of citizens, mostly all loyal and true to the Union's cause. The people turned out from every house to see the soldiers, the ladies waved their handkerchiefs, cheered us on and encouraged us anew. We are now nearly to the Pennsylvania line. The rebels are doing bad work upon Pennsylvania. I hope we will give them fits when we overtake them. I understand that our commander again has been changed.

Edgar W. Clark.

Historical context: Two days earlier, on June 28, President Abraham Lincoln replaced Gen. Joe Hooker with Gen. George Meade. The Battle of Gettysburg ensued, one of the great battles in history, from July 1 through July 3, 1863.

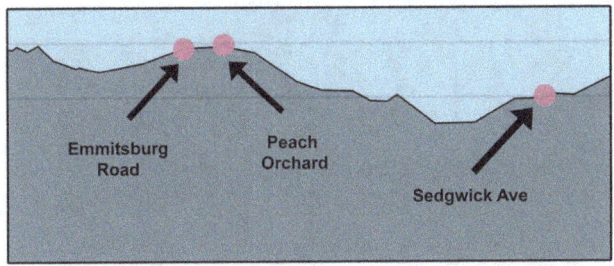

Gen. Daniel Sickles was located to the right at Sedgwick Avenue. But its low elevation led him to move forward to the higher Peach Orchard. (Jonathan James).

GETTYSBURG — July 6, 1863.

My Dear Wife: Through the mercies of a kind providence I am still spared in life, though we have been through tough times since the first of the month. We arrived on the battle-ground on the second of the month and we fought them very hard *(at the Peach Orchard)*. We lost a good many men killed and wounded. Among the wounded is Sgt. Stephens. A shell tore off his knapsack and wounded him so bad that he left the field. Sgt. Bissell from Wacousta was wounded in the hips. Our colonel was wounded. Yesterday we still were supporting the same battery that we did on the 3rd. The rebels made a charge on one of our batteries with 11,000 men who were nearly all captured, killed or wounded *(Pickett's Charge)*.

I counted more than 100 dead and wounded close to me. We had 12 large pieces of cannon firing on them. I went over the battleground the morning of the 4th and was two hours giving the wounded water to drink. I had a very long and interesting talk with one of the eight Virginians we captured. We captured four flags and about 2,000 prisoners. Our loss was not so large as theirs. I found out it makes a good deal of difference if we attack them or they attack us. I got some rebel trophies that I will send to you.

Edgar W. Clark.

Historical context: Edgar's letter was brief and left a huge gap. What was his unit doing? Actually, he was at the point of the most controversial tactic of the battle on the second day. On the first day of the battle on July 1, 1863, when Edgar was not involved, Lee's forces had the manpower and surprise advantage but were slowed by Union Gen. John Buford's troops. Confederates swept through the city of Gettysburg but never gained control of Cemetery Hill or Culp's Hill on the northern end of the fishhook battle line. On the first day, Lee gave Gen. Jubal Early ambivalent orders to take Cemetery Hill "if practicable." Early didn't push forward. Had he won that key location on the Northern flank of the Union lines, Lee could have placed artillery there and won the battle and perhaps the war. It is ridiculous that after the war Early blamed Longstreet for the defeat.

Before dawn on the second day, July 2, Lee sent a scout to survey the Union lines and figured the Union was vulnerable on its left. Lee had a three-pronged plan of attack on the second day at Gettysburg that repeated his tactics at Chancellorsville. He would move infantry through woods that hid his troops and then smash the Union left on its flank. This oblique attack was a classic military maneuver, designed to smash defenders at their flank. Lee wanted to (1) gain the high ground at the Peach Orchard, which would allow him to place artillery there (2) in order to launch an attack on Cemetery Ridge and finally (3) gain the high ground of Cemetery Hill. Once the Army of the Potomac was crushed, Confederates could threaten Washington, D.C. and Philadelphia and force the Union to sue for peace. Gettysburg is only 81 miles from Washington, D.C. and 141 miles from Philadelphia.

Edgar's 3rd Michigan Infantry troops were placed as skirmishers in the Peach Orchard next to the 3rd Maine. They were guarding artillery and protecting gaps in the Union lines. These two regiments, along with the 141st Pennsylvania and 2nd New Hampshire, were formed on the infamous Sickles salient. Many references omit the fact that they were protecting Union artillery in a furious showdown with Confederate artillery a short distance away.

Edgar's fate was directly connected to the leadership of Gen. Daniel Sickles. The relationship between Sickles and his superior, Gen. George Meade, has provided fodder for historians for generations, in part because the life of Sickles was so melodramatic. It is amazing that no movie has been made of the man.

Of all the books written about Sickles, the most complete and balanced I have read was written by James Hessler: "Sickles at Gettysburg: The Controversial Civil War General Who Committed Murder, Abandoned Little Round Top and Declared Himself the Hero of Gettysburg." Hessler masterfully sorted out the confused fighting on the second day. And he knew the controversial background of Sickles, which obscured some of his military maneuvers at Gettysburg.

The high ground is less apparent in books, maps and movies. The side that held the high ground, as well as having interior lines, had a huge advantage in battle. It's obvious in person when viewing the mile-long slope that Confederates had to climb during Pickett's Charge. It's less obvious when it comes to the Peach Orchard, the key to the second day's battle, though there is a significant rise from the Union lines on Cemetery Ridge to the orchard. Hessler, a Gettysburg resident for over 20 years and an official tour guide as well as an author, understands this.

As Hessler said in an interview with the author, Lee surely knew about the importance of holding high ground at Gettysburg. He had been defeated in the mountains of West Virginia and had seen the advantage of holding the high ground at Fredericksburg. During his Malvern Hill assault during the Seven Days' battles in 1862, Lee attacked the retreating Union troops. But attacking up that hill turned into a slaughter for the Confederates. Author Webb Garrison quotes Union Gen. Daniel Hill: "It was not war, it was murder." Garrison wrote that Lee sent couriers to cancel the attack at Malvern Hill, but some messages never got through. At Gettysburg, Lee's forces were spread out along a 6-mile exterior line, which made communications difficult, which was another feature of the Confederate defeat — disjointed attacks. Gen. James Longstreet later complained that he did not have enough support on the second day while Union Gen. George Meade was able to pull reinforcements from several directions to stop Longstreet's assaults.

Meanwhile, on Cemetery Ridge, the 3rd Corps was assigned to no ridge at all but was in a low, rocky, swampy area that left Sickles blind. Sickles was anxious to escape from his vulnerable low position. In front was a higher plateau with a peach orchard that could have reminded Sickles of Hazel Grove at Chancellorsville just two months earlier. If the Confederates were able to place artillery there, they could have pummeled Union forces in several directions.

The high ground beckoned to Sickles "like an inviting mistress," wrote the four authors of "Don't Give an Inch: The Second Day at Gettysburg." The Sickles move forward disrupted both Union and Confederate plans. And so began the controversy.

Meade had a poor relationship with Sickles, who was a fan of the disgraced Gen. Joe Hooker. Meade expected the Confederates on the second day to attack the Union right flank, going after Culp's Hill or Cemetery Hill, following up their first day's gains. So he placed Sickles at the opposite end of the Union line and told Sickles to extend his line to Little Round Top "if practicable." Those two words, "if practicable," were used to justify lack of action by Confederates on the first day and bold or reckless action by Sickles on the second day. Sickles figured he had the flexibility to move forward, but this left Little Round Top and Big Round Top exposed. In addition, Meade pulled cavalry away, leaving Sickles blind, so Sickles sent sharpshooters into the woods in front of the Peach Orchard and discovered the Confederate advance.

Sickles and Lee, it turns out, were on the same wavelength. Sickles and Meade were not, though Meade acted quickly to rush reinforcements to the gaps in the Union line caused by Sickles.

Sickles could have used the Hazel Grove experience at Chancellorsville as a reason to move forward into a salient at Gettysburg, though Hessler wrote that Sickles after the war never publicly used that as an excuse. But Sickles also could have remembered Stonewall Jackson's flank attack through the woods at Chancellorsville that surprised the Union. After all, it had been only two months earlier. In fact, when Confederates emerged from the woods in front of the Peach Orchard, they were surprised to find Union troops and artillery there. The advantage of surprise had been flipped.

Sickles had moved units into an area marked by the Peach Orchard with the Wheatfield behind it. That placed 3rd Corps forces
out front of the main Union lines in the shape of a "salient," an
upside-down V, which meant that forces could be attacked on two
sides, which is generally frowned upon as reckless. However, since
the salient at the Peach Orchard was elevated, it gave the Union
defense a good view of the Confederate advance. And it could also
be used as a kind of "breakwater," dulling the Confederate attack
before it reached the Union lines.

A furious artillery duel ensued, described by one Confederate in "Never Give an Inch" as the most rapid firing he had
ever witnessed: "The earth literally vibrated under the continuous
roar." About 50 artillery pieces on each side were engaged in close
combat, some only a few hundred yards away, amazingly close for
artillery fire. Imagine a duel with shotguns. Confederate artillery
commander Porter Alexander called this the heaviest artillery
duel of the war. An attack by South Carolinians "struggled"
versus the 3rd Michigan, according to James Hessler and Brent
Isenberg in their book "Gettysburg's Peach Orchard: Longstreet,
Sickles and the Bloody Fight for the Commanding Ground Along
Emmitsburg Road."

The sound of the battle on the second day was described by
Francis Adams Donaldson of the 118th Pennsylvania Infantry,
which was assigned nearby in the bloody Wheatfield: "The deafening sounds of the combatants, the crash of artillery, the trem-
bling ground beneath us, the silent and stricken countenances of
the men, the curtain of smoke overall and its peculiar smell, made
up a picture never to be forgotten by any who witnessed it."

When the Confederate attack began, led by Longstreet, Sickles
was with Meade. When Meade learned that Sickles had moved
forward, it was too late to order the 3rd Corps back, so Meade
ordered the 5th Corps led by Gen. George Sykes to move up from

reserve to fill the gaps in the lines while Sickles rushed to lead his men. Meade also used the 2nd Corps, led by Gen. Winfield Scott Hancock, to push back the rebel assault.

De Trobriand, who led the 3rd and 5th Michigan Infantry Regiments, among others, wrote that the Union forces at the Peach Orchard and Wheatfield could have been overwhelmed if the rebels had charged with bayonets. Instead, Union troops fought with desperate obstinacy.

Amid all the confusion of battle, there were many close calls. De Trobriand described a soldier who thought he had been struck in the neck with a bullet, only to find that it had bounded off his leather collar and choked him for a moment. Another soldier had his revolver struck but was uninjured.

Assigning blame is controversial, but clearly, there was a lack of communication between Meade, newly commanding the Army of the Potomac, and the headstrong Sickles. There is evidence that Meade gave Sickles clear verbal orders, including a map, to remain on Cemetery Ridge and extend his lines to Little Round Top. But in defense of Sickles, he came to the headquarters at 11 a.m., seeking clarity.

Would the battle have gone better if Sickles had not moved forward and instead extended his line to the Round Tops? Meade still would have had to move troops to combat the rebel assault. We do know that Meade took operational control of the battlefield, moving troops in order to reinforce the lines. Meade was well suited for this, having been a corps commander until just a few days before Gettysburg, when President Lincoln appointed him to replace Joe Hooker.

At any rate, late afternoon on the second day at Gettysburg, there were three hours of desperate fighting at the boulder-filled Devil's Den, the Peach Orchard, the Wheatfield and Little Round Top. Only nightfall ended the carnage on the second day.

The 5th Michigan in the Wheatfield suffered terrible casualties, about half its manpower. In "Gettysburg's Bloody Wheatfield," Jay Jorgensen wrote that "these men fought under confusing, deadly circumstances. Often, one regiment's activities were unknown to an adjoining regiment, as the terrain, smoke and noise led to rapidly deteriorating combat conditions."

By the end of the second day, though the Confederates occupied Devil's Den and the Peach Orchard, they never gained control of the 26-acre Wheatfield, which became a no-man's land after being "a whirlpool of death," chaos in all directions.

When ordered to fall back from the Peach Orchard, the 3rd Michigan helped to return portions of two artillery batteries to the Union lines so that the rebels could not seize them. Animated battle maps showed the unit rapidly disappearing to the rear of the Union lines.

Ralph Siegel, licensed battlefield guide at Gettysburg, said in a podcast that the Battle of the Peach Orchard was "more important than Pickett's Charge. It's a much larger attack, with more troops involved, it's a longer fight, it's a lengthier battle line, it's the fight on July 2 when Robert E. Lee lost the Civil War." In fact, the second day's battle was "the largest and costliest of the three days," reported the American Battlefield Trust.

Jeffry Wert, biographer of Gen. James Longstreet, also contended that the second day at Gettysburg was pivotal. "The Army of Northern Virginia nearly achieved victory," he wrote. "That it did not can be attributed to internal problems and human failings, and to the performance of the Army of the Potomac." Longstreet praised his troops, which at times reached Union lines on Cemetery Ridge, but complained that he did not receive enough support to follow up their courageous attacks.

Along with the destruction of much of his corps, Sickles was wounded and had a leg amputated. That was it for Sickles in the war. He spent the rest of his life promoting the Gettysburg National Cemetery site, justifying his actions and criticizing Meade. After the battle, the riddled 3rd Corps of Sickles was merged into the 2nd Corps of Gen. Winfield Scott Hancock.

To this day, Sickles' actions are controversial. Glenn Tucker, author of "High Tide at Gettysburg: The Campaign in Pennsylvania," quoted Col. John Batchelder, the official historian of Gettysburg. In a survey of 56 generals, they were evenly divided on the wisdom of Sickles' advance.

Edgecumb Pinchon wrote in his flattering book on Sickles ("Dan Sickles: Hero of Gettysburg and 'Yankee King of Spain'"), that by moving troops forward and forcing a battle in front of Cemetery Ridge, "The Confederate Army had spent its strength and gained nothing." On the other hand, author Richard Sauers concluded in his book, "A Caspian Sea of Ink: The Meade-Sickles Controversy" that he became "biased" in favor of Meade. It wasn't until 3 p.m. that Meade came to Sickles' camp to survey the ground, too late to make changes in the lines.

The contradictions of the Sickles-Meade controversy are illustrated by comments made by Harry Pfanz in his book "Gettysburg: The Second Day." At one point, Pfanz wrote that "General Sickles increased the odds of Confederate success when he advanced his Third Corps from its important and relatively secure position on Cemetery Ridge." Then shortly later, he wrote: "It was only when Longstreet and others reached the attack area that the Confederates realized that Lee's orders were impractical and had to be changed."

Well, the orders were only impractical because Sickles had moved forward and interrupted Lee's plans. Wert wrote that after furious fighting, it seemed to Longstreet that continued attacks were futile. He quoted one Confederate as saying: "Great God! Have we got the whole universe to whip?" Nevertheless, Union casualties were severe on the second day. Pfanz reports that Gen. David Birney was distraught, saying his horse had been killed and wishing he had the same fate.

The fact remains that the Confederates did not win the strategic ground of Cemetery Ridge on the second day's battle at Gettysburg, despite communication breakdowns between Sickles and Meade. Such is the impact of holding high ground with interior lines.

On the third day, Lee didn't decide to follow up on his right flank after gaining control of the Peach Orchard. So it wasn't crucial after all, as Meade believed. But Lee was confident enough to make the catastrophic decision to charge uphill on open ground (Pickett's Charge) in the center of the line, a move that Meade predicted.

That returns us to the fundamental military tactics that were most effective during the Civil War: Commanding high ground or crouching behind heavy entrenchments gave the defense a huge advantage, thanks to rifled muskets and artillery. Having interior lines, inside a semi-circle, allowed the defense to communicate more easily and move reinforcements quickly. At Gettysburg, Lee chose to attack on longer exterior lines of about 6 miles vs. about 3 1/2 miles for the Union. As Union General Henry Halleck wrote to President Lincoln: "To operate on exterior lines against an enemy occupying a central position will fail, as it always has failed in 99 of 100 cases. It is condemned by every military authority I have ever read." According to Confederate Gen. Porter Alexander, who commanded artillery at Gettysburg, Lee should have remained on Seminary Ridge and dared the Union to attack. Similarly, Longstreet proposed a flanking move to the south, which would have allowed the Confederates to choose better terrain for defensive tactics, a move that Meade feared Lee would take. Lee refused that proposal as too difficult, in part because he did not have the use of J.E.B. Stuart's cavalry, but that seems too pat since Lee still had other cavalry and scouts.

An impressive analysis of Gettysburg came from Alexander, who commanded rebel artillery and wrote in his memoirs: "The official reports are a painful record of insufficient attempts at execution ... Between the lines, the apparent absence of supervision excites constant wonder." Alexander described the Confederate position as "an utter absurdity. ... It was simply preposterous to hope to win a battle when so strung out and separated — cooperation between the three corps was impossible except by a miracle. And comparatively little pains were exercised to bring it about either. ... On no other battlefield in the East during the war did the Army of the Potomac defend a position of such natural advantage and with interior lines for troop movement." Similarly, John Bell Hood wrote in an 1875 letter to James Longstreet that the Union position was "impregnable ... they could easily repel our attack by merely throwing and rolling stones down the mountainside as we approached."

Alexander wrote that the key to the Confederate loss was failing to take Cemetery Hill on the Northern curved end of the fishhook of the battle line, which would have put rebel artillery in position to shell the entire Union line and probably force a retreat. That implicates Jubal Early on the first day for failing to follow up advances. Early spent postwar days accusing Longstreet of the defeat.

The terrible irony of the Battle of Gettysburg is that on this rare occasion, Lee was not outnumbered 2-to-1 or more. There was near-parity: about 75,000 Confederates vs. 90,000 Union troops, and the Confederates had the initiative, new supplies and could have dictated a battle on favorable ground. Lee had attacked the flanks on the first two days. By allowing the Union to maintain the defensive advantages of high ground and interior lines, Lee sent his soldiers to be slaughtered on the third day much like the Union soldiers were at Fredericksburg.

Lee's bad decisions at Gettysburg were part of a pattern and were foreshadowed by his military failures in West Virginia early in the war. As described by Edward Bonekemper III in "How Robert E. Lee Lost the Civil War," Lee tended to give vague instructions, use overly complicated plans that often led to poorly coordinated attacks and sometimes failed to supervise execution on the battlefield. Everything worked at Chancellorsville, thanks in large part to the hesitant generalship of Union Gen. Joseph Hooker. Had Hooker been in charge at Gettysburg, perhaps Lee would have won. Give President Lincoln the credit for replacing Hooker with a Pennsylvania native (Gen. George Meade) just in time. Also, after Lee lost Stonewall Jackson at Chancellorsville, he failed to take firmer control of his subordinates at Gettysburg.

Following Gettysburg, the Confederates no longer had the manpower to invade the North, thus the battle is justifiably called the "high water mark for the rebellion." Respected historian Gary Gallagher of the University of Virginia takes issue with the conventional wisdom that Gettysburg was a "turning point," noting that people at the time didn't think so. How could they? They couldn't know how the war would end. The outcome of the war was not inevitable. The war still had nearly two years to go.

Historian Allen Guelzo of Gettysburg College speculated about what would have happened if the Confederates had won at Gettysburg. It would have empowered antiwar forces in the North. After all, there were draft riots in New York City 10 days after the battle. What if Lee and his army were rampaging through the North at that time? In a 2014 speech at UCLA, Guelzo contended that Gettysburg was decisive enough to restore the morale in the Union, to keep at bay opponents of emancipation and indicated that the South could never again take the initiative.

The North needed a big victory. President Lincoln's Emancipation Proclamation was unpopular with a segment of Northerners who weren't fighting to end slavery. A draft was causing dissension and widespread riots. Britain and France were trying to decide if the Confederacy had earned the right to be considered a nation. Gettysburg and Vicksburg provided two big victories. U.S. Grant captured an entire Confederate Army at Vicksburg. If only Meade had done the same by pinning Lee against the flooding Potomac River immediately after the battle, perhaps he could have won a siege.

For Pickett's Charge on the third day, Edgar's riddled 3rd Corps was placed in reserve. According to official statistics of the Michigan Monuments Commission in 1889, the 3rd Michigan Infantry avoided the worst of the Gettysburg action with 45 casualties out of 286 soldiers. Next to the Peach Orchard, the Wheatfield was the scene of 165 casualties for the 4th Michigan and 109 casualties for the 5th Michigan. The casualty rate for the 3rd Michigan of 18.9 percent was less than the 50.5 percent rate for the 5th Michigan. But the greatest Michigan losses occurred on the first day in Reynolds Grove with 363 casualties of 496 men of the 24th Michigan Infantry. Their sacrifices helped to prevent the Confederates from gaining a foothold on the high ground of Cemetery Hill and Culp's Hill. The second day's battle produced the most Union casualties.

According to Karlton Smith, a park ranger and historian, the best estimate of Union casualties at Gettysburg is as follows: 8,955 on July 1; 9,161 on July 2; and 4,160 on July 3.

Michigan provided 3,894 men at Gettysburg and 1,111 (28 percent) were casualties — dead, wounded or missing. There are 10 monuments to Michigan units there. At the Peach Orchard, there is a 12-foot granite monument to the 3rd Michigan Infantry Regiment. It shows a pair of soldiers skirmishing, which was the unit's job on the second day of the battle. It was dedicated on June 12, 1889.

Besides the brutality of war and the looting of dead and wounded on the battlefield, there was kindness, as well. Edgar spent hours giving water to the wounded on both sides. Pfanz described a scene in which a Georgia soldier dragged a wounded Pennsylvanian to shelter on the Wheatfield. The Pennsylvanian lost a leg but survived and married his nurse. After the war, that man, Lt. James Jackson Purman, became a Washington attorney and official in the Grand Army of the Republic. His Confederate Samaritan, Lt. Thomas Oliver, became mayor of Atlanta.

Edgar's experience at Gettysburg is forever tied to the decisions of his Corps commander, Gen. Daniel Sickles. Let's put the Sickles controversy in context.

In favor of Sickles

Due to his experience at Hazel Grove at Chancellorsville, Sickles knew that Lee was likely to try a flanking movement, screened by trees, then head for the high ground of the Peach Orchard to pepper the Union troops with artillery. Hessler wrote: "For all of Dan Sickles' many faults, he was correct on one key point: the primary Confederate attack would occur on his front."

Sickles had to be feeling abandoned and thus empowered to act. First, Meade's son was used as an errand boy, and Meade removed Buford's cavalry from Sickles' troops. On his own, Sickles sent sharpshooters into the woods and discovered evidence of a Confederate movement toward the Peach Orchard.

Though Sickles was overextended, so was Confederate Gen. James Longstreet, who never had enough troops to follow up advances. And when the Confederates were done seizing control of the Peach Orchard and Devil's Den, the Union still held the high ground of Cemetery Ridge. In addition, while Sickles' 3rd Corps was engaged, Meade had time to rally reinforcements to fill gaps in the Union line and on Little Round Top. Longstreet, in a 1902 letter to Sickles, wrote: "I believe that it is now conceded that the advanced position at the Peach Orchard, taken by your corps and under your orders, saved that battlefield for the Union cause."

In opposition to Sickles

Sickles was the only Union commander who had trouble understanding Meade's orders at Gettysburg. Though he didn't have enough troops to man the entire line on Cemetery Ridge, his salient effectively doubled the line that the 3rd Corps had to defend.

Sickles left Little Round Top undefended. He should have put at least some troops there. The heroism of the 20th Maine should not have been required to repel Confederate assaults.

Sickles sacrificed the 3rd Corps, losing about half its strength to death, injuries and missing. Would the result have been better for the 3rd Corps if Sickles had remained in that low, swampy area to be pummeled by Confederate artillery from the Peach Orchard? The rebels won control of Devil's Den, so there is reason to believe they could have gained control of that low area, too.

Conclusions

The Sickles salient worked. It acted like a breakwater. Unlike Chancellorsville, the Confederates did not have the advantage of surprise because Sickles took the initiative.

Troy Harman, author of "Lee's Real Plan at Gettysburg," summarizes it well: "Lee's real plan for Gettysburg was defeated so effectively that its particulars were never completely revealed. If, on the other hand, Longstreet had been able to drive in the Union left obliquely toward Cemetery Hill on July 2, no questions would have arisen about Lee's intent and focus. As had occurred at

Chancellorsville, his two wings would have converged, Cemetery Hill would have been taken, and that would have settled the issue."

Credit for filling in the gaps in the Union line must go to Meade and other subordinates, who acted rapidly. The Union took advantage of holding the high ground with interior lines. Also, the importance of Little Round Top was exaggerated. If the Confederates had taken it, only a few artillery pieces could be placed on the steep, rocky ground.

There were communication breakdowns between Sickles and Meade. Sickles was a fan of Joe Hooker, who Meade had replaced. Hessler makes the good point that, given the tensions between Meade and Sickles, Meade had the obligation to ensure Sickles understood him, ideally by putting his orders in writing. It was poor form for Meade to send his son to Sickles, twice. But the communication breakdown wasn't for lack of effort by Sickles. His aide went to Meade five times.

Meade led well. He correctly predicted that Lee would attack the Union center on the third day (Pickett's Charge) as well as predicting that gaining the Peach Orchard would do little good for Lee. In fact, having gained control of the Peach Orchard, Lee decided to move his third-day assault to the enter of the Union Line. Meade had taken over command of the Army of the Potomac just a few days before Gettysburg. He was awakened on June 28 and told he was in command of the Army of the Potomac, a difficult job if ever there was one. But as a Pennsylvanian, he had a home-ground connection to the battle. As a previous corps commander, he was well prepared to be engaged during the battle, taking an active role in moving reinforcements. Lee, in contrast, was not as engaged near the front lines as he was in other battles.

In recent years, the importance of the second day's battles at the Peach Orchard and Wheatfield have become more appreciated.

Laymen visiting Gettysburg can more easily understand Pickett's Charge when viewing the mile-long slope that the rebel attackers had to cross in contrast to the deceptively innocent appearance today of the Peach Orchard and the Wheatfield.

Give Sickles credit for predicting the Confederate attack on the second day. Give Meade credit for moving his troops to compensate for the Sickles advance.

Historical context: HistoryNet.com reports that one-third of the forces at Gettysburg became casualties (killed, wounded or missing). Lee could not afford to lose so many soldiers. In his first seven months of command, Lee's army inflicted 50,000 casualties on the Union but lost 40,000 Confederates, Bonekemper writes. Given the Union's manpower advantage, those rebel losses could not be sustained.

Statistics, however, cannot describe the terrible carnage of this war. Frank Haskell, an aide to the Union general of the Iron Brigade and a lawyer in civilian life, wrote a poetic account of the Gettysburg battlefield after the conflict. He described "swords, scabbards and belts, some bent and cut by the shot or shell; broken wheels; exploded caissons and limber-boxes, and dismantled guns and all these are sprinkled with blood; horses, some dead, a mangled heap of carnage, some alive, with a leg shot clear off or other frightful wounds, appealing to you with almost more than brute gas as you pass; and last but not least numerous, many thousands of men — the men of South Carolina were quiet by the side of those of Massachusetts, some composed, with upturned faces, sleeping the last sleep, some mutilated and frightful, some wretched, fallen, bathed in blood, survivors still and unwilling witnesses of the rage of Gettysburg. And yet with all this before them, as darkness came on, and the dispositions were made and the outposts thrown out for the night, the Army of the Potomac was quite mad with joy."

On July 4, the Gettysburg battlefield was filled with dead and wounded men and horses. DeTrobriand described a young sergeant resting on his back, natural, even graceful, a stone for a pillow, one knee slightly raised, hands crossed on his breast, a smile on his lip, a New Testament open at his stiffened fingers. He had sought this spot to die. A wounded soldier pointed out the dead near him: "This one lived only till sundown. That one lasted until about midnight. There is one who was still groaning but an hour ago." A young man from Florida said he had tried to escape service in order to care for his aged parents but Confederate agents forced him to join. His left heel was torn off and his right hand was shattered by canister shot. One of DeTrobriand's aides gave him a horse in order to reach a medical facility quickly.

Pfanz describes a scene following the second day's battle. One of the Confederates on the battlefield sang for the wounded, closing with the hymn, "When This Cruel War is Over." Applause sounded from both lines. This was a popular song. Lyrics were adjusted to fit Northern and Southern sensibilities. The same song had a different title in the North, which quoted the song's lyrics, "Weeping, Sad and Lonely." (See the podcast, "Civil War Survivor," for an excellent version of this Civil War-era song as well as other Civil War-era songs).

Gettysburg. The memorial for the 3rd Michigan Infantry Regiment is appropriately located in the Peach Orchard. The inscription reads: "Mustered in Sept. 3, 1861. Engaged in 26 battles including all the important actions on the Peninsula, Fredericksburg, Chancellorsville, Gettysburg, Wilderness, Spotsylvaia, Cold Harbor, Petersburg, Appomattox." Edgar W. Clark survived battles from Fredericksburg to Petersburg. (Darryl Wheeler).

Chapter Ten

Edgar protects New York draft

Edgar follows the Confederates retreating from Gettysburg. He goes to New York after the draft riots. Brother William is injured in camp.

CAMP NEAR MIDDLETOWN, PA. — July 8, 1863.

My Dear Wife: We marched from Pennsylvania back into Maryland. I think we will have another fight in a day or two. I want to whip Lee and his forces so that they will never do any more harm in this rebellion. We gave him a good sound whipping at Gettysburg. I want to give him one more in this state and I think our summer campaign will be ended. We marched yesterday in a very heavy rain and the mud was very deep. I saw quite a sight last night. I saw a man hanged. If I had stayed 30 minutes I would have seen two more hanged. They were found as spies. This is a very beautiful country of land. The farmers are harvesting their wheat.

Edgar W. Clark.

NEAR ANTIETAM CREEK — July 11, 1863.

My Dear Wife: We have had a long and tiresome march since we started from our camp just one month ago today. Just how long the march will continue, I cannot say. For the last 16 days we have been on the go every day. If the rebels make a stand on this side of the Potomac, we will have an awful battle, bigger than the one we have had the other day and the Lord knows that was big enough. You could say so if you had seen the dead and wounded that I have seen. I think that I saw over 1,000 dead on less than 5 acres of ground. There was not a rod square *(5.5 yards square)* without one or two on it.

I would like to see Carrie with her shoes and dress on. I know she will look nice. I think I will one of these days. I do not think I shall be killed but I may get wounded. If I do, I will come home as soon as I can. I hope you have a good time at the camp meeting on the 4th. I know I spent the 4th looking at the dead and giving water to the wounded on the battlefield. I got more than a thousand thanks from the rebels as well as the Union soldiers.

Edgar W. Clark.

Notes: Edgar's letters indicated little action among his regiment following Gettysburg. Though Edgar was consistently wrong about the Union winning the war quickly, he was prophetic about his own fate. Soldiers were indeed more likely to survive their wounds than die on the battlefield.

EIGHT MILES FROM HARPER'S FERRY — July 18, 1863.

My Dear Wife: The war may close before fall if we do our duty on the traitors and Copperheads who do not wish to keep the Constitution as it is preserved and won't keep still and let the president do as he has a mind to with affairs. I was in hope we would not have to go into the state again. You must not worry if you do not hear from me as often as you would like. We are a good way from a post office and the mail is very irregular.

Edgar W. Clark.

Historical context: There has been much debate about Gen. George Meade's failure to force a battle with Gen. Robert E. Lee before Lee escaped across the Potomac River after Gettysburg. As President Lincoln said, "They will be ready to fight a magnificent battle when there is no enemy left to fight."

I benefited from two recent books that place this controversy in context: "One Continuous Fight: The Retreat from Gettysburg and the Pursuit of Lee's Army of Northern Virginia, July 4-14, 1863" and "Lee is Trapped and Must be Taken: Eleven Fateful Days After Gettysburg, July 4-14, 1863." (See the Bibliography.) Both armies were exhausted by hard marching and tough battles at Gettysburg. One estimate is that Union forces marched 266 miles in two weeks. Edgar reported being on the march for two months, marching 10 to 15 miles per day at one point. Judging from the addresses of his letters, Edgar started marching on June 7 at Blackburn's Ford, Va., then to Gettysburg and ending at Alexandria, Va. on Aug. 16 — about 214 miles in stifling heat. Edgar's 2nd Corps was devastated by the second day's combat at Gettysburg and lost its commander, Gen. Dan Sickles, to an amputated leg.

Meade was deterred by night and rain on July 3 and July 4. Lee immediately built entrenchments and dared the Union to attack. Also, Lee's escape was protected by mountain passes. At the Potomac River, Meade was afraid of a frontal attack on a wounded Confederate force at Williamsport, especially once defensive lines were established there. Author Kent Masterson

Brown, author of the book "Retreat from Gettysburg," wrote that Meade's forces were not as well supplied as Lee's were and were less able to pursue immediately. Union horses, for instance, had not eaten in three days. About 12,000 horses died from sheer exhaustion and lack of food, reported Brown. Though much has been written about the Confederate need for shoes, Union Gen. Oliver Howard wrote that his corps needed shoes. After marching about 200 miles, shoes would wear out. Meade feared a Pickett's Charge in reverse if Lee were allowed to build fortifications and establish a good defensive position. I think Meade was correct in not waging a frontal assault at Lee's entrenchments in Williamsport. It was a great defensive position that could not be flanked. Author and historian Eric Wittenberg said a federal attack at Williamsport would have been as awful as Fredericksburg. Lee was a master at building entrenchments. There was some combat after Gettysburg among the cavalry, but these were skirmishes, not the destruction of Lee's army, which is what President Abraham Lincoln wanted. For his retreat, Lee had the benefit of Gen. J.E.B. Stuart's cavalry, which he mostly lacked at Gettysburg.

Brigadier Gen. Henry Hunt, who was not involved in Meade's councils of war, told a congressional committee that the terrain at Williamsport, with its ridges and rolling ground, was perfect for a Confederate defense. But a Union attack from the right could have minimized that difficulty. In addition, posting cavalry and some infantry on the other side of the Potomac could have prevented a Confederate crossing or at least forced them to abandon their extensive wagon trains of supplies.

Meade was in bad shape. Over 10 days, he did not have time to change his clothes or get a night's rest. In addition, an argument can be made that Union forces were more exhausted in their chase North while the Confederates had been collecting provisions in Pennsylvania.

Meade had no regular meals and was in a constant state of anxiety. He had only taken charge of the 90,000 members of the Army of the Potomac three days before the Battle of Gettysburg. And his subordinates were timid. He lost three aggressive corps commanders at Gettysburg: Gen. John Reynolds was killed and Winfield Scott Hancock and Sickles were injured. When Meade asked his remaining corps commanders on two occasions (July 4 and July 12) for their opinions, most voted against attacking Lee. In his memoirs, Col. Regis DeTrobriand wrote that Meade was faced with jealousy by his former colleagues. The five votes opposing an assault came from generals with the longest service. As Troy Hannan has written, Meade was fifth in line for taking over the Army of the Potomac. In order, Darius Crouch left to oversee emergency preparations in Pennsylvania; Henry Slocum, John Sedgwick and John Reynolds didn't want the job; so Meade was ordered to take it. In addition, DeTrobriand wrote that Meade was "modest, reserved" and had neither expected nor sought this command.

Meade was aware of the dismay in Washington that he had not destroyed Lee's army and offered his resignation. It was not accepted. Lincoln wrote a letter to Meade expressing his dismay but didn't send it.

Arguing against Meade is that Lee was trapped on the North side of the Potomac River where levels were swollen high by rain, making the river impossible to ford. Meade had more soldiers left than Lee, but Meade refused to accept accurate estimates of Confederate strength and imagined more enemy troops than existed (similar to George McClellan). Confederate Gen. Porter Alexander, who offered some of the wisest analyses of the battles, stated that Meade was like a mule chasing a grizzly bear: "Chasing us was the last thing he wanted to do." Alexander also said that Meade could have sent forces south of the Potomac at Harp-

er's Ferry, intercepting provisions and ammunition, trapping the Confederates from escaping, forcing a siege and making the rebels attack on ground of Meade's choosing. In his book "Campaigns of the Army of the Potomac," William Swinton wrote that by moving to his right, Meade could have occupied the heights commanding the river. It would have flipped the tactical advantages to the federals. When Union forces finally attacked on July 14th, the rebels had escaped.

In my opinion, Meade was right to fear a frontal assault on entrenched Confederates. As a corps commander he had been willing to use flank attacks and avoid frontal attacks; first at Fredericksburg, where he charged the Confederate right flank but received no support and then at Chancellorsville, where his proposal to strike the Confederate left was denied by Hooker. Given Meade's inexperience leading an army, his troops' exhaustion and his generals' hesitancy, it's difficult to find fault with Meade. Bottom line, when it came to a frontal attack, the risk was greater than the reward.

As for Lee, he waged a successful advance into Union territory where he resupplied his troops and sent panic among the populace. Lee, according to Edward Ayers in "The Thin Light of Freedom," seized over 45,000 head of cattle, 35,000 sheep, more than 20,000 horses and mules and plenty of food. He also successfully retreated back to friendly Virginia. But he will always be remembered for foolishly attacking a Union force at Gettysburg when he could have invited a Union attack on high ground. Lee won the advance and the retreat but lost the battle. And so it took some mighty fancy fiction writing to blame Lee's underlings and make him a hero after the war. Had Lee won the battle of Gettysburg, he could have won Southern independence. Gen. James Rusling, in his book "Men and Things I Saw in Civil War Times," was present for a conversation on July 5, 1863, between President Lincoln and the newly injured Sickles. Lincoln responded to a question from Sickles: Was there great concern in Washington during the battle? Lincoln admitted that several Cabinet members talked of Washington being occupied, ordered a gunboat or two and even sent some government archives abroad. But Lincoln himself said he prayed for victory and was convinced that his prayers would be answered. They were — with high ground, interior lines, brave soldiers and excellent leadership. Edgar was there.

NEAR UPPERVILLE, MD. — July 22, 1863.

My Dear Wife: We are in Virginia and resting up. We came to this place the night before last. How long we will stay here is impossible to say. Probably not long I hope, for I want to keep agoing until this rebellion is put down. The news came to us yesterday that the rebels were largely reinforced and were agoing back into Maryland and to Pennsylvania again. If that is so, we will have to go back and drive them out again. I would rather fight in a loyal state than in old Virginia. But I think it is a false report. I do not think they could attempt to go back there again, they got a good whipping the last time. We are having a good time. The blackberries are ripe and Virginia affords a good quantity this season. We are in good spirits and confident of success before many months.

From your husband, Edgar W. Clark.

BETWEEN WARRENTON AND SULFUR SPRINGS — July 27, 1863.

My Dear Wife: We had a small battle at Manassas Gap on the 23rd of the month. We drove them about 4 miles although our regiment did not fire a gun. We have to support the skirmish line. The balls flew around us but good luck sent them all over our heads. I hope we will cut them off on their retreat to Richmond. We are getting the upper hand on them now, and if we only keep it, we will see peace before many weeks. We are waiting for rations which we will get probably by noon, then we will start out again. I do not think we will get any rest until we get to Richmond or somewhere near that place. We need a little rest. We have been constantly on the march for the last two months. I stand it first-rate, better than I thought I should. We eat about a quart of blackberries every day and they do us a considerable good.

From husband, E. W. Clark to wife, Catherine.

SULFUR SPRINGS — Aug. 2, 1863.

My Dear Wife: We have laid still now nearly one week. Great things are expected of this Army toward putting down the rebellion. Time has passed very fast. I wish it would pass faster. I don't know if I can stay away from you two years longer without deserting. If I cannot see you in any other way, I suppose I will have to if this unholy war does not end sooner than that. I have great confidence it will not last one year longer.

Edgar W. Clark.

WARRENTON, VA. — Aug. 10, 1863.

My Dear Wife: I am glad to hear your health is good and was sorry to hear the children have been sick. But I am glad they got over the scarlet fever as well as they did. We have been in camp now for nearly two weeks. I think we will stay in camp until the hot weather is over. You cannot hardly imagine how warm it is here. To keep from suffering from the heat, our company last Saturday built a shade 100 feet by 12 feet high and 7 feet high, covered by pine boughs.

This place is about as big as Detroit but somebody set fire to the best part of the town and burned it up before we came here.

You can hardly go over any part of Virginia but you will find graves of the Union Army and some of the rebels, too.

It was one year ago today that I last saw you. To me, the year has passed very quick. To you, it has probably been too long. I will try to get a furlough and come home and see you this winter. I cannot tell if I will be discharged next spring when the regiment is. When the Army of the Potomac gets filled up with conscripts and gets them thoroughly drilled I think they will make a move that will end the rebellion by fall. If this Civil War will close by this summer, I could come home and put on new siding and make a nicer job than can be made now on those weather-beaten boards.

No more from your husband, Edgar W. Clark.

Historical context: Edgar briefly mentioned that the children had scarlet fever. It may be difficult to realize how many serious illnesses affected children in previous eras. In fact, measles often swept through soldiers' camps. Scarlet fever, a bacterial illness, was common among children, usually following strep throat. There were no antibiotics for treatment. It was deadly. Other common epidemics in the 1800s included smallpox, typhus, yellow fever and cholera.

ALEXANDRIA, VA. — Aug. 16, 1863.

My Dear Wife: I hope we will not go to Charleston. I would rather go to New York to enforce the draft. There are too many troops coming here to think we're coming home. The war news is encouraging. I think they are on their last legs and are getting weaker.

Edgar W. Clark.

Historical context: The new Union draft law made all White men eligible for duty between the ages of 20 and 35 and all unmarried men between 35 and 45. A lottery was used to determine which men to draft. Though Edgar was in his late 20s and eligible for the draft, he likely would not have been drafted because so many Michigan men volunteered. By volunteering a year earlier, he was making a principled decision. States received quotas for the number of men to be drafted into the service. The Army of the Potomac near the end of the war was filled with men who did not want to be there — those paid a bounty, draftees or malingerers. Thus, the impact of Black Union volunteers late in the war went far beyond their numbers.

New York was a strong Democratic Party state, full of Copperheads and did not fill its quota of volunteers. The draft was so unpopular in New York City in the summer of 1863, Carl Sandburg wrote, that there were only 4 volunteers for every 100 draftees. Compare that with Michigan's 95 volunteers for every 100 draftees.

Broken down: 164,394 were exempted from the draft, 52,288 bought exemptions at $300 each, 39,877 did not report and 26,002 hired substitutes.

On July 12, names were drawn in New York City's first draft, reported in the Sunday papers. That afternoon, protesters began forming, and by Monday morning, the number of protesters had grown to 50,000 people. The poor, many of them new Irish immigrants, were infuriated by the exemptions for the rich.

The draft riots were described in detail in the book by Iver Bernstein, "The New York City Draft Riots: Their Significance for American Society and Politics." Over five days, the New York City violence claimed 1,000 civilian lives and great property damage. This is far greater than the official death toll of about 120. The Tulsa race riot of 1920 resulted in from 50 to 300 deaths.

In any case, the 1863 New York City draft riot was the worst riot by death toll in U.S. history.

Bernstein describes the draft riots as involving several factors: Irish-Catholic hatred, lower-class racism by Whites, Confederate or Copperhead sympathies and resentment of the poor to the entire draft process. By the end of the first day of the riot, some citizens fought for justice, such as protecting a Black man from a lynch mob. Bernstein wrote that not all of the rioters were Irish or Catholic.

The draft riots often turned into race riots. Attacks on African Americans were common, based in part on the use of Blacks to break strikes on the docks. Irish longshoremen sought to keep those trades Whites-only. Racially mixed couples were targeted. The police superintendent was beaten and dragged through the mud. Police officers were stripped of their clothes and beaten. Also, a crowd set fire to a postmaster's house and a police station. Even a Negro children's orphanage was burned down, though the children were safely evacuated. Later, Irish mobs attacked German and Jewish shops. They even went after the mayor's house.

By the fourth day of the riots, Union troops arrived from Gettysburg, set up artillery, took control of blocks and limited civilian access. Up to 10,000 troops were rushed to New York City, including the 26th Infantry Regiment from Michigan. Union troops shot artillery shells into the mobs, wrote Herbert Asbury in "The Gangs of New York." But the scope of the unrest was startling. Practically every police officer was injured. About 50 soldiers were killed and 300 wounded. Eighteen Blacks were lynched and about 70 were reported missing.

Edgar was sent to New York City about a month after the draft riot, part of 20,000 troops protecting a resumption of the draft. Then he was sent to Troy, N.Y. to guard those draft offices. Draft riots in Troy had occurred on July 14, reported the Times-Union newspaper of Albany in a 2013 article. A mob erected a scaffold and promised to execute anyone involved in carrying out the draft. Also in Troy, 300 employees of the Albany Nail Works and Rensselaer Iron Works went on a rampage, destroyed a pro-Lincoln newspaper office and sacked the town jail, reported David Williams in his book, "A People's History of the Civil War." The National Guard put down the violence.

Williams documents Northern draft violence in about 30 cities. Some draft officers were assaulted or killed in draft riots. In President Lincoln's home state of Illinois, a mob of 400 in DuQuoin assaulted a provost marshal and freed several deserters.

Detroit had an anti-draft race riot in March of 1863, reported the Detroit Free Press. Two civilians were killed, one White and one Black, while 35 buildings were burned down. More than 200 people, mostly Black, were left homeless. The Detroit City Council refused to grant compensation to the victims.

Though heavily Democratic New York continued to oppose using Black soldiers — New York Gov. Horatio Seymour especially so — the federal government stepped in. By March of 1865, the 20th U.S. Colored Infantry marched down Broadway unimpeded.

Following the war, widespread Northern opposition to the draft was underplayed. Williams reveals that 90,000 young men in the North fled to Canada to escape the draft. And 31 percent of all draftees avoided the draft by using medical exemptions. In 1863, some Northerners joined draft insurance societies. For instance, a group of men would pay $10 or $20 each to hire a substitute in case any of them were drafted. Thus, the statement that the North had a 4-to-1 manpower advantage is an exaggeration. The actual advantage was 2-to-1. If Gen. Robert E. Lee had won at Gettysburg, followed by draft riots in New York, perhaps European nations would have recognized the Confederacy.

GOVERNOR'S ISLAND — Aug. 23, 1863.

My Dear Wife: I am happy to say we landed safe in this harbor and on this land last night after a beautiful and pleasant passage on board a large government steamer. Though we had a pleasant passage, most of us were glad to get our feet on land once more. We are now encamped on some of the pleasantest places that we ever were in. This island comprises about 40 acres in New York Harbor. There are some very fine and costly residences — a very pleasant place generally. When I stand outside our tent, I can count 25 or 30 vessels from all parts of the world. We were in the City of New York yesterday for about four hours. It would take a man a week to go all through the city. We have tents large enough to accommodate four people comfortably. I came here to help the government support the laws and uphold the Constitution of the U.S. We are going to protect government property from foes without and traitors within. We may stay here the remainder of the regiment's time. I hope so. I am tired of old Virginia.

Edgar W. Clark.

NEW YORK CITY — Aug. 23, 1863.

My Dear Wife: I hope we stay here quite a while for this is a beautiful place. There is so much to be seen. I think the war is coming to a close. I think the downfall of Charleston will round the thing up. There are a great many fine girls in this city but that makes no difference to me. I have got it at home and that is enough for me. I think peace will be declared by winter and, if not, we will come home by spring. You wrote that you have a fine garden. I am glad of that. I wish I was there to help you eat some of it and I wish you were here to see some of the sights on Broadway.

There are very few of the Lansing boys in the company for they were almost all killed or are wounded in a hospital. Whit Miller is in Alexandria getting rich making cider and selling it to people.

Edgar W. Clark.

Notes: In any war, there are fortunes to be made, some legal, some illegal. For instance, Sen. Harry Truman led a Senate investigation into corruption during World War II. The trip to New York City was like a furlough for Edgar. The draft riots had already been put down. Edgar still had two years left on his enlistment. And the terrible bloodshed of the Overland campaign was still to come. He clearly was aware of his good fortune given the casualties of his Lansing neighbors. Meanwhile, his friend was profiteering.

NEW YORK CITY — Aug. 29, 1863.

My Dear Wife: We got the news about the fall of Fort Sumter this morning. That is the place where the rebellion commenced. I hope that with its downfall it may end this war. Then I will come home to see you. I think the rebellion is on its last legs. I went to one theater and into Barnum's Museum, which is the best I have ever seen. We have men from all parts of the world and thousands of things that are impossible to name. I wish you could go in there with me.

I hope you will pick a good lot of berries so that if we stay here this winter you may be able to spare us some. I hope we may be at home early but I am afraid this war will not be closed as soon as fall but I think it will be in the spring. The draft is over in the city. Everything passed very quietly.

From your husband, Edgar W. Clark.

TROY, NY — Sept. 1, 1863.

My Dear Wife: We left New York last Sunday night and went up the Hudson River about 100 miles on a steamboat. The draft is to commence in this place tomorrow. There are some hard feelings on account of the draft but I don't think there will be any trouble. The people give us a good deal of praise.

Edgar W. Clark.

TROY, NY — Sept. 6, 1863.

My Dear Wife: I was glad to hear from you that you are well. I am very sorry that you have not received that money. I am afraid you never will. I will never send any more by mail so nobody will get any more of my money. We are having nice and easy times. The draft has passed quietly although the Copperheads threatened to clear us out. I think sometime I would rather shoot a Copperhead than a rebel because they are doing more harm to their country. It seems hard to be separated from those we love for so long. I hope a just retribution will fall on all those who are the cause of it.

Edgar W. Clark.

TROY, NY — Sept. 11, 1863.

My Dear Wife: The boys are going to have a military social tonight. I do not think I will go. The price is $2.50. You need the money too much. If the boys will let me get in for nothing, I will go to see the others enjoy themselves, though you know I would never dance.

Edgar W. Clark.

Notes: Edgar never mentions this to his wife other than assuring her of his love, but large numbers of prostitutes followed the armies. Edgar's letters make it clear that there were long periods of inactivity. The term "hooker" is credited to Union Gen. Joseph Hooker. And the U.S. Army Medical Department reported in 1861 that 1 in 12 soldiers had venereal disease. Imagine returning to your wife with VD.

TROY, NY — Sept. 13, 1863.

My Dear Wife: We leave this place this afternoon for New York. It is rumored that we will soon go from there to our old place in Virginia. I would rather do that than go to any other place such as Texas. This is a very nice place to live. I wish we could stay here until our time is out. I would have you come and make me a visit but the fortunes of war are continually moving us from one place to another. My health is excellent. I would not wish for better. We have the best of living.

If you do not hear from me in quite a while you need not think that I have forgotten you but think of you every day.

Edgar W. Clark.

WASHINGTON — Sept. 16, 1863.

My Dear Wife: We have had a nice time in the state of New York. I wish it had been to Michigan. Some of the boys found some nice girls and one in our company found a girl and married her. He only stayed with her for two days after they were married. Some of the boys found girls and made engagements; when they get out of the war, they would marry them. About 30 men in our regiment got married in Troy. The newspaper states that our Army of the Potomac is fighting and I think that we will soon go there.

You must write often. Let me know about your affairs. Give my love to all of your friends and save a double share for yourself. Kiss the children for me.

No more from your husband, Edgar W. Clark.

CULPEPER, VA — Sept. 19, 1863.

My Dear Wife: This morning finds me with the Army of the Potomac in our old corps, division and brigade. We are about 3 miles from Culpeper and within 4 miles from the rebels. Our cavalry is fighting with them every day. The first thing I heard yesterday was cannonading. We thought we would have a battle before we got into camp.

No one can tell what this advance toward Richmond will amount to but I hope we will be successful and conquer that stronghold and end the rebellion, sure. I am willing to take my chances and will come out alive and someday come home and I think I will when the fall campaign is over, which will be in about three months or less, and if I am alive and well.

There is no excitement in camp, no fighting this morning. The boys are cooking their meals and cleaning up their guns and some are writing to their wives and sweethearts in Troy and Lansing and other places and all seem to be enjoying themselves first-rate and telling about the good time they had in their pleasant excursion to New York State in enforcing the draft.

You must take good care of yourself and the children.

I remain your husband, Edgar W. Clark.

CULPEPER, VA — Sept. 23, 1863.

My Dear Wife: All is quiet on the Rapidan River. Our forces occupy the north bank of the river and the cavalry scours the south bank. Yesterday we got an order to prepare to march with eight days' rations. I hope this war will close before long and then I could come home and see you all. Give my love to all and save a double share for yourself.

Edgar W. Clark, to his wife and children.

CULPEPER, VA — Sept. 26, 1863.

My Dear Wife: We cook our rations and do our guard duty and drill one hour each day to keep in practice. I have had a promise of my discharge next spring when the regiment's time is out. Then I can come home and see you and stay as long as I have a mind to. If I can do it I will try to get a furlough this winter. I could have a good visit with you. How I would like a good meal this morning with biscuits and good butter to put on them. I have not had a good warm biscuit of any kind since I was at Upton Hill about a year ago.

Give my love to all and retain the largest share for yourself. Please write as often as convenient.

From your husband, Edgar W. Clark.

Notes: Edgar has made many references to furloughs, discharges and even deserting, none of which he took. It seems cruel to constantly offer false hope to his wife, Catherine.

CULPEPER, VA — Sept. 28, 1863.

My Dear Wife: We are having very fine weather though the nights are very cold. We have to have blankets over us to keep us warm. Our roof is two small pieces of shelter tents and that is not much protection. It keeps the frost and rain from us and that is about all. Our Army has stripped them of everything. It does not take long for 100,000 men to lay waste. I tell some of them when they complain about hard times to use their influence to stop the rebellion and then we will go home and not trouble them. For just as long as they keep us here we calculate to have the best the country affords if we can find it.

No more from your husband, Edgar W. Clark.

CULPEPER, VA — Oct. 4, 1863.

My Dear Wife: We see a good many soldiers and hear a good deal of music. I wish you could see one of those reviews. You would like it. We hear no heavy cannonading nor anything to excite alarm. I think it will be impossible for us to have another battle in these parts, for the government has taken away two of the three corps of the Army. We have built up a nice little house about six logs high and 7 feet square and it is covered with our shelter tents. We have a very good living, beef every other day and pork every other day. We have potatoes once in three days and beans once in three days and dried apples and onions. I must stop and help the boys clean up the street and then my day's work will be done after getting dinner.

No more from your devoted husband, Edgar W. Clark.

CULPEPER, VA — Oct. 7, 1863.

My Dear Wife: We have moved our camp about 1 mile. We have a nice little house. I think we will move in a day or two back toward the Rappahannock where we can hold our front line to a better advantage. We have had a long line to hold and it is rather hard work. The biggest part of the Army has gone West. Our regiment numbers nearly 300 and over 200 put down their names to reenlist. We get orders one day and the next they are countermanded. I must close this and say goodbye from your devoted husband.

Edgar W. Clark to Catherine Clark.

FAIRFAX, VA — Oct. 17, 1863.

My Dear Wife: We left camp about a week ago today and marched about 2 miles and formed in lines of battle and waited there for the rebels to attack us. But they did not come, so the next morning we marched across the Rappahannock and stopped for 36 hours where we again got in line and marched toward Alexandria.

Our brigade had quite a sharp skirmish with the rebels on Tuesday. We had one in our regiment wounded. My health is not very good. We had to wade the Rappahannock River and I took a very hard cold and had a slight fever. I went to the doctor and got some quinine and feel better today than I did yesterday. William met with quite an accident last Sunday. He was splitting some kindling wood when the hatchet made a glance and cut his big toe bad. So they sent him to the hospital in Washington.

I got a letter from my mother last week. She wrote that your mother made all sorts of complaints about me, said that I was not fit to have a wife, that I did not care for you, I had gone off and left things in bad shape. I am sorry that money was lost that you needed very bad. I have sent you all the money that I could spare and I went without myself to send it to you. If I get out of the service I should be better off and can say that I helped save our country. As long as your folks try to help you along, they will get my thanks, for it makes no difference what they say about me. I can stand it. Give my love to all and I will write again in a short time.

No more from your husband, Edgar W. Clark.

Notes: Edgar had issues with his mother-in-law. And Edgar was writing to Catherine about the lovely weather in Virginia.

CAMP IN FIELD — Oct. 24, 1863.

My Dear Wife: This cold and stormy afternoon finds me well. We have traveled 20 miles to get 5, the reason unknown. I wish I would be with you today before a warm stove instead of sitting here with this cold damp rain. We have to go to bed to keep warm, which is very unpleasant to sleep this time of year. We have very easy times, no duty, only guard now and then. William is in Washington at Stanton Hospital. His foot is not well.

You must kiss the children for me every day for when I come home one of these days I want to see as nice girls as the country affords. You must write as often as you can and I will do the same.

Edgar W. Clark.

CAMP BRATTON — Oct. 30, 1863.

My Dear Wife: We have orders to move, so accordingly we got up this morning at 4 o'clock and cooked our meat and coffee and were ready to start at daylight. So we are in line of battle, ready to have the rebels pitch on us if they want to, but I guess they will keep off and we will not have any fun today. If I could get into a regiment of cavalry or mounted infantry for the remainder of my term, I believe I could do it. I have got tired of carrying such heavy loads. If I could have a horse to carry them, I would get along better.

You must give my love and respects to all friends and keep a share for yourself. I will write in three or four more days.

No more from your husband, Edgar W. Clark.

Historical context: Cavalry usually was involved in raids or reconnaissance, not direct action. Therefore, casualties in the cavalry were lower, as Edgar seemed to say. Gen. George Meade scored a few victories in Northern Virginia by doing the unexpected, such as attacking at night at Kelly's Ford. Meade did not follow up, however. Meanwhile, Lee was forced to use defensive tactics for his reduced forces.

BRANDY STATION — Nov. 11, 1863.

My Dear Wife: We have marched about 30 miles, crossed the Rappahannock again, and fought a large battle. Our brigade was in advance. We took 300 prisoners, killed quite a number and wounded a large number. There were none killed nor wounded in our regiment and it was a wonder, for the balls whistled around us in every direction. Men were killed in other regiments around us but we have a good colonel and he looks out for his men better than any that I ever saw.

Edgar W. Clark.

Historical context: This apparently was a reference to The Battle of Rappahannock Station on Nov. 7. A dusk attack overran the Confederates, capturing more than 1,600 prisoners from Jubal Early's division. Fighting at Kelly's Ford was less severe but the Confederates retreated. Edgar's reference to his good colonel is instructive because if the Civil War taught us anything, it was the importance of leadership. This was life or death. DeTrobriand wrote that soldiers were aware of the dangers: "The same men fight very differently depending on who commands them. If they have confidence in their commander, they will dash upon the enemy without reserve, for they know that the regiment will not be compromised without necessity, and that, if they must die, their death will at least be useful to the cause to which they are devoted. But if they feel they are poorly led, and if they are afraid of being sacrificed without result, from lack of judgment or by an intellect obscured by the fumes of whiskey, their enthusiasm gives way to indecision." The corollary of this is the fact that Union soldiers fought bravely despite poor generalship early in the war.

BRANDY STATION — Nov. 13, 1863.

My Dear Wife: We heard heavy cannonading this morning but a few miles off. The first thing that we know is that Lee will try to drive us back across the Rappahannock and so it goes. First, we drive him to his fortifications and then he will drive us to ours. I wish this war would come to an end.

Edgar W. Clark.

Notes: Edgar probably didn't want to admit it, but he had written previously that the rebellion would have to be firmly put down. Neither side was going to give up unless forced. But the Union now had generals who could stand up to Robert E. Lee.

BRANDY STATION — Nov. 18, 1863.

My Dear Wife: I think this rebellion is playing out as fast as it can. I will send you $15. There is no possible way to express it. I will try it once more by mail. I have not much time to write, only that I am in the best of health.

Edgar W. Clark.

BRANDY STATION — Nov. 22, 1863.

My Dear Wife: I wish that we could whip them so badly this fall that they will be compelled to lay down their arms and come back in the Union. We have been on regimental inspection and I am now cooking beans and pork for dinner. I have some hard crackers, which we have to thump to shake the worms out, which are long and white with a red streak around their necks. You may be thinking that I am joking but I am not. You must give your respects to your father and mother and all the rest who wish to hear from me. Tell them to come and help us put down this rebellion and not stay at home and wait to be drafted. They do not know with what contempt a drafted man is looked upon by the volunteers.

Edgar W. Clark.

Notes: Winter was arriving. The previous winter, Edgar was so sick that he lost 15 pounds and was hospitalized. The lousy food wasn't helping. Weevils from hardtack were a constant nuisance. Sometimes soldiers dipped hardtack in water or coffee and then scooped off the weevils from the surface.

BRANDY STATION — Nov. 25, 1863.

My Dear Wife: We are under marching orders. I think we will have some very hard marching and it may be some hard fighting but I guess not, for I don't think Meade will risk a very heavy engagement this time of year. The weather is so uncertain. I think we are agoing to abandon this part of Virginia and try to take Richmond again. Everything looks like peace would be restored by the beginning of next summer. I begin to think there is no place like home and kind friends with plenty to eat and drink and a good bed to sleep in. Here we eat on the ground, sit on the ground and sleep on the ground. More men have got to come and help us put down the rebellion. Another draft takes place in January and it will take what is left of Detroit.

Edgar W. Clark.

Historical context: Edgar was involved in the Mine Run Campaign from Nov. 26, 1863, to Dec. 1, 1863. The Army of the Potomac probed Confederate defenses south of the Rapidan River. Lee threw up defenses along the banks of Mine Run Creek. Meade withdrew and went into winter quarters. That was no respite for Edgar, who nearly died of illness the previous winter.

BRANDY STATION — Dec. 3, 1863.

My Dear Wife: Since I wrote you last *(Nov. 25)*, this Army has been across the Rapidan and fought a battle every day. We were under fire from the enemy for days. Our regiment has lost 40 men killed and wounded or taken prisoner. Our regiment has done the best it ever done and if we get the amount of praise we deserve we will be praised very highly. We arrived at our old camp at 3 yesterday afternoon very tired and I am in good health and spirits, thankful that through so many dangers in so many days that William and I came out safe while many of our comrades fell from rebel bullets. Though our company never lost a man, companies on either side lost quite heavily. I feel quite confident that we will close all the fighting this year unless we are attacked by the rebel Army.

This regiment saw a deserter shot. He was shot kneeling on his coffin. Death on the battlefield is preferable to the death of a deserter.

William sends his love to you and all the rest and I do the same.

From your husband, Edgar W. Clark.

Notes: Edgar had no mercy for deserters, Copperheads or rebels, so long as the rebellion was in effect.

BRANDY STATION — Dec. 6, 1863.

My Dear Wife: The weather is quite cold here today but probably not so cold as you have it there. The sun shines all day but a cold North wind blows. We will change camp soon and then we will build good winter quarters. Time flies very fast. We have no duty nor drill, we have a good fry pan and a good coffee pot.

Edgar W. Clark.

BRANDY STATION —Dec. 11, 1863.

My Dear Wife: My health has been very good. I have been on duty building comfortable winter quarters, but not as good as last winter. The only excitement in camp is with reenlisting, which a great many of them are doing. I shall not reenlist. I would like to see you for Christmas and New Year's. I think we would have a gay old feast of fat things. I think everything looks encouraging for the war to close. I cannot see how they can hold out any longer than spring.

Edgar W. Clark.

Notes: The 3rd Michigan was formed in 1861 about one year before Edgar joined, so those early three-year enlistments would be ending in 1864, while Edgar's three-year enlistment would not end till August of 1865.

BRANDY STATION — Dec. 14, 1863.

My Dear Wife: I know that you must feel lonesome for I do myself with thousands around us all the time.

Edgar W. Clark.

BRANDY STATION —Dec. 17, 1863.

My Dear Wife: My health has never been better. I weigh more than I ever did, 160 pounds. We have plenty of clothes to keep us warm and plenty of hardtack and pork. I must again express the wish that I would see you. I have written that sentence so much that I presume you are tired of hearing it. I would like to see you very much but I would rather see this rebellion closed.

Edgar W. Clark.

Chapter Eleven

Welcome goods, lonely holidays

Edgar spends a second Christmas in the Army of the Potomac. He wishes for tea. Edgar again expresses optimism about the end of the war. Confederate guerrillas are a nuisance. He supports total war and tough treatment of rebel leaders.

BRANDY STATION — Dec. 22, 1863.

My Dear Wife: Your letter with a box and contents was very gladly received last night. I was pleased with those pictures. If you carry out your determination to learn, I think you will feel more enjoyment in writing to me than you will in telling others what to write. Time passes very fast. We ought to be thankful that our lives are spared through so many dangers.

Edgar W. Clark.

Historical context: Loneliness must have been worse during the holiday season. Thus the box of food from home was huge for Edgar's morale. Edgar's wife Catherine was trying to learn to read and write, which she did eventually. In 1870, accord-

ing to the National Assessment of Adult Literacy, 20 percent of Americans aged 14 and older were illiterate. Among Blacks, the illiteracy rate was 80 percent for understandable reasons since literacy was outlawed in many enslaved areas.

For instance, in South Carolina, someone caught helping a slave learn to read was subject to a steep fine, according to a 1740 law. Thus, it was difficult to find many letters written by African Americans during the Civil War, one of the main regrets of historian and author Bell Irvin Wiley. However, during the New Deal, the Federal Writers Project conducted valuable oral interviews with about 2,300 ex-enslaved people.

BRANDY STATION — Dec. 26, 1863.

My Dear Wife: Yesterday was a very quiet day for me. The sun shone all day and the weather was quite warm. The officers tried hard to get a furlough for all of us. My time will come one of these days. I will have only one year and two months to stay from Jan. 11. I think the war will close before my time is out.

Edgar W. Clark.

Historical context: Edgar never gets his furlough. Again, he was overly optimistic about ending the war. Gen. Robert E. Lee, trained as an engineer, was able to build strong defensive earthworks and hold out against Union attacks in the Overland campaign. If Confederate President Jefferson Davis had not replaced Confederate Gen. Joseph Johnston for his defensive tactics in favor of more assaults, the Confederacy probably would have been able to hold onto Atlanta through the 1864 presidential election. More on that later.

BRANDY STATION — Dec. 28, 1863.

My Dear Wife: A number of the boys reenlisted for three years longer and they are expecting to start for home any day on a furlough of 35 days. A person cannot calculate on anything in the Army unless he has it in his hand and sometimes not then. It has rained for the last 48 hours and there is no sign of stopping yet. I hope our health will continue to be good while we may be separated in this cruel war.

Edgar W. Clark to wife, Catherine A. Clark.

Notes: Between December of 1863 and March of 1864, 206 men in the 3rd Michigan Infantry reenlisted. Company G, Edgar's company, had the highest proportion of reenlistments — 24 men or 13.4 percent of the total, according to official records. Since Edgar joined a year after the war started in 1862, he was not involved in reenlistments.

BRANDY STATION — Jan. 1, 1864.

My Dear Wife: The first day of this year finds me enjoying myself as well as circumstances will permit. It has been lonesome, although we try to put on a cheerful aspect. I calculate to try hard to get a furlough when the boys come back in February. Yesterday I got the book that included a description of every man in the company. I will send it home to be kept as a future reference. It may have a good deal of importance in future years. Tell William not to forget to fetch me an ax and I would like to have you send me some green tea. I have not had tea since I have been in the Army.

Edgar W. Clark.

Historical context: Edgar was well aware of the historic importance of this war. It was apparent that Lincoln's Emancipation

Proclamation, which took effect one year earlier, would have a profound impact on the war. The South needed enslaved people to compensate for the more populous North. After the first battle of Bull Run, Gen. Richard Ewell proposed enlisting enslaved people in the military, which Confederate President Jefferson Davis called "stark madness" because it would "revolt and disgust the whole South." Confederate Gen. Patrick Cleburne in a detailed memo on Jan. 2, 1864, proposed the use of enslaved people in the Confederate Army with the promise of freeing them. Cleburne reported a drop in morale and increasing desertions in the rebel Army. Cleburne wrote: "Slavery is a source of great strength to the enemy," and "it is our most vulnerable point, a continued embarrassment and in some respects an insidious weakness." Union forces were raiding Confederate areas and then freeing the enslaved people, and there weren't enough rebel forces to stop it. Cleburne wrote that the Confederacy had to choose between independence or slavery. In addition, neither England nor France would help the South so long as slavery was in play. England, for example, paid hundreds of millions to emancipate enslaved people in the West Indies and break up the slave trade. Cleburne wrote that freeing the enslaved people would solve the Confederacy's manpower issues and improve its standing throughout the world. Cleburne's proposal met deaf ears because the leaders in the Confederacy were married to the slave system.

On the Northern side, Robert Penn Warren wrote in "The Legacy of the Civil War" that Blacks were needed in the Union Army because Northern volunteering had plunged. In fact, about 70 percent of Northern African American men of military age served in the Union Army by the end of the war, reported Ira Berlin and Leslie Rowland in "Families and Freedom: A Documentary History of African-American Kinship in the Civil War." While racism was certainly present in the North, many

White Northerners were more than ready to accept "Sambo's Right to be Kilt," the title of a popular song. President Lincoln said in 1864 that without Black troops "we would be compelled to abandon the war in three weeks." Not only were Black soldiers needed at the end of the war, they served during the postwar occupation of the South.

The need for the labor of the enslaved people continued to pressure the South. In November of 1864, Confederate President Jefferson Davis proposed enlisting Black laborers and then freeing them when their terms were finished.

One year after Cleburne's proposal, in January of 1865, Gen. Robert E. Lee wrote that enslaved people be offered participation in the Confederate Army along with the promise of eventual emancipation. On Jan. 11, 1865, Lee asked for permission to raise and organize "colored troops," stating that with proper training "they can be made efficient soldiers." His plan would include gradual emancipation. That was a change from his previous view that emancipation was "a savage and brutal policy ... which leaves us no alternative but success or degradation worse than death."

Opposition was strong, though, as illustrated by a letter from Georgia politician Howell Cobb to the Confederate Secretary of War on Jan. 8, 1865: "I think that the proposition to make soldiers of our enslaved people is the most pernicious idea that has been suggested since the war began. ... The day you make soldiers of them is the beginning of the end of the revolution. If enslaved people will make good soldiers, our whole theory of slavery is wrong — but they won't make soldiers."

Lee surrendered on April 9 before his plan was put into effect. In short, the South chose slavery over independence and then lost both.

The fact is that Black people had proved their worth in battle since Crispus Attucks was killed in the Revolutionary War. In a

petition by the "colored citizens of Nashville to the Union Conven-
tion of Tennessee," the freedmen stated: "We hold that freedom is
the natural right of all men, which they themselves have no more
right to give or barter away than they have to sell their honor, their
wives or their children."

BRANDY STATION — Jan. 6, 1864.

My Dear Wife: I am well and enjoying myself first-rate. I have
been out on picket for three days, 7 miles from camp. We have
a good time. The weather was rather cold and the snow was 3
inches deep. One of our company is missing this morning. He
left his post with two others from our regiment and was not
heard from. It is supposed that he went out to find a pig or sheep
and probably has been captured by guerillas.

Edgar Clark.

Notes: It is easy for us to forget how close the armies were to
each other in Northern Virginia. It was possible for troops to chat,
exchange items or be shot by sharpshooters.

BRANDY STATION — Jan. 13, 1864.

My Dear Wife: Our brigade changed camp yesterday. We
moved about 2 miles from where we have laid for the last two
months. We need teams to haul off our stuff. You would have
laughed to see a brigade move the way we did. It looked like
moving in the North. You wrote that you wish I could have been
with you on Christmas and New Year's. I wish I could, too. I
think the time is fast approaching when we will meet again. I
am quite anxious for the time to come.

Edgar W. Clark.

CAMP BULLOCK — Jan. 13, 1864.

My Dear Wife: Your kind and welcome letter found me well. I thought something was the matter. I did not get a letter from you in so long a time. But your excuse is a reasonable one and I cheerfully submit. I would like to have come home with the boys, but circumstances would not let me. I am sorry you were so disappointed in not seeing me. A good many are confident that this war will close before fall.

We finished our tent yesterday and I think we have as nice a one as there is in the regiment. We have a good warm fireplace and a very comfortable and convenient home. I never enjoyed better weather than I do this winter and I cannot ask for easier times — once in a while a little picket duty or guard duty. I was on guard last night so that excuses me from picket today. One of the first things a soldier learns is to get rid of all duty he can and then he leaves other things as fast as he can. I would not have you think I am lazy but I calculate to get along as easy as I can, consistent with honor and military description.

Edgar W. Clark.

Historical context: Building shelters that kept soldiers off the cold and wet ground was a key to their health. Some of the shelters are described by John Billings in his book "Hardtack and Coffee: The Unwritten Story of Army Life." During winter months in the camp, soldiers often built structures with logs for walls and mud filling the gaps. The coverings were Army ponchos, which were made of vulcanized India rubber with a hole in the center for the head. Some companies had masons who could build fireplaces made of brick, stone or mud-treated wood. So far as not receiving a letter from his wife, I imagine she was busy with her two infants during those cold winter months in Michigan.

CAMP BULLOCK — Jan. 19, 1864.

My Dear Wife: Lucky for me that you have seemingly got along as well as you can. I wrote to you about sending home the names and descriptions of everyone who have been in the company. I will send it to you to preserve until I come home. My description will be on it so you can see where I enlisted — age and everything — which you will need if I desert so you can find me by advertising in some paper and get the authorities after me, but I guess I never will trouble you in that way.

Edgar W. Clark to Catherine A. Clark.

Notes: Desertion? Dropping bombshells to his wife was not wise, especially since Edgar recently wrote about the death penalty for a deserter. It might have been tempting to leave when there was no military action and others in the company were on furlough. In fact, desertion rates were as high as two-thirds in the Confederacy and one-third in the Union, wrote David Williams in "A People's History of the Civil War." Dissent in the South has been underplayed by the Lost Cause myth. For instance, historian Walter Fleming estimates that by 1863 at least half of Southern White males were associated with the Peace Society.

CAMP BULLOCK — Jan. 21, 1864.

My Dear Wife: The guerrillas made a raid on our corps' trains and have captured a few guns and a few mules. A few straggling guerrillas are dressed in our uniforms and move among us, and pounce on anyone they can find.

Since the regiment has left, we have lived bully. I suppose they are trying to get us in good order for they got some big work for us to do in the spring and that is to take Richmond. We are about 70 miles from that place now.

The weather has been very warm and pleasant. It looks like spring. I would like to spend my days in this country. It is a pleasant and beautiful country. I cannot tell you what my pursuit in life will be after I get out of this. I think I can do better than to follow what I did before I came to this war. I am confident that this war will be closed sometime in the early part of summer. All it needs is for us to hold them tight as we have and they most certainly will yield before long.

Edgar Clark.

Historical context: Actually, Gen. Robert E. Lee did not surrender until April of 1865, almost 15 months from the date of Edgar's letter. Lee didn't give up until his supply train was captured. Speaking of guerrillas, the Confederacy would not have been able to conduct a guerrilla war after Appomattox. Millions of ex-enslaved people would have been present to inform on them. The Union's repeating rifles would have become more numerous. Mountains would have not provided safety for rebels, they were full of Union supporters. The Confederacy's inability to prevent West Virginia from seceding is one example of Union support in the mountains.

CAMP BULLOCK — Jan. 24, 1864.

My Dear Wife: I was sorry to hear you have taken a bad cold, I hope you are recovered. I was also sorry to hear our mother was sick. I hope she will get well for I would like to see her and all of my kind friends in Lansing and DeWitt when this cruel and inhuman war is over. No person can realize the comforts of a good home until he is deprived of it. I think when I get out of this they will not catch this chicken again. If I was a girl, I would never marry anybody but a soldier, one who thinks enough of this country to try to help save it from rebellious hands. So I say it is the duty of every man to help put this rebellion down and the sooner it is put down the better it is for everybody and the nation at large. I am no Copperhead. I am for the Union, one and inseparable, now and forever.

Give my love to all and save a good share for yourself. Kiss the children for me. I must bid you goodbye. Write often.

Edgar W. Clark to wife, Catherine Clark.

Notes: The Union was less than 100 years old when Edgar wrote this letter. But his commitment to it was as deep as ever.

CAMP BULLOCK — Feb. 1, 1864.

My Dear Wife: I would be very glad to see all the faithful friends who have given us kind wishes and constant friendship, who have done all in their power to gladden a soldier's life by writing to us. I wish them to see prosperous and happy times now and for all time. And may your father live to see the country restored to its original purity when peace and industry may once more visit our country, which is now being deluged by a Civil War. I see every day men who are older than me who are battling all the trials and hardships of camp life and marching through rains and storms with guns on their shoulders, trying to save their country.

You must get along as well as you can and I will do the same. Kiss the children for me often and often think of your husband who is fighting to maintain a good and acceptable government. Give my love to all and write often.

Edgar W. Clark to wife, Catherine A. Clark and children.

Historical context: During the Civil War, the federal govern-ment approved the building of the Transcontinental Railroad, which had been stalled by disagreements over whether it would take a Northern or Southern route. The federal government also approved land grant colleges, in which land was provided for colleges that focused on teaching agricultural and technical lessons to working people. The federal government also approved a first income tax, which helped to pay for the war.

CAMP BULLOCK — Feb. 18, 1864.

My Dear Wife: I was pleased to hear from you but sorry to hear that you were sick with a sore throat. It seems that you have had a very hard time. I wish I could be with you. I would try to come if I could. I have never enjoyed better health. I am getting as fat as a pig. Since I got that box I have lived first-rate.

I do not think the war will last longer than one year more but still no one can tell how long it will last. This spring will tell, for both governments are putting forth every exertion to try to conquer one another this spring. I think we will see some of the hardest-fought battles of the war and lucky will be the man who comes out alive. I for one feel confident that I will live to see my wife and loved ones once more on this side of the grave. No one can tell what the fortunes of war may disclose but one thing is for certain — the rebellion must be put down. I hope we will be successful and that peace may be restored to this now-agitated country.

I got my first cold this year and those handkerchiefs are good about now. I am a thousand times obliged to you and Mina for sending them. I am glad to hear that Mina learns so fast. I hope she will be a good girl and keep on learning until she can beat her father in reading, writing, spelling and all other branches of education. If I live to get out of war safe and sound I will try my best that she and Carrie will have as good an education as can be got, for if there is anything needful in this life it is a good education.

I often think of the past in pleasure and wonder and hope that more enjoyment and pleasures may be our lot to enjoy in this world after the war is over. I must bid you goodbye for this time hoping to hear from you as often as convenient.

Yours as ever, Edgar W. Clark.

Historical context: Edgar foresaw some of the hardest battles of the war in 1864, and he was right. The Union suffered massive casualties in the Overland campaign as Gen. U.S. Grant kept moving left and south toward Richmond, repeatedly assaulting strong defensive positions. Edgar's unit was in some of the most famous and bloodiest battles of this campaign, especially the Bloody Angle at Spotsylvania.

CAMP BULLOCK — Feb. 21, 1864.

My Catherine: I am still enjoying good health although I have a slight cold and yesterday I had an earache all day but I went and got something to put in it and it cured it. I hope you will take good care of yourself and the children. I would like to see the children first-rate. I am glad to hear they are making good use of their time by agoing to school. You must keep up good courage and all will up well. I must finish this letter by saying goodbye from your husband,

Edgar W. Clark, to his wife, Catherine A. Clark.

CAMP BULLOCK — Feb. 24, 1864.

Dear Lydia: I am glad that Catherine's health is getting better. I hope that she will be well so that she can take good care of the children. I hope she will not get discouraged. The motto is to try again and if you do not succeed, then try, try again. I think the work in which she is engaged is worthy of a good trial before it is given up. She must learn to spell as well as write.

There is no war news in these parts. The boys somehow caught a big black crow and then got a stout string and tied his legs together and then tied him to the top of a big tree and then threw stones at him almost all day to see how many times they would hit him. After they got tired, someone climbed the tree and got him down and tied his feet close together and then let him go. He flew and tried to light on a tree some ways off but could not. Then he went to another and kept on until he got out of sight. I can't say but he is still trying to light. That is how the boys keep up sport and fun.

I am glad to see the improvements in which you make in writing and composing. I must close this by giving my love to all and save a share for yourself.

Edgar W. Clark.

Notes: Lydia was Catherine's sister who apparently was teaching Catherine to read.

CAMP BULLOCK — Feb. 27, 1864.

My Dear Wife: I am well and we will probably move tomorrow to try our strength with the rebels across the river. Kiss the children for me and be a good girl and will try to be a good boy. You must try to get along as well as you can.

No more from your husband, Edgar W. Clark, to his wife, Catherine Clark.

CAMP BULLOCK — Feb. 29, 1864.

My Dear Wife: Your first letter I think done well. So let me urge you to keep studying. You will find it will be a great advantage to you in later years. Give my love to all and save a share for yourself.

Your constant and faithful husband, Edgar W. Clark.

Notes: So wife Catherine has sent her first self-written letter! It has been about 18 months since Edgar joined the 3rd Michigan Infantry.

CAMP BULLOCK — March 3, 1864.

My Dear Wife: We did not see any rebels nor nothing that looked like any, only some women who have husbands in the rebel Army. We found a family of a man who has three sons in the rebel Army. When we came to this place, he had a large tannery but when we came only a few ashes remained. They had better be at home tanning leather than be fighting against us, who are trying to preserve the Union. He had a large farm and I guessed he owned a sawmill close by, which is also destroyed with all of his wagons. All of the fences on this farm were burned up. If they still continue to have their sons fight, then their property must suffer. Give my best wishes to all and keep a share for yourself and the children. Kiss them for me once a day and consider me your husband till death.

Edgar W. Clark.

Historical context: Edgar realized that the only way to put down the rebellion was to wage total war. As the year 1864 dawned, units of Black soldiers would begin to make their presence felt. Not only did they want to earn respect for their fighting ability but it soon became clear that the Confederates would kill many of them rather than take them prisoners. "Arms in the hands of enslaved people constituted the South's ultimate nightmare," wrote James McPherson in "Abraham Lincoln and the Second American Revolution. "The enlistment of Black soldiers to fight and kill their former masters was by far the most revolutionary dimension of the emancipation policy." Rebel soldiers often gave

Black soldiers "no quarter," which meant killing them on the battlefield rather than taking them prisoner. In a typical Civil War battle, there were two wounded soldiers for every one killed. When that ratio was flipped with more killed than wounded, the cause often was soldiers being executed on the battlefield. There were several prominent examples, such as Fort Pillow in Eastern Tennessee, Poison Springs in Arkansas and Olustee in North Florida. At Poison Springs in Arkansas, there were 117 Black soldiers dead and half as many wounded. Given that African Americans were likely to be killed rather than taken prisoner, African Americans had every incentive to fight ferociously.

In "Finding Florida," T.D. Allman wrote about the after-action report of Union Gen. John Hatch after the Olustee defeat, about 50 miles inland from Jacksonville. The number of Union missing outnumbered Confederate missing by 84 to 1. "It is now known," Hatch reported, "that most of the wounded colored men were murdered on the field," but in the process, the brave Black soldiers allowed retreating Union forces to escape back to Union-held Jacksonville.

At Fort Pillow, famed Confederate Gen. Nathan Bedford Forrest either ordered the slaughter of Black Union soldiers or failed to control his men. In demanding the surrender of the outnumbered Union forces at the fort, Forrest promised to treat them as prisoners of war. Union Lt. William Clary arrived at the battlefield the next day: "I rode all around the battleground and saw some of our men half-buried and saw five Negroes burning. I asked Colonel Chalmers, the general's brother, if that was the way he allowed his men to do. He concluded that he could not control his men very well and thought it was justifiable in regard to Negroes; that they did not recognize Negroes as soldiers and he could not control his men." But there was evidence that Forrest could control his men. A White soldier who was captured said he heard that Forrest had issued an order the evening after the battle not to kill any more Blacks because Forrest wanted them to help haul artillery.

A congressional investigation followed the Fort Pillow massacre on April 14, 1864. It produced vivid and shocking accounts of the Confederate atrocities from Union survivors. That report is still available in book form. The report from the congressional investigation concluded that at least 300 Union soldiers were "murdered in cold blood." Confederates criticized the report as inaccurate but the specificity of the descriptions makes it unlikely that the witnesses were making up stories. In fact, a letter from a Confederate shortly after the incident confirms it all. From Achilles Clark: "The fort turned out to be a great slaughter pen. Blood, human blood, stood about in pools and brains could have been gathered up in any quantity. I and several others tried to stop the butchery and at one time had partially succeeded, but Gen. Forrest ordered them shot down like dogs, and the carnage continued."

Forrest, a slave trader before the war, became a leader in the Ku Klux Klan after the war. He left the group after it turned too violent for him.

Following the executions of Black Union soldiers at Fort Pillow, Tennessee, President Lincoln issued General Order 252: "For every soldier of the United States killed in violation of the laws of war, a rebel soldier shall be executed." The order also stated that for every Black soldier placed in slavery, a rebel soldier would be placed at hard labor. Lincoln did not follow through on these promises; however, the Confederates in January of 1865 finally agreed to treat Black soldiers equally in POW exchanges while they were debating whether to place Black soldiers in combat units and free them.

However, the brutality was not one-sided. There were reports that an all-Black division murdered prisoners at Petersburg, "They can hardly be blamed," wrote Capt. Charles Francis Adams Jr., quoted by James McPherson in "The War That Forged a Nation: Why the Civil War Still Matters." At Resaca, Ga., a White Wisconsin soldier wrote that 23 rebels surrendered but were killed as the Union troops asked if they remembered Fort Pillow.

CAMP BULLOCK — March 5, 1864.

My Dear Wife: Our cavalry surprised a rebel camp and captured 100 prisoners and about 500 horses besides destroying three or four flour mills and property too extensive to mention.

William got a letter from his dear wife last night. She feels quite bad for she says Alice Collins has reported a story that he slept with three girls one night and she does not like it much. I would not if I were in her place. I think there must be some mistake, for I do not think he would cut up such a caper as that so near home, much less tell Alice of it. I do not know what is the matter with him nor do I care much. He knows that I do not like his Mary nor never did see how he can, but you know love will go where it is sent and you know somebody must like her and he may as well be the victim. Give my love to all.

Edgar W. Clark.

Notes: Rumors of wild partying by his brother, William. Steve Soper reported that William and his wife Mary had at least two daughters after the war. Soper writes it is possible that William and Mary separated after their second daughter, Gertrude, was born in 1876. William moved to California and married a California woman in 1883.

CAMP BULLOCK — March 7, 1864.

My Dear Wife: My cold is all gone since we went off on that march the other day. I never enjoyed better health than in the last year. Yes, I think it would cure about any cold to sleep in a nice feather bed with a nice woman by one's side. I am sorry there will not be a draft in DeWitt for I would like to see some of the chaps come who are at home hindering others from going. I wish every man who is able to shoulder a gun to come and help put down the rebellion so we can all come home. Give my love to all your folks and save a share for yourself.

From your husband, Edgar W. Clark.

CAMP BULLOCK — March 9, 1864.

My Dear Wife: I wish I could see you on my birthday. I think the president is getting in earnest about this war. He will soon call out for 200,000 more men and I think we will bring this rebellion to a close. I think that they would surrender now if it was not for the president's last proclamation, all but the leaders, and then he calculates to make them swing by the neck and I think the punishment will be just. I think the war will open pretty early in the spring.

Edgar W. Clark.

Historical context: More Union soldiers were needed. As described by Paddy Griffith in "Battle Tactics of the Civil War," within six months a regiment of 1,000 could be reduced to 600 people. Some were killed or wounded, some were not tough or brave enough, some were disabled, some were sick, some were absent on furlough or assigned to support duties like nurses or bakers. Edgar had his doubts but he persisted as a soldier.

Spotsylvania. Fighting was most intense at the Mule Shoe salient on the right of this photo. The Bloody Angle occupied a small knoll. Of the 17,000 men killed or wounded, most occurred within sight of this photo. (Michael P. Clark).

At 4 a.m. on May 12, the 3rd Michigan Infantry was involved in a surprise attack on rebel forces. The charge resulted in mass confusion. Hand-to-hand bloodshed lasted over 20 hours. (National Park Service).

Chapter Twelve

Bloody battles, brutal campaign

Edgar is in good health. Catherine has started writing her own letters and appears to have moved from Lansing to her parents' house in DeWitt. Gen. U.S. Grant takes over; no more retreats. Edgar hopes the war will end by summer. Edgar describes familiarity with the dead.

CAMP BULLOCK — March 15, 1864.

My Dear Wife: I am glad to think you are going to have a good neighbor around your house. I guess you will find out the name of your neighbor. I am quite anxious to know what his name is. Give my best wishes to your father and mother and all the rest and do not forget to kiss the children for me every day.

Edgar W. Clark.

CAMP BULLOCK — March 16, 1864.

My Dear Wife: Today we have been on review. The corps was reviewed by its commander. There were 20,000 soldiers in review. It was a grand sight. There were about 25 ladies with three officers riding around seeing the troops of the 3rd Army Corps. I wish you could have seen them. I think you are improving very fast in writing. Keep on and you will soon write good enough for anybody to read.

Edgar W. Clark.

CAMP BULLOCK — March 21, 1864.

My Dear Wife: I am still enjoying the best of health and able to eat my allowance on what the government furnishes to us. We have a little duty when the weather is pleasant. We drill two hours a day and that is beneficial but we try to get out of all that we can. I will hardly know how to go to work when I get out of this. I will be so lazy that I cannot work, I am afraid.

The rebels are only 10 miles off but they do not seem to have a desire to come out and attack us and continue to prepare themselves to fight us when we advance on them when the weather becomes favorable in the spring. I think we will be successful because we have a new commander who the people and armies have the fullest confidence in. I am sure we must be successful and if so the war cannot last another year.

Edgar W. Clark.

Historical context: The war lasted slightly more than another year. Edgar's new commander was Gen. U.S. Grant, who Robert E. Lee could not intimidate or outthink. Former U.S. Gen. David Petraeus described Grant as one of the rare generals in U.S. history who was expert in operations, tactics and strategy. For example, at Vicksburg, Grant showed brilliance by finding a way to attack the city by leaving his supply lines and confronted the city from rebel territory in the south. He faced two Confederate armies and won five battles. At Chattanooga, he broke a Confederate siege and then ordering successful attacks up the side of Lookout

Mountain, driving Confederates into Georgia. By pinning Lee outside Richmond, Grant prevented Lee from sending troops to stop Gen. William Sherman's March to the Sea. Grant, by refusing to retreat, gave his troops confidence. However, Grant was not exempt from criticism, specifically with a suicidal assault at Cold Harbor and a mysterious failure to provide hands-on direction at Petersburg.

CAMP BULLOCK — March 23, 1864.

My Dear Wife: I am glad you remember the many happy hours spent in one another's society and I hope they will not be the last. You have had more deaths in your community than we have had in our regiment in the last six months and we have been in two battles since that time. So you see that men die out of the Army as well as in. We had one man die the other day with the measles, and that is the first death by disease that has been in the regiment since last spring. You must not worry about me. As long as I am well I can eat government rations. The idea of sending to you for money — I would starve before I would do it if I was well but if I was sick in some hospital it would make a difference. In doing so, you show your interest in my happiness and welfare and it shows that you are true and faithful to your husband. Be a good girl and consider me your husband.

Edgar W. Clark.

CAMP BULLOCK — March 25, 1864.

My Dear Wife: I will tell you how we work our victuals. Our meals are primarily pork and beef twice a week. We cook them as we would any meat, but make our coffee as you would make tea. We put as much water in our dish as we want and then we put the coffee on at the same time. We put in the water and as soon as it boils, we think it is done. We have a loaf of bread every day.

It weighs a pound-and-a-half. But I think we will soon come down on our hardtack and pork, sugar and coffee. I think we will soon commence an active campaign. You must be a good girl and I will be a good boy until death.

Edgar W. Clark.

CAMP BULLOCK — March 26, 1864.

My Dear Wife: I am glad that you can write your own letters. I am most overjoyed at your handwriting. Your own letter writing looks well and now you should practice. I think we will soon see stirring times. Our Army is to be reorganized. The corps to which we have been in is to be broken up and put in the 2nd Corps. The president of the United States will be in the Army next week with a new commander, U.S. Grant, who will review us. I hope we will have good luck and whip the rebels this summer and then I think we will see the end of the rebellion by fall.

My time is more than half out and time is passing away fast. If we can keep up good courage we will see each other some time or other. I have a great hope that we will see each other and enjoy ourselves again as we used to when we were together. I hope Mina is a good girl. I am glad she thinks she is getting to be quite a girl. Take good care of them and kiss them for me and write often.

Your husband, Edgar W. Clark.

CAMP NEAR BRANDY STATION — April 3, 1864.

My Dear Wife: The regiment moved about 2 miles last Thursday. We are camped near the railroad. I think it is more pleasant than it ever was. William and I tent together. We have got as nice a tent as there is in the regiment. There is not much news in camp. All seem confident that the war cannot last any longer than this summer. You must give my love to all and save a share for yourself.

Edgar W. Clark.

BRANDY STATION — April 10, 1864.

My Dear Wife: I think you write well for a new beginner. I could read every word of it. I am glad the children are tough and healthy.

Edgar W. Clark.

BRANDY STATION — April 14, 1864.

My Dear Wife: There is no one who wants this war to close any more than I do, but when it will be, time must tell the story. I hope by fall, if not sooner. You wrote about so many dying around you in the last six months. That is more than have died or been killed in our regiment in the last year. We have been in six battles, and two of them the heaviest of the war, Gettysburg and Chancellorsville.

Edgar W. Clark.

BRANDY STATION — April 15, 1864.

My Dear Wife: I am well and enjoying myself first-rate but am lonesome. I have not slept on a feather bed since the last night I slept with you. I have not had a warm biscuit since you made them for me that Sunday before I left you. I try to lead an honest and virtuous life — do unto others as I wish they would do by me and in so doing I find no trouble in getting along here in the Army.

Edgar W. Clark.

BRANDY STATION — April 17, 1864.

My Dear Wife: Your kind and affectionate letter found me well as usual. I was very glad to get such a letter from you; they do me a great deal of good. I read it over two or three times and then did as you requested and burned it. You must not be afraid to write such letters to me for no one will see them but me and I am sure they will not hurt me. You must not keep anything from me that you think I should hear. I think you improve every letter you write.

If I come out all right I will be very glad and I am confident that I will and that we will see each other again. I know the value of a good house, being deprived of one as long as I have. I wish you could peep into our shanty today and see how we live comfortably; we enjoy ourselves here in old Virginia. My dear, it is expected that we will move soon and then we will see some pretty hard times and some very stirring times. If I come out all right I shall feel very glad.

Mr. Peter Clark of Lansing has had bad luck losing so many children. I have not seen a dead person since last fall and he was a rebel, and I gave him a kick and picked his pocket. I love to roam on a field of battle at night and see if they need any water or help.

I am sorry to hear that Mina has the ague. I hope it will not last very long. I also hope she will get well and be a good girl. You must kiss her for me and take the best kind of care for her. I hope to see them very much and I hope to when this cruel war is over. I wrote to you last Friday because I was so lonesome. I know the value of a good home, being deprived of one so long. I wish you could peep inside our shanty and see how comfortably we enjoy ourselves in old Virginia. Dear, it is expected that we will move soon and there will be some pretty hard times. I wish the war was over with. I must say goodbye for the present and a kiss to you and the children.

Edgar W. Clark.

Notes: Symptoms of ague are marked by fever and chills. Mina would have been about 3 years old.

BRANDY STATION — April 21, 1864.

My Dear Wife: Your kind and loving letter was received with pleasure. Today we were reviewed by General Grant. There were nearly 50,000 soldiers and it was a splendid sight. Catherine, we expect to move soon. Warm weather is coming, the roads are getting in good condition and I soon think that we will make an advance and try our fortune with the traitors. This Army is in splendid condition with plenty of rations and clothing. I expect all communications with Washington will be cut off for a short time.

I know you must feel very anxious about me being exposed to so many dangers. Your thoughts will wander when you hear of a big battle and if I was killed or wounded. You must not worry yourself about me. I will try to do the best I can to write to you as often as there is mail to go out. I hope you will do the best you can, be a good and faithful woman, honest and virtuous and write as often as you can. Catherine, you must accept my warmest love and devoted kiss from your husband.

Edgar W. Clark.

BRANDY STATION — May 3, 1864.

My Dear Wife: I was glad to hear that you were getting along as well as you are. I think you can settle better down home than you can in Lansing all alone and a good deal safer. I am afraid you will not hear from me often this summer because we expect to move every day and then our communications will be cut. A forward movement will be made, then you will find out by the papers about our movements quicker than we can write. I wish you were with me to fix my pants and sew some buttons on my clothes and do a little cooking for me.

I will escape the Sunday morning inspection which is considerable for one who is as lazy as I am. I think we will commence a march about the middle of this week. The weather has been very warm and pleasant for the last two or three weeks. Peach trees have been in blossom for nearly three weeks. Apples and cherries are beginning to bloom. Grass is large enough for cattle to get a good living. There has got to be some hard fighting due this spring. I feel as though I will come out all safe and sound. I do not believe a person will die until his time comes, and if he is to be killed by a ball or by disease, it might as well be for the defense of his country as any other way.

Catherine, tell my mother I hope she may live to see the end of this wicked rebellion and see peace and happiness again restored to this country. Tell her I hope that I may live to enjoy many happy hours with you and the children and the rest of my dear friends and relatives in a united and peaceful country that I have tried to save. I hope this summer will settle this rebellion and if it does I will come home by fall and see you all. Give my love to all inquiring friends and save a share for yourself and the children.

No more this time from your husband, Edgar W. Clark.

Notes: Apparently, Catherine and her two toddlers moved in with her parents in DeWitt, a small town just north of Lansing in Clinton County. Once again, it is clear the depth of personal duty that Edgar felt toward saving the Union and the hardship this placed on his family at home. These are not the words of a new recruit, full of innocent eagerness to see war. Having witnessed the impact of terrible battles, Edgar's commitment to die for his country comes with full knowledge and awareness. Apart from combat, familiarity with death was far more common in the mid-1800s when Americans were generally helpless against cholera, yellow fever, tuberculosis and other diseases. Life expectancy at birth was only 40 years. There were shocking rates of both infant and maternal mortality. For instance, the first two wives of Michigan Gov. Austin Blair died in childbirth.

BRANDY STATION — May 3, 1864.

My Dear Wife: I am on duty today, helping draw some wood to cook our rations. I shall not work very hard, I can assure you, for I am getting too lazy to work. I don't know how I can get a hireling after I get home. Soldiering spoils a man for work. A year ago today I fought the battle of Chancellorsville. Our captain and a good many others were killed. This world has many tempting evils to allure and destroy the happiness we ought to enjoy but we must set our price high and strive with good deeds and a strong resolution to win and we will surely do it.

Edgar W. Clark.

Notes: Long days of inaction broken by days of horrible war are the lot of the infantry soldier. Nevertheless, Edgar shouldn't be commenting about his laziness when his wife is struggling to keep the home fires burning. In any case, Grant kept Edgar and others in continuous battles all summer.

Historical context: With Edgar's former commander of the 3rd Corps, Gen. Daniel Sickles, laid up with an amputated leg, and the Corps itself devastated by casualties, the entire corps was merged in March into the 2nd Corps led by Gen. Winfield Scott Hancock. Grant chose to attack the Confederates in the Wilder-

ness along the same familiar territory as Chancellorsville. The heavy undergrowth hampered the Union's manpower advantages and also limited the use of artillery and cavalry. The Battle of the Wilderness from May 5 to 7 turned into another bloody firefight for the Union, which was flanked by the Confederates.

In the Wilderness, the 2nd Corps under Hancock was busily fighting in a hellish dense woods: There was a red, smoky haze, rifles flashing in the gloom, vision blocked by trees and brush in cramped quarters with few roads. No great advantage was gained by either army but based on the past tendencies of Union generals, a retreat would have come next. Instead, when Grant led an advance to the south and east of the Confederate position, his troops cheered.

The next battle was at Spotsylvania. Had the Union arrived first, it would have been between the rebel Army and Richmond and would have forced the rebels to attack. But Lee had the advantage of shorter interior lines, arrived first and built defensive positions. The battle from May 8 to May 21 had similarities to the Wilderness with one major exception. A young Union colonel, Emory Upton, spotted a weak spot called the Mule Shoe — a salient that jutted out from Confederate lines. It would be vulnerable to an attack. Worse for the Confederates, Lee became confused and figured that Grant did not intend to attack the position, wrote Thomas Buell in "The Warrior Generals: Combat Leadership in the Civil War." Lee had pulled artillery from the salient. A part of the salient was called "Bloody Angle." Upton planned an attack with an innovative formation. Rather than use wide lines, he used narrower lines to puncture the rebel lines like a needle. Beginning at 4:30 a.m. on May 12, 1864, a Union column attacked. Edgar's 3rd Michigan Infantry was in the second line directly behind the 5th Michigan Infantry. In a shroud of mist and darkness, as Buell wrote, there was a "mad rush" of

Union troops, for once having the advantage of surprise. Within minutes, several thousand Confederate soldiers were captured along with two senior officers. Quickly, the battle turned into bedlam, "a struggling, flailing arena of pandemonium," Buell wrote.

"No tongue can describe the scene around me," wrote Daniel Holt, assistant surgeon with the 121st New York Infantry, in a letter to his wife. "Dead and dying men by the scores and the hundreds lie piled upon each other in promiscuous disorder."

Jedediah Hotchkiss, a Confederate topographer, wrote: "Infantrymen, from opposite sides of the works, climbed up and fired into the faces of their opponents; they grappled one another and attempted to drag each other across the breastworks; bayonet thrusts were made through crevices; the continuous musketry fire cut off large trees standing in the line of the works; the dead and the dying had to be flung into the rear to give room for the living, fighting ones ..."

For over 20 hours, so many bodies piled up that they could be used as breastworks. The sheer brutality of the battle was described in the book, "For Cause and Comrades: Why Men Fought in the Civil War" by James M. McPherson. Said a Union officer: "I never expect to be fully believed when I tell of the horrors of Spotsylvania because I should be loath to believe it myself."

For instance, an oak tree stump was so riddled with bullets that it appeared to have been whittled down. That jagged stump has been preserved by the Smithsonian, a dramatic example of the firestorm. It looks like a hand with an index finger pointing up. You can see it by making an Internet search for "Spotsylvania stump."

As Union and Confederate forces surged back and forth, Lee led a counterattack to halt the Union advance. Finally, Lee pulled *back his forces from the Mule Shoe to a new defensive line. The fighting claimed about 17,000 casualties.*

By May 21, Grant moved south and east toward the North Anna River.

CAMP IN BATTLEFIELD — May 13, 1864.

My Dear Wife: Through the mercy of a kind providence, I am permitted to write you a few lines to inform you that William and I are still in the land of the living. We have been in a battle every day for the last nine days. Our company has lost very heavy in killed or wounded. We went in the first battle with 39, and this morning we can muster only eight.

Yesterday was the worst day we ever had. Our division charged the enemy's stronghold and captured about 3,000 prisoners and 30 large cannon and gained a large victory. Our forces are following them up and I think will find them not a great way off. We have lost about half our regiment in killed, wounded and missing.

You must not worry about me. I am doing as well as I can. The dead and wounded are lying around on both sides. I must stop for the mail is going out.

Edgar W. Clark.

Historical context: In just two battles, at the Wilderness and Spotsylvania, Edgar's company was reduced from 39 to eight survivors, including Edgar and his brother, William. Edgar had been winning the battle lottery over and over. It had to be difficult for his wife to read about all the casualties and not worry.

CAMP IN WOODS — May 15, 1864.

My Dear Wife: We have not had any fighting since the 12th of the month but we have been in sight of the enemy all the time. Our pickets are continually fighting with them. We keep on the go most of the time, up about every night holding breastworks and rifle pits to protect us from their sharpshooters. It has rained every day and when it rains in Virginia it is muddy, so we are a very dirty-looking lot.

On the 12th we had not over a half-mile march when we came onto them. We took them by surprise on their flank or in their rear so their guns could not bear on us. We charged up to their breastworks and took a large amount of prisoners. As soon as we captured their guns, horses and ammunition, we turned their own guns on them and I tell you we made them light out on a double quick. Our wounded and killed were very slight on that charge.

Edgar W. Clark.

Notes: This was another reference to the Bloody Angle at Spotsylvania. In contrast to his earlier letter, this makes it appear that the battle was an easy Union victory. The surprise attack certainly was, and that is when the 3rd Michigan was involved. But a Confederate counterattack extended the battle for an exhausting 20 hours.

CAMP — May 19, 1864.

My Dear Wife: William and I have passed through very tough times lately. We have not been in a heavy engagement since the 12th. We are in good spirits and confident of ending this cursed rebellion before many months. Today is the first day of rest we have seen since we left camp (*on May 5, two weeks earlier*).

Yours forever, Edgar W. Clark.

Historical context: Grant moved his Army again south and west to the North Anna River (May 23-26). Lee's forces were entrenched on the other side of the river. Grant had to split his forces in three parts. Edgar's 2nd Corps led by Gen. Winfield Scott Hancock seized the Chesterfield Bridge over the North Anna River.

RIFLE PITS, SOUTH OF NORTH ANNA RIVER — May 26, 1864.

My Dear Wife: I received a letter from you dated May 14 in which you said you never expected to hear from me again. You must not give up so easily as that. If you do, you will not enjoy yourself much I am afraid. We have not been in much danger since I wrote to you last. We advanced down to this river and gained a very important point where the rebels tried their best not to let us come down, but we were bound to stay and we did. They shot a good many balls at us from their cannons and rifles but that could not scare us, although we lost about a dozen men killed and wounded. We are now about 2 miles from Richmond. When we get there it will be hard to tell, for the rebels are in a strong force about a mile from us behind strong works. It will be hard to get them out of their works.

William wanted I should tell you he killed a rebel yesterday. He has a Sharps target rifle that will kill a man as far as you can see. He went out to the skirmish line and got a good shot off, and after he shot, he saw four men carrying a man off.

Some nights we will advance and then build breastworks and fortify our positions and work all night. There has not been a day we have not had our knapsacks on since we left camp, nor do I think we will have much rest until Richmond is in our hands, which I hope will not be long but none can tell how long it will be. I cannot write to you as often as I would wish. You must not worry about me for I will try to take good care of myself and you must do the same. I will write to you as often as I can. Kiss the children for me and accept my warmest love and well wishes.

From your husband, Edgar W. Clark.

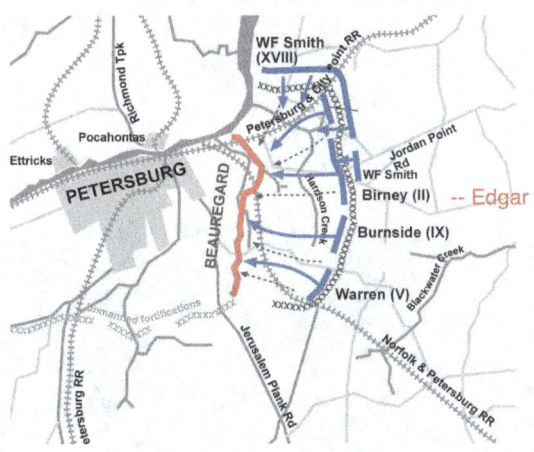

The second day at Petersburg was a fiasco, a delayed attack on a weakened rebel position. Union forces assaulted sections filled with Confederate soldiers. Had the attack occurred earlier with a reconnaissance to find weak sections, Union forces could have walked into Petersburg and shortened the war. Instead, it continued for about 10 months. Edgar Clark was a victim of the poor generalship. (Jonathan James).

Entrenchments at Petersburg provided excellent cover for rebel troops. After a summer of ferocious Union assaults, some soldiers were reluctant to attack. After more failed assaults, a siege ensued. (Ray Richardson).

Harrison Creek at Petersburg was the site where Edgar Clark was wounded on the second day's attack, June 16, 1864. (Ray Richardson).

City Point June 20th 1864

My Dear Wife

I thought I would write you
a few lines to let you know how I get along.
about an hour after I wrote the first part of this
letter our Division went in on a charge about
sundown and I was severly wounded in the left
leg, shattering the bone in my knee joint.

Chapter Thirteen

'Bloody fiasco' at Petersburg

Edgar sprints from Confederate captors. The Overland Campaign moves south of Richmond at Petersburg, where Edgar's luck runs out. Also, a look at Andersonville Prison as well as the Union's hospital and medical system.

PAMUNKEY RIVER — May 29, 1864.

My Dear Wife: The last two days we have been on the march all the time. We are nearer to Richmond but we have changed our base on the peninsula. Our company is now so small we have got only eight men on duty. I have only 14 months left to stay and when that time expires you will see me at home without fail for I would not stay in the service any longer for all the greenbacks Uncle Sam has got. We must keep a stiff upper lip and all will come out safe one of these days. We will see some heavy fighting yet before this rebellion is through but I think I will come out all safe.

From your husband, Edgar W. Clark.

Notes: Edgar's optimism about his fate generally comes true.

CAMP — May 31, 1864.

My Dear Wife: You must not worry about me for I think I am lucky and I will come out all safe one of these days. I must tell you how near I came to be taken prisoner the other day. I would have been taken but for a bully pair of legs. I had to throw down my knapsack with my portfolio and all of my writing papers and the house knife that mother made. It had a nice pair of scissors in it.

Edgar W. Clark.

Historical context: Given the many casualties in his regiment, Edgar was feeling lucky. But his wife must have been wondering when his luck would run out. As close as the armies were to each other, with all the confusion, it is no surprise that being captured was always possible. He certainly wouldn't want to be sent to Andersonville in Georgia about 125 miles south of Atlanta. According to the National Park Service, 45,000 prisoners were held there in total and nearly 13,000 died from disease, poor sanitation, malnutrition, overcrowding or exposure. Many of the prisoners were transferred from prisons in Richmond and were already in poor condition. At one point, 33,000 prisoners were in a stockaded area built for 10,000. Andersonville was marked by open sewers and tainted drinking water. Even today, Andersonville is in a secluded area far from most cities. The prison was so badly designed and supported that it is a wonder that so many prisoners survived. As noted by Walter F. Smith of the 16th Connecticut Infantry: "The introduction of disease into the camp, the pollution of the water supply, inadequate medical care, lack of shelter, short and defective rations and overcrowding — all these contributed to the terrifying mortality rate, which in August reached 100 a day."

The lack of supplies was ridiculous. For instance, there weren't enough nails to construct barracks or enough sheet iron for baking pans.

A good book about the conditions there was written by a former newspaper employee from Jackson, Mich . — "John Ransom's Andersonville Diary." On March 14, 1864, two months before Edgar avoided capture, Ransom was sent there. Ransom was not a journalist, he worked in the composing room of the Jackson Daily Citizen, placing lead type on the pages. But he certainly was literate. He managed to acquire paper and pencil.

He described in his diary how a small group of Union soldiers enforced strict dietary and cleanliness rules that were largely responsible for keeping them alive. His first impression was that the Andersonville prison was "a dismal hole." On June 8, he wrote that over 100 were dying each day. By Sept. 7, Ransom and some others were allowed to leave for a hospital in Savannah, but only soldiers who could walk were allowed to go. Ransom barely made it out, helped to walk by a friend. On Nov. 1, he was moved to a camp at Millen, Ga. After several more moves, in early December Ransom and several others jumped off a train car near Savannah and were rescued by enslaved people in the woods. "The Negroes were fairly jubilant at being able to help genuine Yankees," he wrote. After a series of adventures and the continued aid of enslaved people, Ransom and his fellow soldiers were able to meet the Union Army led by Gen. William Tecumseh Sherman near Savannah. Ransom, seeing people he knew from the 9th Michigan Cavalry, danced and yelled in the middle of the road. Then he saw his old company from Jackson, Mich. They thought Ransom was dead; funeral services had been held for him. Officers who read portions of his diary said some of the scenes he described were "incredible." They still are incredible today.

Ovid Futch in his "History of Andersonville Prison" quoted Eliza Frances Andrews, who passed through the prison: "It is dreadful. My heart aches for the poor wretches, Yankees though they are and I am afraid that God will suffer some terrible retribution to fall upon us for letting such things happen." Though attempts have been made to excuse the conditions, Futch concluded that "the Confederate government should not have permitted the terrible conditions that existed at Andersonville." One reason for the large numbers of prisoners there is that Confederate leaders repeatedly would not agree to prisoner exchanges that included Black troops. It is curious that respected books on Andersonville never mention that fact. Futch wrote, "If the Confederacy could no longer provide for its prisoners and was yet unwilling to surrender, it should have released them on parole," as two Confederate officers overseeing the prison recommended. In fact, paroles were common in the Civil War on both sides.

Surely the prisoners from Andersonville were little threat to rejoin their units in combat. Walt Whitman described the Union prisoners arriving in Washington in April of 1865: "Can those be men — those little livid brown ash-streaked monkey-looking dwarfs? Are they really not mummified, dwindled corpses? ... Probably no more appalling sight was ever seen on this earth." Those responsible deserve "endless damnation," Whitman wrote.

In fairness, Union prisons weren't much better, and the Union had more resources. The Elmira, N.Y. prison, the largest in the Union, had 2,970 deaths out of 12,100 prisoners — a death rate of 24.5 percent compared to the 29 percent death rate at Andersonville. The Union retaliated for the bad conditions in Confederate prisons. In total, the percentage of soldiers who died in captivity was 15.5 percent for Union soldiers in rebel prisons vs. 12 percent of Confederates in federal prisons. A comprehensive evaluation of the Civil War prisons was conducted by James Gillispie in his book "Andersonvilles of the North: The Myths and Realities of Northern Treatment of Civil War Prisoners." Gillispie documents many instances when prisoner exchanges were offered but denied because Confederates refused to include African American troops in the exchanges. The Union had good reason to insist on including Black troops because they were needed. It wasn't just altruism.

A postscript: I always wondered why Gen. William T. Sherman did not send troops to free the prisoners at Andersonville. He did. He described in his memoirs that he sent the cavalry of Gen. George Stoneman to destroy a railroad and then go to Macon and Andersonville. Instead, Stoneman went to Macon first where he destroyed some railroad cars but found his retreat obstructed. "There he became bewildered," Sherman wrote, "and sacrificed himself for the safety of his command." Stoneman surrendered and about 700 troops were captured while the rest escaped to Sherman's main army. In short, the attempt to rescue Andersonville prisoners was bungled.

CAMP FIELD ON ROAD TO PETERSBURG — June 4, 1864.

My Dear Wife: It is noon now and the cannons begin to roar. I must hurry for the colonel will say fall in pretty soon.

Edgar W. Clark.

Historical context: In just two months, from May 5 to July 4 of 1864, the Army of the Potomac lost two-thirds as many casualties as in the three previous years in battle. And Edgar was in the middle of this. The devastating frontal attack on June 3 at Cold Harbor was the only one that U.S. Grant regretted in his memoirs. Estimates of Union losses ranged from 3,000 to 7,000 in about 20 minutes. Lee's attack on the third day at Gettysburg, Pickett's

Charge, was inexcusable because Lee knew what soldiers could do in a fortified position on a hill. By the same token, Grant should have known better than to order an assault at Cold Harbor where legend has it that soldiers pinned their names and identifying information to their uniforms — Union soldiers did not wear dog tags. Luckily, Edgar's unit was spared from the devastating Cold Harbor attack. As Thomas Buell wrote in "The Warrior Generals: Combat Leadership in the Civil War," after a summer of casualties the soldiers were zombielike, their assaults were weakening. Replacements for the thousands of veterans who had been lost were draftees and bounty jumpers, "ill-disciplined cannon fodder who often either deserted or were quickly killed by their inexperience." Soldiers, fearing suicidal assaults on Confederate entrenchments, simply hit the ground after being ordered forward and fired from a prone position. Stephen Minot Weld of the 56th Massachusetts Infantry wrote that "the feeling here in the Army is that we have been absolutely butchered, that our lives have been periled to no purpose and wasted. In the Second Corps, the feeling is so strong that the men say they will not charge any more works." The Army of the Potomac had been devastated by losses at this point. James McPherson in "For Cause and Comrades" wrote that modern research shows that an army unit is wrecked psychologically if it twice loses casualties equal to one-third of its strength. Many units during the Overland Campaign had suffered such losses. During Edgar's tenure, the 3rd Corps was merged into the 2nd Corps. The 3rd Michigan Regiment was merged into the 5th Michigan Regiment just days before he was shot. His Company G was merged with Company H.

BIVOUACKED FOR NIGHT — June 4, 1864.

My Dear Wife: Since I wrote you, we have been under fire every day but our regiment has lost but a few men, none in our company. I think we are very lucky but our time will come in a few days. We are so near Richmond that we cannot expect anything else. We hear the cannons roar in every direction but cannot tell with what success. We stop during the day to fortify and march at night to gain new positions.

I tell you this is the country to live in. There is not a field 10 acres big but what has a beautiful spring on it. The rivers and small streams are good enough to cook with and drink.

Edgar W. Clark.

Historical context: Edgar described bullets whistling around him on several occasions. Leander Stilwell in his book "The Story of a Common Soldier," described an incident during the Battle of Shiloh. He hid behind a tree that was too thin to offer much protection. Nearby, another Union soldier, behind a much thicker tree, was shot. Stilwell wrote: "But all at once, there he was, lying on his back, at the foot of his tree, with one leg doubled under him, motionless — and stone dead!" On another occasion, Stilwell discovered a bullet had made nine holes in his clothing and overcoat and never touched his body. Recall that an artillery shell exploded over Edgar's head at Chancellorsville and another artillery ball bounded over his unit at Fredericksburg. In his reports to a local newspaper, Wilbur Fisk of the 2nd Vermont wrote that close calls were numerous. He saw a gun shot out of a soldier's hands, a bullet stopped by an account book in a soldier's pocket and a soldier's nose scratched by a bullet. Fisk wrote that one gets used to death and the "extreme peril" of battle. Soldiers often took death calmly. One soldier, shot in the jugular vein, was asked what to say to his friends. "Tell them that I was a good soldier." As Fisk wrote: "It is difficult in the time of action, the extreme peril one's life is in. Death there seems of less consequence than anywhere else, one gets used to it. ... But when the excitement is over and we go back to camp and see so many comrades whose society was our pleasure, missing, we feel very keenly the loss we have sustained." That explains why PTSD would strike a veteran long after combat.

CAMP TEN MILES FROM RICHMOND — June 6, 1864.

My Dear Wife: We are making slow but sure progress. I think if we do not meet with a reversal we will go into Richmond by the 4th of July. If we do, we will have a good time.

Last night we marched and worked all night. We went within 10 rods (55 yards) of the enemy picket line and took a strong position and fortified it stronger and this evening they had to fall back. In this way, we will gain the advance and gain a grand victory over the rebels. We are every day under fire from the rebel guns and sometimes in a good deal of danger, but fortunate. You are in my thoughts all of the time. Give my respects to Lydia and a double share for yourself.

Your husband, Edgar W. Clark.

CAMP NEAR COLD HARBOR — June 9, 1864.

My Dear Wife: You must not worry to make yourself sick, which I fear you will do. There will be plenty of time enough to feel bad when you hear I am killed or wounded. We are constantly in danger though for the last few days, I have laid still for the first time since we started.

Yesterday there was a flag of truce and our boys and the rebels talked. They are right sick of fighting and they allow that we are, too. We tell them that we have no grudge against them but we must preserve the Union at all hazards. A good many of them say they hoped we would but they say they would have given up long ago if it was not for the president's proclamation freeing all their slaves and his proclamation punishing all traitors above the grade of lieutenant colonel.

Edgar W. Clark.

Historical context: Catherine's worries reached a crescendo — and for good reason. There was no formal way to notify the next of kin when a soldier was wounded or killed. As James McPherson wrote in "The War That Forged a Nation," more than half of the soldiers who died in the war were buried without identification. Meanwhile, the rebel soldiers confirmed to Edgar this was a war about slavery. Or to use a finer point, slavery was the single issue that could not be compromised. How do you compromise on free-dom? Abraham Lincoln and the 1860 platform of the Republi-can Party stated that they only opposed extending slavery to new territories. This was unacceptable to the seceding states. After the Confiscation Acts and the Emancipation Proclamation freed en-slaved people in the seceding areas, there was no turning back. In December of 1863, Lincoln proposed a Proclamation of Amnesty and Reconstruction. The proclamation is best known for Lincoln's proposal that when 10 percent of voters in a state took a loyalty oath, that state could be readmitted to the Union. He offered full pardons and restoration of property (except for enslaved people) for those Confederates who take an oath to "faithfully support, defend and protect the Constitution" as well as acts of Congress referring to enslaved people. Exceptions were officers or agents of the Confederate government, those who left the judiciary to aid the Confederate government, all those above the rank of colonel in the Army or lieutenant in the Navy, all those who left seats in the U.S. Congress, all those who resigned commissions in the U.S. Army to join the rebellion and all those who treat Black people other than prisoners of war.

CAMP — June 10, 1864.

My Dear Wife: We are laid now where I wrote to you the day before yesterday. The cannons keep on roaring, telling the enemy we are bound to stay with them and not to give up until this rebellion is crushed. Our company has been consolidated with Company F. The two companies now number over 80 men. We are commanded by a first lieutenant who none of us like. I do not look for as good times as we have had. Our commander will not be so kind and good. I hope this regiment will retain its good name and not bring a dark spot in its history. Green berries are getting good to eat. I went yesterday to get a lot of huckleberries and cooked them. I have had green peas and green apples.

From your husband, Edgar W. Clark, to his wife, Catherine Clark.

CAMP TEN MILES FROM RICHMOND — June 12, 1864.

My Dear Wife: We have been in this camp now one week. I am very anxious for this rebellion to come to a close. I hope my life will be spared to return home and see you all one of these days. We have seen a good many pass by on stretchers but think nothing of it. We are constantly in danger but none of our regiment has been hurt for a number of days. We keep down behind our works where the balls fly over our heads. But in some parts of our lines, men are getting hurt. Both sides are protected by small earthworks. As soon as a man shows his head above the works, the one who sees it first will shoot. A man would stand no chance at all to stand up. Imagine yourself as a target for a thousand shots a minute and then think what a slim chance a soldier has to come out of this all safe. On our part of the line, the boys on both sides have agreed not to fire unless we or they advance, so we are safe. You must not worry too much about me for I have been in danger for most of two years and been in some of the hardest fighting of the war and not been hurt yet.

Edgar W. Clark.

Notes: It is interesting that soldiers informally agreed not to fire on each other unless they were attacked — a small, unofficial ceasefire of sorts. As usual, Edgar told his wife that he had been in hard fighting but not to worry. On June 13, 1864, Edgar Clark's 3rd Michigan Infantry Regiment was merged with the 5th Michigan Infantry. The 3rd Michigan Infantry Regiment was devastated during the Overland Campaign. In official documents, Edgar is sometimes listed as a member of the 5th Michigan, including on his gravestone, because that was his unit when he was discharged from service. Yet he spent 99 percent of his combat experience with the 3rd Michigan. Both the 3rd and 5th Michigan Regiments often fought next to each other, including at Fredericksburg, Gettysburg and Spotsylvania.

Historical context: After the disastrous assault at Cold Harbor, Gen. U.S. Grant did not take the next predictable move to the south, the Union left. He made a daring move, brilliantly executed. The goal was Petersburg, a key railroad and supply location south of Richmond. It was protected lightly by a militia composed of many teenagers and the elderly. The attack was overseen by Gen. Benjamin Butler, who had made little progress in the Carolinas. Grant's engineers built a pontoon bridge 2,200 feet long in less than 48 hours. Grant also sent a diversion toward Richmond to keep Gen. Robert E. Lee convinced that Richmond was the real target. Lee's cavalry was occupied by the diversion, which would normally be used for reconnaissance. On June 12, Grant stealthily began pulling out his forces over four different roads. From June

14 to 17, he successfully moved his entire Army across the James River, using pontoon bridges.

The earthworks at Petersburg, called the Dimmock Line, looked impressive but housed only about 2,500 men on the Eastern end. Yet, Gen. William "Baldy" Smith hesitated. He personally scouted enemy lines. Perhaps he was intimidated by the sight of the earthworks — redans connected to rifle pits, ditches that could be used as moats — and the memory of the disastrous Union assault at Cold Harbor.

As evening fell, June 15, Petersburg was at the mercy of the Union. About 13 hours after he arrived, Smith's assault began at 7 p.m. After two hours of fighting, the Union forces opened a 1.5-mile hole in the Dimmock Line. According to the National Park Service, the attack on Petersburg on June 15 by about 15,000 Union soldiers, many of them Black troops, took the Confederates by surprise.

By 9 p.m., the troops had taken five redans, the connecting rifle pits and artillery. A White officer said of the Black troops, "I am now prepared to say that I never ... saw troops fight better, more bravely and with more determination."

John David Smith in the book "Black Soldiers in Blue" reported that the Black troops took six batteries, nine artillery pieces and 200 Confederate prisoners. It was a victory but not a walkover. The 4th Colored Infantry unit suffered wounds of about half its members. The Rev. William Hunter, the chaplain of the 4th, wrote that the unit's performance on June 15 represented the day "when prejudice died in the entire Army of the United States of America."

Gen. Benjamin Butler sent a scout to order Smith to continue the assault: "Petersburg could be taken that night," as Noah Andre Trudeau wrote in "The Last Citadel: Petersburg, Virginia June 1864-April 1865." Then, in a tragedy of errors, the scout couldn't find Smith. He had gone to sleep in a tent far from the troops. Meanwhile, the soldiers realized that they had out-flanked and outfoxed Lee. The moon was bright, 83 percent illuminated. Confederate Gen. P.T. Beauregard said after the war, "Petersburg at that hour was clearly at the mercy of the federal commander, who had all but captured it." (Quoted by James McPherson in "Battle Cry of Freedom").

The Union soldiers were eager to attack the thinly manned works. They knew that Lee's troops were only four to five hours away. True, the Union soldiers were tired, but they could have walked into Petersburg. Yet they were held back from a night-time attack. "The rage of the enlisted men was devilish. The most bloodcurdling blasphemy I ever listened to I heard that night uttered by men who knew they were to be sacrificed on the morrow," wrote Private Frank Wilkeson of the New York Light Artillery in his book, "Recollections of a Private Soldier in the Army of the Potomac. "They were supremely disgusted with the display of military stupidity our generals had made."

Believing his men were exhausted, Smith waited for rein-forcements from Gen. Winfield Scott Hancock's 2nd Corps, including Edgar's newly merged unit, the 5th Michigan. That delay allowed the Confederates overnight to beef up their troops in the trenches from about 2,500 soldiers to about 14,000. Confederate Gen. P.G.T. Beauregard had swiftly reinforced his lines.

Still, the wait continued. The second day's attack on June 16 didn't start till 6 p.m. when Union forces launched a series of piecemeal assaults, resulting in from 2,000 to 2,500 Union ca-sualties, which is when Edgar was shot. They failed to break the Confederate line at Harrison's Creek. Edgar was carried off the field by his brother, William. When Edgar charged, feder-al troops outnumbered Confederates by 50,000 troops to 14,000 rebels. It took a combination of incompetence and miscommunication to bungle the assault.

In his memoirs, Grant noted that the Confederate fortifications were just 2 miles outside of Petersburg. Had Baldy Smith attacked early on June 15, "Petersburg could have been easily taken," Grant wrote. Blame for Smith's delay has to be placed at the feet of Grant, who was strangely uninvolved in the attack. As Ron Chernow wrote in his book on Grant, "Perhaps distracted by the James River crossing, Grant was not as deeply engaged at Petersburg as he should have been." That's incredibly generous. At this point, late in the war, there is no excuse for Grant's inaction. Where were his orders? One of Grant's strengths, in contrast to Lee, is that he wrote clear directions. That did not happen here. Jeff Shaara wrote that Grant's plan was a "flawed and inefficient system." Grant should have ordered all available Union forces to assault the lightly defended Petersburg lines as soon as possible. Hesitancy was not Grant's usual battle plan. Beauregard wrote the Union conveniently attacked exactly where his rebel troops were placed. Why wasn't there a reconnaissance in force, followed by an attack on the weakened sections? The rebels were outnumbered 3 to 1 or more.

Thomas J. Howe, in his masterful book, "The Petersburg Campaign: Wasted Valor: June 15-18, 1864," reported that Smith was confident that he "held the key to Petersburg." That proved to be overconfidence. Howe called that "one of the greatest command blunders of the war." As Howe wrote, "Petersburg represented the best and the worst of federal staff work." The Union moved a massive army across the James River, outflanking and surprising Lee, yet never took advantage of surprise. It was chaos like the Union disasters earlier in the war. Troops got lost, they ran out of ammunition and staff ignored ground reconnaissance and *artillery support. Soldiers like Edgar were forced to charge across open ground toward protected entrenchments.*

As a result, Howe wrote, in just four days the Union lost about 11,000 troops killed, wounded or missing in comparison with about 4,000 Confederate casualties. Howe summed it up as "a bloody fiasco."

Edward Bonekemper III, in his book "The 10 Biggest Civil War Blunders," includes the failures at Petersburg. "Grant's army needed only competence and aggressiveness to break through at Petersburg and virtually end the war," Bonekemper wrote, traits that Grant usually showed. Grant and his generals, however, demonstrated neither. Bonekemper called the assaults at Petersburg from June 15 to June 18 this way: "Inept, tepid, tardy, uncoordinated, unfocused and unsuccessful." Shockingly, it was the kind of poor generalship that occurred before Grant took over the Army of the Potomac.

Summing up the failures, Allan Nevins wrote: "Everybody blamed everyone and everyone else was to blame. ... A comedy of errors and general ineptitude combined with skillful Southern leadership prevented a Northern success ..." By the time Edgar charged on June 16, Grant wrote that the federal advantage had been "squandered." Grant replaced Baldy Smith, who received most of the blame. But in fairness, Grant deserved criticism for his timid underlings at Petersburg just as Lee deserved the blame for his timid underlings at Gettysburg.

Those fateful early days of the Petersburg campaign have largely been ignored by historians, who focus on the siege and the ultimate Union victory. The siege of Petersburg qualified as the longest military campaign of the Civil War, lasting about 10 months from June 1864 to April 1865. As a comparison, the Petersburg campaign lasted almost 10 months while Sherman's march to the sea lasted just over one month and the siege at Vicks-

burg was one-and-a-half months. The Petersburg campaign cost 70,000 casualties (42,000 for the North, 28,000 for the South). For those who want to call Grant a butcher, this will do. The war could have ended in June of 1864 rather than April of 1865.

Gen. James Rusling in his book, "Men and Things I Saw in Civil War Times," quoted Grant: "In war, anything is better than indecision. We must decide. If I am wrong, we shall soon find out, and can do the other thing. But not to decide wastes both time and money, and may ruin everything." As Gen. William Sherman wrote in his memoirs, "Every attempt to make war easy and safe will result in humiliation and disaster."

So Baldy Smith was trying to make the assault on Petersburg easy and safe, when Grant had shown that the army that attacks first usually succeeds. Sadly, Grant was not around to force an immediate assault at Petersburg. In fact, he decided that assaulting entrenchments was useless. One month after the disastrous Petersburg attacks, in July of 1864, he ordered Meade, "I do not want Hancock to attack entrenched lines." (Quoted in "The Last Citadel" by Noah Andre Trudeau.)

Edgar Clark could have been wounded in a great Union victory rather than in a forgotten assault that turned into a lengthy siege. Petersburg was just one of the bloody fiascoes in which Edgar participated: Fredericksburg; the friendly-fire night attack at Chancellorsville; the Peach Orchard at Gettysburg; and the second day's assault at Petersburg. Bloody Angle at Spotsylvania was terrible but not exactly a fiasco since it was an initial Union victory that was not followed up. Nevertheless, Edgar was at all of these battles.

It is worth mentioning that in fighting associated with the Petersburg Campaign, Black regiments would participate in six major engagements. By the end of the war, more than 180,000 Black soldiers served in the Army and about 20,000 served in the Navy. Fifteen Black soldiers and eight Black sailors earned the new Medal of Honor, most of them near the end of the war. As President Lincoln said in 1864, "Abandon all posts now possessed by Black men and we would be compelled to abandon the war in three weeks. We have to hold territory." The war that began to save the Union was converted to another goal to eliminate slavery. The ex-enslaved people themselves helped to save the Union and fulfill the promise of the Declaration of Independence.

TWO MILES FROM PETERSBURG — June 16, 1864.

My Dear Wife: We stopped at sundown Monday night on the banks of the James River and lay there all night in line of battle. The next day we crossed the river and again laid on the bank. Yesterday we came to this place. We heard heavy fighting in this direction. We got here about 11 o'clock last night and found that a regiment of Negro troops had charged and taken the outer rebel works about 1 mile from Petersburg. This place is south of Richmond and quite a large place from the number of steeples that we can count. We have confidence in our commander, U.S. Grant. We think he will bring this rebellion to a close this summer.

The country through which we passed on this side of the river is the best I have seen in Virginia and the richest. There are plenty of all kinds of fruit. Chickens, hogs and sheep are plenty and the soldiers feast generally very well, not caring who they belong to. They go up to a man's house and shoot down a hog or anything they want. We do not see many men in these parts. They are all in the rebel Army fighting against us. If they were at home they would not be fighting against us and could take care of their own property. Our commander places guards on these homes where the people are at home to save their property if they say they are good Union men. But I hope we will conquer them so that we may go home and not molest their property.

We have all kinds of vegetables which grow in the garden since we have been on this side of the river. I hope we will conquer them so we can go home and not molest their property. Catherine, I wish I could see you this afternoon. I would like it very much. You must give my love to all inquiring friends and save a share for yourself. Kiss the children for me and accept a thousand from me.

Yours until death, Edgar W. Clark.

Notes: Edgar ended his letter with a rare reference to death, which appears to have been on his mind and his wife's.

CITY POINT — June 20, 1864.

My Dear Wife: Our division went on a charge about sundown and I was severely wounded in the left leg, shattering the bone in my knee joint. William was close by. I got on his back and he carried me back over a slight rise of ground. Then another soldier was there to help him. I got astride a gun and they both took me to where the ambulance was waiting to carry me back to the field hospital.

After laying on the ground all night under a tree, I was put on the table about 9 in the morning to be examined by the doctor. I was told if it was necessary they would have to take my leg off, which they did. I was carried to a large brick house this same day and the next day I was taken to this place. You must not worry for I am getting along first-rate. There are about 2,000 here under the U.S. Sanitary Commission and everything they can do to relieve the wound they will do. We expect to leave in a day or two for some general hospital. You need not answer until you hear from me. I can sit up about half the time.

No more from your wounded husband.

Edgar W. Clark.

HAREWOOD HOSPITAL, WASHINGTON, D.C . — June 23, 1864.

My Dear Wife: When I wrote you last, I was at City Point near Richmond. About 300 left that place the next day on a large steamboat from his place. You can imagine a fellow must feel sore with a leg off, jolting in ambulances and steamboats for six days without much care. But I am here and my leg is doing well. I was at the very front when I was hit. I lay on the ground while waiting for someone to take me out. They said they could not but if they were obliged to fall back they would carry me with them. At that moment I got sight of William. I made a loud noise calling his name. He heard me, then I knew I was all right.

I was carried to the division hospital. The next morning I had my leg taken off without the least particle of pain. My dear, it is a sad misfortune to me now to be deprived of half a leg but it is one of the misfortunes of war for which none are to blame. It would be an honorable misfortune. I would rather it be a leg than an arm.

I cannot tell you how long I will remain in the Army. I have fought my last battle. I have stood my last guard duty. I am totally disabled from all military duty in this war and all wars to come. I think I shall make a living in some way. How it will be done I have not made up my mind yet. I conclude to stay my time, which will be a year from next August. All soldiers get $16 a month and I know I could not make that at home.

Edgar W. Clark.

Notes: Apparently this was the letter that informed Catherine that her husband had been shot. And Edgar planned to stay in the Army for over a year just to collect his pay? It turned out that he was discharged the following February. His estimates of the length of the war and his discharge were wildly erroneous.

Historical context: The Minie ball was shot at a relatively slow speed, which often caused gaping holes, thus the need for amputations. Drugs and herbal concoctions used during the Civil War were not much different than in the time of Hippocrates, wrote Ira Rutkow in the book "Bleeding Blue and Gray: Civil War Surgery and the Evolution of American Medicine." A soldier might have to wait for a day or two for an amputation. Treatment was often done without antiseptic care. Surgeons did not even wash their hands before operating. Bruce Catton wrote that it was common for a surgeon to clean his scalpel on the sole of his shoe before operating. Doctors wore clothes spattered with blood. Sponges were dipped in cold water before being reused. Training and standards for doctors were spotty; there were no licensing boards. Chloroform was usually used, so that the soldier normally was unconscious for the operation. The surgeon typically used a tourniquet to cut off blood flow before cutting through flesh and tissue with a scalpel. Then a special knife cut through muscle and a bone saw would complete the task. Edgar reported no pain. A skilled surgeon could perform an amputation in 10 minutes.

Massive numbers of the wounded in the Civil War led to advances in medical care. Major Jonathan Letterman, called the "Father of Battlefield Medicine," was credited with many advances. He was born in Canonsburg, Pa., just southwest of Pittsburgh, the son of a surgeon. Letterman served in Florida during the Seminole Indian wars and also served in 1860 and 1861 in the West during wars with the Utes.

Letterman's medical advances were described in the book "Surgeon in Blue" by Scott McGaugh. Medical knowledge was primitive. Bloodletting still was practiced. Blood poisoning was common and there was a high mortality rate. Letterman discovered deplorable outhouses, patients cramped together with poor venti-lation and treatments like mercury that could poison a patient.

Using practices from Europe, Letterman recommended pavil-ion-style hospital designs that allowed for fresh air and plenty of space for patients. To combat widespread malnutrition, Let-terman recommended more fruit and vegetables. Scurvy was so widespread that it affected the fitness of thousands of soldiers. About 3 in 10 soldiers were so weak and ill that they were unfit for service.

In addition, organized ambulance units were created to speed the wounded to treatment. McGaugh wrote that "Letterman re-defined battlefield evacuation from a post-battle scavenger hunt to one marked by military discipline."

In less than four months, Letterman organized hospital care, improved the medical supply systems and created a professional medical corps. He enforced better hygiene and sanitation. Troops were required to bathe regularly. Better care was taken with la-trines.

The result is that the mortality rate for the wounded dropped from 26 percent to 10 percent in two years. Edgar was lucky that he was injured so late in the war when conditions were better. Sad to say, many of the hospital attendants had been worthless in combat, dumped by officers as no good in combat, Catton wrote.

HAREWOOD HOSPITAL — June 24, 1864.

My Dear Wife: I just had my leg done. The doctor says it looks well and if I am careful there is no danger, but I have got to keep still, which comes hard, especially to lay on my back all the time. The weather is very warm here and the flies are very thick. I do not know but they would eat me up if I do not keep fighting them. I have sent William to get me my mail. I hope you will not let this sad misfortune worry you or make you sick. It does not worry or trouble me yet, nor do I calculate to let it. I can sit up until I get tired and then I lay there until I get tired of that and then I sit up again. This is the way I pass many long and lonesome days and the way I calculate to spend many to come. I wish you could be with me but that is impossible. Stay where you are and take good care of yourself and the children.

Our regiment lost a good many men this time. We have good attendance and plenty to eat. We have a good hospital for the men who have been in the Army and got slightly disabled. Once in a while, a woman comes through the ward to see and assist the soldiers and to write their friends but I save them all that trouble. I will not bother them at all unless I get worse. I am at the top side of my bed in good spirits and good courage.

Edgar W. Clark.

HAREWOOD HOSPITAL — June 26, 1864.

My Dear Wife: The doctor says my leg is doing as well as can be expected. I think so myself. It pains me a good deal but no more than is expected with a leg off. I am in good spirits and have a strong constitution and am determined to live so that I can see you and the children and enjoy a good many days with them in peace and happiness.

Catherine, this wound brings about a good many queer transactions. A few days ago I was whole and sound. Today I am three-quarters what I once was. The scene looks odd to me as I look at myself, one leg half as long as the other. I imagine it will look odd to you and more so when you see me wobbling around on crutches. The government furnishes all soldiers with wooden legs. I think that I can get a cork leg so I will not need any crutches for a very long while. There are a good many in this ward who have lost their arms and a good many have lost legs in worse condition than I am.

Catherine, I guess I will have you send me 10 dollars because it's hard to tell when I will get any pay from the government. I have not a particle of clothing, only a coat that was in my knapsack. I lost my pants, drawers and shirt, they all got so bloody that I had to throw them away. All I saved is my portfolio and haversack. All I have on belongs to the hospital. As soon as I can wear clothing I can draw all that I want but there are a good many little delicacies that a person can buy which will help a sick fellow amazingly.

Tell my mother that I have met a sad misfortune and need her sympathy and prayers. Tell her to look on the bright side and not worry too much about me. I shall get along I think without any trouble. We have everything handy and nice and comfortable. Tell Mina her pa has not forgotten her and never will. Tell Lydia to often think of me in my misfortune. Give my love to your father, tell him he must sympathize with me.

I must close by saying please accept my warmest and affectionate love and consider one your loving and unfortunate husband.

Edgar W. Clark to Catherine Clark.

HAREWOOD HOSPITAL — June 28, 1864.

My Dear Wife: My leg has begun healing slow. It has itched so I can hardly keep my hands off it. I always heard that when a sore of any kind itched, it was a good sign. I have a piece of beef steak and a good piece of bread and butter and a cup of tea at noon. Or I get the same and three teaspoons of custard sauce. At night I get bread and butter and a fried egg with a cup of tea.

I dread the nights. My leg pains me more than it does in daylight so I do not get much sleep. The days are long or seem so. I am afraid that you are worrying too much about me for I think I will get along without any difficulty now. The worst days are past. Give my love to all who wish to hear from me and often think of your unfortunate husband.

Edgar W. Clark.

HAREWOOD HOSPITAL — June 30, 1864.

My Dear Wife: It is two weeks to the day since my leg was taken off. I got off the bed last night all alone and have my bed made up. I think I can get around first-rate in two weeks with crutches. I probably will need them for quite a while before I can put on a cork leg. It will be sore and tender for a long time.

I'm thinking of getting my discharge on the first of September and coming home and fixing up the house nice and comfortable, putting a good brick foundation under it and fix up the kitchen good. I will have nearly $200 to fix it up with. Then I will get $100 a year so long as I live.

Edgar W. Clark.

Historical context: Edgar quickly put away the idea of staying in the military and collecting his pay. He was making about $200 a year in the Army. But considering Edgar had a garden and livestock, he would be somewhat self-sufficient.

HAREWOOD HOSPITAL — July 9, 1864.

My Dear Wife: My leg is doing fine. I sit up in the rocking chair for about an hour every day. I can get up from my lounge into the chair. I think in three weeks if nothing happens I will go around on crutches. I saved those pictures you sent last fall and the case is nearly as nice as when you sent it. I made a pocket out of some rubber cloth and put it in my blouse coat. I look at your picture you sent me almost every day. I think I will see you in about six weeks.

Edgar W. Clark.

HAREWOOD HOSPITAL — July 10, 1864.

My Dear Wife: You write you thought as much of me now as you once did. I am glad to hear you think that. You know I was not obliged to go to war, for I had a good home and middling easy circumstances. I thought to myself if we have a country worth saving, it was the duty of every able-bodied man to try to help save his country. I have been in 13 battles and been under fire for 40 days where musket balls and solid shot were flying over our heads in all directions all day long. I thought I was lucky and I should have been wounded long before. I have been under heavier fire of muskets than I was that night but that time I got right square in the way of a bullet. I think by putting $25 with the government's $50 I can get a good cork leg, one that I can walk around very comfortable without a cane or crutches.

Edgar W. Clark.

Historical context: Union soldiers had every right to be furious with the delayed attack on Petersburg that cost so many casualties. Private Frank Wilkeson described the human impact of that terrible delay. After the battle, he found a sergeant sitting under a pine tree, a bandage over his eyes made from a shirt sleeve. Blood was oozing from under the bandage. Sitting by his side was a drummer boy, his blue eyes wet with tears, waiting for an ambulance. Wilkeson pointed toward a field hospital and watched as the boy led the soldier by the hand toward the operating table. They were father and son. As Wilkeson wrote: "I hastened on, swallowed my tears and cursed the delay to take Petersburg."

Edgar Clark spent his initial treatment at Harewood Hospital in Washington, D.C. Note the cramped conditions, which would have contributed to gangrene. More open hospital designs maximized air circulation. (Universal Images Group North America LLC / Alamy Stock Photo.)

Chapter Fourteen

Edgar rehabs amputated leg

Edgar survives gangrene. He keeps a positive attitude as he looks forward to a cork leg. The 1864 election looms. A stalemate continues at Petersburg and Atlanta. As casualties mount, President Abraham Lincoln is told he won't be reelected.

HAREWOOD HOSPITAL — July 13, 1864.

My Dear Wife: My health is good, my appetite is good. I think I can eat anything in the shape of eatables. A different doctor saw me this morning and he said it looked first-rate. He said the man who took my leg off understood his business.

There is great excitement in the city now about the great raid of the rebels. They were fighting all day yesterday within 6 miles of this city. They did not succeed in getting inside. We could plainly hear musketry and heavy cannons. This morning there is no firing and I think the rebels are falling back. The 6th Corps of the Army of the Potomac is here. There are enough without any further help to drive them back but the city authorities are calling on all to put forth every effort to defend the national capital. It would be a sad disaster for this city to be captured or fall in the hands of the enemy.

I will be glad when my leg gets well so I can come home to see you. Nothing would please me better and I think you would like to see me, as bad a cripple as I am.

Edgar W. Clark.

Historical context: Gen. Robert E. Lee sent Gen. Jubal Early to threaten Washington, D.C. with a raid via the Shenandoah Valley. The nation's capital was well defended, yet the raid did upset the Union. It is said that President Abraham Lincoln went to view the battle and was told to duck. Confederate sharpshooters had shot several Union generals. In response, Gen. U.S. Grant sent his cavalry commander, Gen. Philip Sheridan, up the Shenandoah to put down Early. Despite initial setbacks, Sheridan rallied his troops and defeated Early. By the end of the war, Union generals like Sheridan were growing in expertise, helped by weapons like repeating rifles.

HAREWOOD HOSPITAL — July 16, 1864.

My Dear Wife: I am still on the gain. My health continues good and my appetite is first-rate. I don't think I will come home till the last of September or the first of October. Then I think I will have time to fix up the house before very cold weather sets in. My wages and bounty, about $181 in all, will fix up the house and keep us a long while. I will also get a yearly pension of $100 that in ordinary times will support us. I don't know when times will be as good as they once were — probably not in a long while, but we must live in hope.

Edgar W. Clark.

HAREWOOD HOSPITAL — July 19, 1864.

My Dear Wife: My leg has been quite painful for the last two days but it is natural. I cannot expect to feel bully every day with a leg off but I think it is healing all the time and if it only gains a little every day, I will be satisfied.

Edgar W. Clark.

Historical context: Edgar was lucky to have this much medical care. During the Battle of the Wilderness a few months earlier, there were only 30 doctors for 7,000 wounded soldiers.

HAREWOOD HOSPITAL — July 24, 1864.

My Dear Wife: I must tell you that my leg has worsened. A poison got into it. It is not dangerous but this will put it back for quite a while. The doctor has to burn it with a powerful medicine.

Edgar W. Clark.

Historical context: Harewood Hospital, according to a photo of the interior, was crowded with little ventilation, which would have promoted infection. Louisa May Alcott, author of "Little Women," served as a nurse at Union Hospital in Washington, D.C. As quoted by David Williams in "A People's History of the Civil War," Alcott described the place as "a perfect pestilence box — cold, damp, dirty, full of vile odors from wounds, kitchens and stables." In fact, Alcott came down with typhoid fever. So it is no wonder that Edgar's amputated leg developed gangrene. This was common in the unsanitary conditions at the time. Among the gangrene treatments were hand washing, whiskey, cathartics, poultices, and topical agents. Also used were chlorinated water, strong sodium hypochlorite solutions, nitric acid, tinctures of io-

dine and turpentine. Many of these treatments were painful and most of them did not work.

Medical care during the Civil War was unbelievably archaic to modern eyes. As James McPherson wrote in "Battle Cry of Freedom," Civil War doctors were not aware "of the exact relationship between water and typhoid, between unsterilized instruments and infection, between mosquitoes and malaria."

According to a paper from the University of Texas at San Antonio, a report from Civil War surgeon Middleton Goldsmith showed that almost half of the soldiers (45.6 percent mortality rate) with gangrene died. Goldsmith didn't know exactly why but his experiments with bromide cured gangrene infections. His research predated Joseph Lister's 1867 work linking microbes with surgical infections and Louis Pasteur's similar work. Goldsmith applied bromide topically with a second application if the gangrenous odor returned. Bottom line: Only 8 of 304 of Goldsmith's patients receiving bromide therapy died, a mortality rate of 2.6 percent. When bromide was applied topically to a wound, it was painful and could cause tissue damage. The burning described by Edgar could have come from bromide.

According to Kenneth Davis in his book "Don't Know Much About the Civil War," good records existed for the Union in what was "the first bureaucratic war." An amputation performed within 48 hours was twice as likely to be successful. Edgar's was performed in about 24 hours. Most fatalities resulted from amputations at the thigh. Edgar's was at the knee. After the Civil War, thanks to English surgeon Joseph Lister's research in antiseptics, death from surgery was reduced from 50 percent to 15 percent. A total of 56 in every 400 wounded Union soldiers died. During the Vietnam War, 100 years later, just 1 in 400 wounded soldiers died.

HAREWOOD HOSPITAL — July 29, 1864.

My Dear Wife: This morning finds me gaining rapidly. The gangrene could hardly be seen. There are about 60 cases of this disease in the ward. There is only one doctor in the hospital who knows how to treat this disease. You recall I told you that I found a watch. I sold it yesterday for $12. I calculate to take $10 of it and buy me a pair of crutches.

Edgar W. Clark.

HAREWOOD HOSPITAL — July 31, 1864.

My Dear Wife: I would very much like to see you this morning. On wings of a dove, I would fly to your sweet bower and find a resting place with you. I must look odd without whiskers.

Edgar W. Clark.

HAREWOOD HOSPITAL — Aug. 3, 1864.

My Dear Wife: This fine morning finds me still on the gain and doing well. My leg is healing very fast, you can hardly realize how fast. Days pass very slow. Time drags heavily. I must come home next month if it is possible because it does not seem that I can stay away from home any longer. My leg does not pain me much anymore but it itches all the time.

Edgar W. Clark.

HAREWOOD HOSPITAL — Aug. 14, 1864.

My Dear Wife: I am out of doors today, laying on the green grass. It is much cooler than it is in the house. I have been penned up for so long that I am very glad to get in the open air once more.

Edgar W. Clark.

HAREWOOD HOSPITAL — Aug. 14, 1864.

My Dear Wife: My leg is going bully now. I can go anywhere I have a mind to on my crutches. I went yesterday about a half-mile.

Edgar W. Clark.

Notes: Guy Hasegawa in his book, "Mending Broken Soldiers: The Union and Confederate Programs to Supply Artificial Limbs" noted that the use of artificial limbs can be traced at least to ancient Roman times when Gen. Marcus Sergius had a right hand made of iron. The Civil War's massive number of amputations led to a surge in both patents and businesses. The leader of this industry was Benjamin Franklin Palmer, who lost a leg in a bark mill accident as a child, fashioned a limb from a section of a willow tree, earned two patents and built a business. The typical willow limb was hollowed and sometimes covered with cork, thus the "cork leg" that Edgar mentioned. Cork itself was too fragile to be entirely used. For amputations at the knee like Edgar's, the artificial limb would be laced around the thigh to a leather upper section. According to the American Battlefield Trust, 1 in 13 surviving Civil War soldiers was missing one or more limbs. That meant that it was common in the second half of the 1800s to see a man without a limb, knowing that man probably was a Civil War veteran.

SOUTH STREET HOSPITAL, PHILADELPHIA — Aug. 23, 1864.

My Dear Wife: You will see I have changed my hospital, I hope for the better. We have just arrived at this place. We left Washington yesterday. How long I will stay in this place it is impossible to say. I can tell you better in my next letter. I stood my ride first-rate. It did not hurt me a bit. I could ride clear home without hurting me and I calculate to try as soon as I can. My leg is going well and if it continues I will be able to travel first-rate in a few days. You need not make any calculations on when I will be coming home for I do not know myself. I will come home as soon as I am able. If I cannot come on a furlough, I will come on a discharge. You must get along as well as you can. I will write in a few days. I cannot think much to write this time. I thought I would write so you would not direct a letter to another hospital. I wish I could see you today; I would not be so lonesome. Give my love to all and save a share for yourself.

No more from your husband, Edgar W. Clark.

Notes: South Street Hospital at 24th and South Streets in Philadelphia was sometimes called "stump hospital" for the large number of soldiers recovering from amputations. According to Steve Soper's book, Edgar remained in Philadelphia until he was transferred to Detroit on Nov. 26, 1864. He was discharged on Feb. 27, 1865.

Edgar W. Clark spent 2 ½ years away from home — from Aug. 11, 1862 to Feb. 27, 1865. He was far off on his predictions of a brief war; he almost completed his three-year enlistment. By 1870 he was working as a clerk in a state government office. His address was listed in an 1888 city directory as 1102 N. Capitol Ave. in Lansing, a residential neighborhood today less than 1 mile from the state capitol.

Edgar died of blood poisoning at the age of 68 on Jan. 10, 1902, and was buried at Mt. Hope Cemetery in Lansing in an area reserved for veterans. The $40 cost of the burial was handled by the local government. According to the official form, widow Catherine Clark was "in indigent circumstances and unable, for want of means, to defray the expenses of his funeral or burial."

Catherine applied for and received a pension. In 1920, the pension was $30 per month, which is $438 in 2022 dollars. She died after a brief illness in 1924 at the age of 90 at the home of her daughter Mina on Moores River Drive in Lansing. According to the typewritten death announcement, she was a life member of the Women's Relief Corps. "Always interested in patriotic work, she loved the American flag. Her life was symbolic of all that the flag holds within its folds, right and righteousness." At the time of Catherine's death, two of her four children, Amos and Carrie, had not survived.

Before the war, Edgar and Catherine had two daughters: Mina (born 1859) and Carrie (born 1861). After the war, they had two sons: Amos (born 1866) and Milo (born 1869).

Amos Clark is my great-grandfather. He lived about 43 years. Amos became a firefighter in Lansing, as mentioned in a Lansing State Journal article on Oct. 3, 1937, regarding firefighting 45 years earlier in 1892. A photo of a horse-drawn firefighting wagon included Amos. As the story reported, to be a member of a local firefighting company "was considered a real honor."

Amos married Agnes McCourt. They had a son, Stanley J. Clark Sr., who owned and operated Clark Cleaners on Michigan Avenue in Lansing. Stanley Sr. married Mary Kathleen Fahey. They had four children, Stanley Jr., Mary Caroline, Richard and Mary Kathleen.

My father, Stanley Jr., and mother, Suzanne Graham Clark, had five children (me, Candace, Peter, Thomas and Elizabeth), which was common for an Irish-Catholic family during the Baby Boom. Dad ran a State Farm Insurance business in three different locations on the west side of Lansing.

Also worth mentioning is that on the maternal side of my father's family, Philip Kennedy was killed in the Battle of Front Royal on Aug. 16, 1864. Kennedy was a member of the 5th

Michigan Cavalry, led for a time by Gen. George Armstrong Custer. Kennedy was a native of Ireland.

There are innumerable memorials to the heroes of America's Civil War — over 1,300 at Gettysburg alone — but the personal stories of people like Edgar W. Clark and his wife Catherine deserve to be remembered by those who benefited from their sacrifices.

— Michael P. Clark, great-great-grandson of Edgar W. Clark.

Edgar W. Clark was discharged as a member of the 5th Michigan Infantry Regiment but he spent 99 percent of his combat time in the 3rd Michigan Infantry Regiment. The two regiments were merged just before Edgar was shot. (Matthew VanAcker).

*Mt. Hope Cemetery in Lansing, Mich. includes graves of
Civil War soldiers, including Edgar W. Clark's grave. U.S.
flags were included on a Memorial Day weekend. Edgar
lived to the age of 68, outliving two of his children. He died
of blood poisoning. (Matthew VanAcker).*

Chapter Fifteen

Epilogue

"It takes everything to make an Army, all sorts of men from the lowest to the highest, from the Black Negro to the White man," Edgar Clark wrote to his wife, Catherine. He was more right than he knew. It was that diversity that resulted in the superiority of the Union's numbers on the battlefield.

As David Williams wrote in "A People's History of the Civil War," there were 1 million native White Americans in both Union and Confederate armies. The Union's 2-to-1 troop advantage came from 500,000 immigrants and 500,000 Southerners — Black and White — who fought for the Union and for the elimination of slavery. There was a military advantage to being on the right side of history. As Lincoln said, "Let us have faith that right makes might; and in that faith, to the end, dare to do our duty as we understand it."

Still, it wasn't easy. Though the North had a 4-to-1 manpower advantage, it only was able to use half of it. Williams documented opposition to the war in the North, widespread anti-draft riots and thousands of draft-age Northerners who fled to Canada. Northerners were reading about the massive casualties during the summer of 1864. From May to July of

1864, the Union lost over 60,000 casualties, as many soldiers as Gen. Robert E. Lee's entire Army of Northern Virginia. In the summer of 1864, there was a weariness about the lack of victories since Gettysburg a year earlier. Lincoln biographer David Herbert Donald quoted Horace Greeley's letter to the president, dreading "the prospect of fresh conscriptions, further wholesale devastations and new rivers of human blood."

Complicating matters was President Lincoln's proposed 13th Amendment to the Constitution that would ban slavery. In the spring of 1864, the measure failed to gain the two-thirds majority needed in the House. Was there so much opposition to freeing enslaved people in the North to threaten Lincoln's re-election that fall? After all, no new Constitutional Amendment had been passed for 60 years.

As the summer ended in 1864, President Lincoln was looking at the need for a new draft that would include middle-class men because Congress had abolished the $300 payment to avoid service. Military service was far less popular in 1864 than in 1861. Fewer than 15 percent of eligible Union soldiers reenlisted between Nov. 1, 1863 and Nov. 1, 1864.

Military defeats early in the war cost Republicans dearly in the midterm elections of 1862. The number of Democratic congressmen nearly doubled from 44 to 75. Edward McPherson, the Republican congressman from Gettysburg, blamed his defeat on tardiness and incompetence, mostly due to poor leadership of Gen. George McClellan, as Carl Sandburg recounted. Lincoln replaced McClellan after the 1862 election.

By August of 1864, New York political boss Thurlow Weed said Lincoln's reelection was doomed. Lincoln was told that he was sure to lose New York, Pennsylvania and even his home state of Illinois. Lincoln told a friend that he would be "badly beaten" without a great change, Donald wrote. The New York Herald editorialized that Lincoln should resign or else he would be dishonored worse than Benedict Arnold, Carl Sandburg wrote.

So on Aug. 23, Lincoln wrote a "blind memo" to his Cabinet members that stated that it was probable that he would not be reelected, so the Cabinet must seek the end of the war before the inauguration of the next president. Cabinet members were not allowed to read it but simply signed the outside of the envelope.

A great change did occur one week later: Atlanta fell to Gen. William Tecumseh Sherman, which gave the Union the victory that the North needed. Confederate President Jefferson Davis had replaced Gen. Joseph Johnston with Gen. John Bell Hood, because Davis wanted more aggressive tactics, which led to the Confederate defeat. If the South had been able to hold onto Atlanta till the November election, just two more months, Lincoln may have lost the 1864 election. If Lincoln had lost reelection, could he have won the war by the inauguration in March of 1865? It's possible since Lee surrendered in April of 1865. But that's the meat of historical fiction.

According to Yale history professor David Blight in one of his Civil War classroom lectures, "It is amazing how long the South held out and amazing how close they actually came to winning their definition of victory." All it would have taken was for President Lincoln to lose the 1864 election. That nearly happened.

So it is not true, as the Lost Cause myth says, that it was inevitable that the North would win the Civil War by the sheer weight of its resources. Williams in "A People's History of the Civil War" points out that internal divisions in the South were just as responsible for its defeat. By 1864, two-thirds of Southern soldiers had deserted, largely under pressure from the homefront. Food shortages created stress at home, leading to food riots in Richmond.

A second presidential term wasn't easy even in normal times. No president had served two terms since Andrew Jackson (1829 to 1837). For instance, President James Polk (1845-1849), despite winning the war with Mexico, declined to run for a second term.

So Lincoln and the Republicans used every device possible to ensure his reelection. (1) The Republican Party changed its name to the National Union Party in order to attract pro-war Democrats. (2) Lincoln replaced his abolitionist vice-president, Hannibal Hamlin of Maine, with a pro-war Democrat from Tennessee, Andrew Johnson. (3) Nevada was rushed to statehood to provide three electoral votes. (4) Lincoln pressed states to ensure soldiers had a chance to vote, such as allowing furloughs or voting by mail. Though 75.8 percent of Union soldiers did vote for Lincoln, they did not provide the only reason for Lincoln's victory over George McClellan.

Lincoln won with 55 percent of the vote in the Union states. He barely won New York State and Connecticut. Nevertheless, he dominated in the Electoral College (212 to 21), winning all but three states. He lost his birth state of Kentucky by a huge margin (Lincoln won just 30.17 percent of the vote there); he lost another border slave state of Delaware; and the heavily Democratic state of New Jersey. Not coincidentally, all three states did not ratify the 13th Amendment that abolished slavery in 1865. Kentucky was the only state that at the time refused to ratify any of the three civil rights amendments (13, 14 and 15). In fact, Kentucky waited till 1976 to ratify them (the Bicentennial year). Mississippi waited until 1995.

It has become popular in recent years to criticize Lincoln for not being sufficiently abolitionist in his policies. It is true that he professed support for sending enslaved people overseas even into his presidency; however, it always was a voluntary policy and clearly, there was no desire among most African Americans to leave a country they had helped to build — for no pay.

But Lincoln was skeptical that Whites would accept equality with Blacks. Even in the North, full equality for Blacks was not common. The North at that time was much like the Jim Crow South of the 1900s with Blacks restricted from the vote, prevented from serving on juries or testifying against Whites in many states. In a Philadelphia speech on Dec. 4, 1863, Frederick Douglass said the nation in the Civil War was fighting for a more perfect Union, not the old Union, "a solidarity of the nation, making every slave free and every free man a voter." That happened for about 12 years in Reconstruction but not until the Voting Rights Bill of 1965 did all American adults of all races and genders have real voting rights.

Lincoln was a politician in the best sense of the word. Only a moderate could have been elected in 1860 and only someone with the ability to deal with pressures from all sides could have survived and won reelection in 1864. Col. Regis De Trobriand summed up Lincoln as "a man of perfect honesty and rare good sense." Common sense meant that Lincoln came to a decision carefully, never too far ahead of the people.

William T. Sherman in his memoirs wrote that Lincoln "seemed to possess more of the elements of greatness, combined with goodness, than any other." Sherman wrote that Lincoln's tall, gangly figure and his haggard look changed when he began to talk. "His face lightened up, his tall form, as it were, unfolded, and he was the very impersonation of good humor and fellowship." The common people trusted Lincoln. Poet Walt Whitman, who volunteered in Washington hospitals, saw Lincoln often and one day got a close look. Lincoln looked him straight in the eye. Whitman saw something deep behind Lincoln's smile that a poet could recognize. Without Lincoln's wisdom, empathy and political skill, Reconstruction never had a chance.

The best summary of Lincoln's political genius came from Frederick Douglass in 1876. Douglass had earlier criticized Lincoln for slow progress on civil rights and eventually became a friend: "Viewed from the genuine abolition ground, Mr. Lincoln seemed tardy, cold, dull and indifferent; but measuring him from the sentiment of his country, a sentiment he was bound as a statesman to consult, he was swift, zealous, radical and determined." Douglass later said that Lincoln was the rare good man "who could entertain a Negro and converse with him without in anywise reminding him of the unpopularity of his color."

Edgar Clark predicted rough treatment of Confederate leaders after the war. That was not Lincoln's intention. After the assassination, President Andrew Johnson went far beyond Lincoln's merciful tendencies in treating former Confederate leaders. For instance, Confederate President Jefferson Davis was indicted for treason and imprisoned. Rather than jailed in a prison cell, he was given an apartment in an officers' quarters where his wife and family were allowed to join him. After two years in the prison apartment, he was released on $100,000 bail provided by a few friends. Davis was never prosecuted.

Confederate Vice President Alexander Stephens was elected to the Congress in 1866 along with other former Confederates but was not allowed to join the Senate due to restrictions on former Confederates by Republicans in Congress. In 1873, Stephens was elected to the U.S. House and served until 1882. He then served briefly as governor of Georgia; he died in office. Individual pardons were needed for high Confederate officials, which Johnson provided en masse — over 13,000 of them.

In 1868, President Andrew Johnson issued a pardon to every person who participated in the rebellion.

Both Davis and Stephens, like so many others after the war, wrote memoirs stating that the Civil War had nothing to do with slavery, thus disowning their previous statements and the Articles of Secession. For instance, in a speech to the Confederate Congress regarding secession, Davis detailed a list of grievances against the North for "rendering insecure the tenure of property in enslaved people." But after the war, Davis wrote that slavery was an "incident," as if once your house burns down, the fire is an incident. That is not what the Charleston Mercury wrote in 1860 — that uncertainty about the future of slavery under President Lincoln created "distrust" and "uneasiness" that would "greatly depreciate slave property." Emancipating enslaved people would be like "the loss of liberty, property, home, country — everything that makes life worth living." The definition of liberty in the Confederacy included enslaving people. So after the Civil War, the myth of the Lost Cause was promoted while Northern opinion leaders went on with life. Thus, the South disproved the cliche that history is written by the victors. The Lost Cause myth converted a mountain of evidence that slavery caused the war into a molehill of fiction.

President Lincoln referred to the Civil War in Biblical terms: "The judgments of the Lord are true and righteous altogether." In fact, the devastation to the South caused by the war was Biblical in scope, as James McPherson wrote in "The War That Forged a Nation." The South lost two-thirds of its assessed wealth and one-quarter of the White men of military age. Wealth in the Confederate states decreased by 60 percent from 1860 to 1870, while wealth increased in the North by 50 percent. But in order to see the awful death and degradation of the Civil War as a form of repentance requires an acceptance of the evils of slavery and racism — which the entire nation shares. The Lost Cause mythology nullified that connection. Indeed, this nation has never undergone a full accounting of the effects of slavery or its aftermath with terror lynching and Jim Crow laws, as South Africa did with its Truth and Reconciliation Commission.

As for the enslaved people — the real reason for the war and a major reason why the Union won — they were left to fend for themselves after the war, with no land to call their own and no compensation for years of unpaid labor.

President Lincoln planned for Reconstruction to be conducted in various forms suited to the cultures of the individual states. In one example, in Field Order No. 15, Gen. William Tecumseh Sherman, in consultation with Black leaders in Savannah, provided 40 acres of former Confederate land to freed enslaved people. Some of the freed enslaved people also received surplus Union mules, though that was not mentioned in the order. Sherman's order specified "the islands from Charleston south, the abandoned rice fields along the rivers for 30 miles back from the sea and the country bordering the St. Johns River, including Beaufort, Hilton Head, Savannah, Fernandina, Jacksonville and St. Augustine." Imagine former enslaved people being given access to elite Southeastern tourism areas. Sherman's order had the immediate effect of providing land to about 40,000 formerly enslaved people in the Sea Islands, many of them having followed Sherman's army. President Lincoln never overruled that order.

By the end of the war, there already were several forms of support for freed enslaved people in the former Confederate areas controlled by the Union, such as in Louisiana and South Carolina. As described by Bell Irwin Wiley in "Southern Negroes: 1861 to 1865," freed enslaved people in Port Royal, S.C. were paid to pick cotton by the Union as early as 1861. Freed enslaved people in North Carolina were provided farmland, schooling and wages. By Feb. 1, 1865, of 90,000 freedmen under the care of the Bureau of Free Labor, 89,000 were self-supporting. But President Andrew Johnson, one of the worst presidents in history, rescinded Sherman's order and others like it and allowed the Confederate landowners to regain ownership if they took a loyalty oath to the Union. So slave owners received unjustified mercy while justified aid for the ex-enslaved people never came. With the death of Reconstruction in 1877, formerly enslaved people were thrown into an underclass as sharecroppers while civil rights and voting rights were stripped from them.

I also wondered why freed slaves rarely benefited from the Homestead Act, which provided 160 acres of public land in exchange for a small fee and a commitment to live on and improve the land. Well, it's the same old story. Many former slaves were destitute and could not afford the fee while Southern Whites used devices to obstruct African Americans from participating. Instead, they sought to keep Blacks as tenant farmers. The Homestead Act was repealed in 1876, right around the end of Reconstruction, and few Blacks benefited from it.

During Reconstruction, African American votes gave U.S. Grant his presidential election victories. Black elected officials were numerous in the former Confederate states. Then Jim Crow laws combined with widespread White opposition diabolically suppressed Black votes. After Reconstruction ended, the former states of the Confederacy had even more power. The principle of White supremacy lingered as Jim Crow laws placed African Americans into a lower caste. They were able to count formerly enslaved people as 5/5 of a person, obtaining more congressmen and electors for the former Confederate state, and then stripped voting rights from African Americans.

For instance, in Mississippi, following an 1892 law, only 8,615 of the state's 76,742 Black voters were qualified to vote, reported The Washington Post. In Louisiana, from 1898 to 1904, the number of Black voters plunged from 130,000 to 1,342, reported Henry Louis Gates Jr.

Terror lynchings were used to enforce disenfranchisement; a total of 4,440 Black people were victimized by lynchings between 1877 and 1950, reported the Equal Justice Initiative. These terror lynchings occurred mostly in the South, though a few occurred in the North. A lynching of a Black Civil War veteran occurred in Mason, Mich., in 1866. You can't get much more Northern than Duluth, Minn., where three Black men were lynched in 1920. The murderers involved in lynchings were almost never held accountable by the local justice system. The NAACP campaigned valiantly during the 20th Century for a federal anti-lynching bill but Southern political power helped prevent its passage. Finally, on March 29, 2022, a federal antilynching bill became law.

On the subject of alternative history, what if the South had not seceded? The gradual elimination of slavery could have taken many decades. Kenneth Stampp, in his book "The Imperiled Union," suggested that the South panicked after Lincoln was elected. After all, Lincoln in 1860 was a minority president with less than 40 percent of the popular vote (39.9 percent), the lowest winning percentage in presidential history; the Republican Party was divided; Republicans were in the minority in Congress; Lincoln's appointments could be blocked by a hostile Senate; and the Supreme Court due to the Dred Scott decision would be no help. But the South, worried about losing control of the government, seceded before giving Lincoln's moderate policies a chance. So Lincoln was able to use war measures to amass immense powers.

By the same token, what if the South had successfully seceded? It could have led to separate nations in New England, the Middle West and the Pacific West. Then the United States could have become like Europe.

What if the Confederate States expanded to Central and Southern America, Cuba and the Caribbean? What if the Mason-Dixon line became an Iron Curtain to protect against slave escapes? There would be continual Kansas-style border skirmishes and perhaps a second Civil War. A slave empire that included Cuba and Central and South America would have expanded slavery when the rest of the civilized world had abandoned it. Imagine the human suffering and evil.

Col. Regis DeTrobriand, a Frenchman who led Union troops, wrote in his memoirs that this was a war for "national integrity," for "free institutions," for "progress and liberty," for "civilized nations" and for "the supremacy of the government of the people, by the people." These causes were worth the sacrifice, he wrote. The United States accomplished "a work of power and patriotism, a victory for humanity."

To quote the Cincinnati Commercial of May 5, 1861, as the Civil War was starting: "The great battle which is now joined is to prove whether a republic, founded on the will of the people, is capable of exerting power enough to enforce its laws and maintain its existence, or whether it contains within its existence the seeds of its own destruction."

That answer was written in blood. It showed future generations that their crises could be overcome. It proved that a republic of the people, by the people and for the people can survive the most serious threat to its existence. It proved that there is no compromise when freedom is at stake. And it proved that good can triumph.

Chapter Sixteen

Interview with Lansing author

Matthew VanAcker is a native of Lansing, Mich., like me. He is the Director — Capitol Tour, Education & Information Service and the Director/Curator of Save the Flags. He wrote the book, "Lansing and the Civil War." In fact, VanAcker mentions Edgar W. Clark in his book. Therefore, I took the opportunity to interview him for my book. The following is a lightly edited transcript of our conversation.

Michael Clark: What was Lansing, Mich. like during the Civil War?

Matthew VanAcker: It was a small city in 1860. The census listed Lansing's population as approximately 3,000 people. It was a really small community where there weren't 6 degrees of separation, it was honestly maybe 1 or 2 degrees. They worked together. They went to church together. They attended school together. They worked on farms together. And though it was politically divided as the country was between Democrats and Republicans, people pulled together to try to help each other out. Political differences, and religious differences aside, when the war came, the community pulled together to support the war effort, including contributing a large number of volunteers.

Clark: What were some of the surprises as you researched this book?

VanAcker: I was personally surprised by how attached I became to all of these people. As a historian, I try to stay a little detached from my subject, but it's hard to do when you're reading about their sacrifices and what their families were enduring. There's a really sad story of a man who fought with one of the U.S. Sharpshooters companies that formed here in Lansing, and while he's gone his son is tragically killed, thrown from a horse and dies of a fatal brain injury. It broke my heart when I read that. I did a lot of my research by reading the Republican, the local newspaper, a forerunner of the Lansing State Journal. I read seven years of the Republican, and got to know these people, and it broke my heart when I would read about these tragic things that were happening to them. I could tell you what they were growing in their gardens, and where they worked and what church they went to, and you really get an emotional attachment to these folks.

Clark: You wrote there were 500 volunteers from Lansing in the Army.

VanAcker: Most of them were from the city, but there were some men who came from other areas surrounding Lansing to enlist with companies that were forming in the city. So I did include them in that number. But the overwhelming majority of that 500 number were men who were actually living in Lansing, and listed in companies that formed here in Lansing.

Clark: According to the 1860 census, there were 1,500 men between the ages of 20 and 29 in Ingham County. So 500 of them volunteered for the Union. That's one-third of all the men in prime military age. That's incredible.

VanAcker: Michigan sent over 90,000 soldiers from a state population of about 750,000. That constituted well over half of our eligible male population who fought in the Civil War. On a per capita basis, Michigan's contribution was one of the largest of any of the Northern states. This was an all-in affair and those who weren't fighting were back home supporting the war effort in a number of ways.

Clark: Michigan probably didn't need to use the draft much because they were filling their quota with volunteers. Right?

VanAcker: The draft was necessary with the attrition rates in the Union Army. The municipalities and states really did not want to have to resort to the draft, so they did everything in their power to try to entice men to enlist, including offering pretty substantial bounties and bonuses for men who would enlist of their own free will. I mentioned we'd sent 90,000 soldiers from Michigan. About 85,000 were volunteers, and we really only resorted to drafting about 5,000 men. I don't know exactly how many men were actually drafted from Lansing, but it was very, very few.

Clark: Well, I can tell you that my ancestor Edgar Clark wrote that he received a nice bounty, and his Army pay, which was $16 a month, was more than he could make at home. So when he left his wife and his two babies, ages 1 and 3, he figured they would be well taken care of, and the war would be brief. Edgar didn't think much of the draftees and the bounty jumpers. Near the end of the war, the draftees and the bounty jumpers were filling up the ranks. I got the sense that the quality of the Union soldiers from 1864 on was pretty poor.

VanAcker: I've gotten the same impression. Some of the later recruits were not the same quality. Some people have disparaged men who signed up to receive the bonus, but I don't fault them one bit. As you mentioned, they had families at home that were dependent on that money, and if you could enlist and get a pretty sizable bonus you could ensure that your family would be well cared for while you were gone. And there was a little bit of shopping around, too. Some men would enlist in other municipalities that were offering larger bonuses, and I don't fault them for doing that.

(My comments: Nothing wrong with taking bounties as Edgar did but bounty jumpers were a special category. They enlisted several times, collecting multiple bounties. The implication is that they didn't make good soldiers. Men who were not interested in battle could easily find ways to avoid it.)

Clark: Think of the women at home. Most of them had a garden at least, and Edgar had a little livestock, and here you had a wife with babies, ages 1 and 3, trying to take care of everything while the husband was gone.

VanAcker: My wife and I have talked about this in the course of my research, and I would share with her that a fellow enlisted with five kids at home. We have four children. My wife and I have joked about what her reaction would be if I came home one day and told her I'd enlisted in the Union Army and was gonna leave her to fend for our four children.

Clark: Edgar writes that his wife didn't want him to leave, and at one point Edgar's mother-in-law accused him of abandoning the family.

VanAcker: Oh, my goodness!

Clark: I mean that was tough to hear but in a way it was true. His wife actually received government payments. My father and I went to the Library of Michigan and found documentation.

VanAcker: They apparently had a special levy that had been raised to create a fund to help these families. The level of sacrifice that took place during the war is a little hard for us to imagine

Clark: So there were about 40 members from Lansing in the 3rd Michigan Infantry with Edgar and within about a year he wrote that everybody he knew was gone, and the company, which started at 100 people, was whittled down to 39. By the summer of 1864, there were just eight left. Edgar was almost the last man standing in his regiment to the point that they had to merge the 3rd Michigan Infantry Regiment into the 5th Michigan Infantry Regiment and Company G into Company H.

VanAcker: Yeah, I found a reference to a gentleman from Lansing, Edward Flower. He fought with the 8th Infantry Regiment. In one of his letters home he wrote to his folks that of all the men who came with him, he was the only one left. Everyone else had been killed, wounded or captured. And what a thing for these men to realize they were the last of the group.

Clark: Two veterans committed suicide after the war, and you know we're aware of that danger today, but certainly that had to have been happening back then.

VanAcker: I brought this to the forefront to make people realize the incredible baggage, emotional and physical, for these boys, and young ladies from the war. Back then there was more of the mentality to buck up, face life, get over it and pick up the pieces. We have a monument to the 1st Michigan Sharpshooters and a group of boys from Lansing fought with that regiment. I've walked past that monument thousands of times in my time here at the Capitol and noticed the plaques, and read the names periodically, not fully realizing that two of the names on the plaque were two young men who came back from the war and just really couldn't cope with what they had experienced. They were brothers-in-law and brothers-in-arms. Asa Nichols took his life about a year after the end of the war, and then a couple of years later his brother-in-law did the same thing. And I really wanted to let people know that these men coped with the same kind of difficulties that our soldiers in modern times have. Most of these young men hadn't traveled more than 20 or 30 miles from their hometowns, and then enlisted to fight and were sent down South. Their bodies hadn't developed natural immunity to some of the diseases that they encountered down there, and of course, sanitation was deplorable during the war and the camps. Men were drinking out of the same streams that men upstream were defecating in. So yeah, I think we have plaques in the Capitol Rotunda, where our replica battle flags are. I'd be giving a tour up in the rotunda, and people would wander over to look at the plaques, and they're always surprised that the majority of the Michigan regiments had more men die from disease than actually died of battle injuries.

Clark: Yeah, twice as many died of disease. Edgar Clark spent his first winter in the Army of the Potomac in a hospital, suffering from diarrhea. He was being treated with opium. And if he didn't take opium, he was right back in the hospital. He was lucky to survive his first winter in the army.

VanAcker: And it's amazing that he didn't develop an addiction to the opium

Clark: If you were well enough to travel 1,300 miles back to Lansing, then you were well enough to be back in your unit. So there was a Catch-22.

VanAcker: I've read about a number of boys from Lansing who were released and then died en route; apparently they weren't well enough to travel home. So in your research on Edgar, does he write about his reasons for enlisting? Was it to save the Union? Was it to end slavery? That subject has come up quite a bit in my research on the Lansing boys.

Clark: He pretty much followed almost exactly Abraham Lincoln's views. He mentioned matter-of-factly that there were Black people in his regiment. Then, once the Emancipation Proclamation came out, he supported it entirely. He wrote: "The president has issued a proclamation freeing all the slaves after the first of January in the revolting states. I like that first-rate."

VanAcker: A lot of my research was based on reading the Republican, which was obviously a very Republican newspaper, so they made no secret about their feelings. A lot of the letters that the men wrote home to the Republican made it very clear that an overwhelming majority of the boys from Lansing were fighting to end slavery and uphold the Union. I found one reference to an officer in the 8th Michigan, one of the men who formed that company, and he made it very clear that he was fighting to uphold the Constitution, and basically says in one of his letters to his uncle that he would shake hands with the rebs tomorrow, and not change a word in the Constitution, if they would agree to put down their arms. He was clearly fighting to uphold the Constitution and the Union, and really not so much to end slavery.

Clark: Edgar mentioned several instances when he talked to the rebels on picket and a couple of times the rebels said they would quit this war if it weren't for the Emancipation Proclamation and Edgar basically says, well, tough. That was part of the deal. Also, when the soldiers actually saw the South and saw what slavery looked like in person, that radicalized a number of them.

VanAcker: There was no doubt in their minds the horrible things that they witnessed, and the way the enslaved people were being treated. One of the quotes I think I use from the 3rd Michigan Infantry that Edgar fought with was that they were on a reconnaissance mission in Virginia and they marched past an old slave pen, and they said that the Union soldiers had whitewashed out the name of the slave traders. But the soldier made a comment that you can't whitewash this institution and its impact. And he said the blood on the hand cannot be washed off. And there was no doubt in their minds that it needed to end.

Clark: I'll mention a few things I learned from your book that I never learned in school. I learned about a lynching in Mason in 1866.

VanAcker: I have a coworker here, a colleague who wrote a really incredible article on John Taylor for the Michigan Chronicle and I had a good friend who's a reenactor with the 102nd Colored Infantry Regiment from Michigan. So both of those gentlemen shared their knowledge of that case. John Taylor fought with distinction with the 102nd, a regiment that formed here in Michigan, and came back and took a job with a local farmer. The details are a little unclear, but he was arrested for a supposed attack on the family of a farmer over disputed wages. A lynch mob broke him out of the jail and hanged him just outside of the county courthouse. Very few people in Ingham County are familiar with that story. We think of lynchings and we Northerners tend to get on our high horse. They're not happening in the Northern States like Michigan.

Clark: Obviously, the vast majority of lynchings happened in the South. But there were some as far north as Duluth, Minn., for crying out loud. They had a lynching, but I think they've also put up a plaque or memorial to recognize that fact. I know Lansing has recognized Malcolm X who spent his youth there.

And maybe there ought to be some sort of memorial to that lynching as well.

VanAcker: It's a sad and notable bit of Ingham County history that not many people are aware of.

Clark: Another weird fact that I've discovered in your book is that the first uniforms for the 3rd Michigan Infantry Regiment were the color gray.

VanAcker: Yeah, I found that remarkable, too. I knew there were some Union troops that were uniformed in gray at the start of the war and led to some friendly fire casualties at the first battle of Bull Run. Now the 3rd Michigan, before they went into action, were issued blue blouses.

Clark: Edgar was involved in a very famous friendly fire incident at Chancellorsville during a night attack when the 3rd Michigan literally captured another Union group of soldiers.

VanAcker: Friendly fire led to one of the biggest losses in the Confederate army, the shooting of Gen. Stonewall Jackson by his own troops at Chancellorsville.

Clark: Another surprise was that there was a women's college in Lansing at the current location of the Michigan School for the Deaf and The Blind.

VanAcker: There was a full article on Michigan Women's College in Michigan History Magazine on the female college and its founder, Abigail Rogers. It was a really groundbreaking institution because the Michigan universities were not accepting female students at the time. There are a number of notable young ladies who went on to incredible careers in Michigan.

Clark: And Gov. Austin Blair spoke about a reform school in Lansing at that time.

VanAcker: So there were a number of goals that were achieved by encouraging these young men to enlist. One of the youngest boys to enlist, I think, was 14. And a number of the Reform School boys were killed, wounded or captured.

Clark: And there's a famous story about a 12-year-old drummer from a Michigan unit who actually wound up being a hero in a battle.

VanAcker: That was Johnny Clem. There was a well-known Disney TV movie ("Johnny Shiloh," 1963). They sort of played pretty fast and loose with the facts. But yeah, he started out as a drummer boy and by the end of the war was fighting alongside the other men of his regiment. He actually was from Ohio but he connected with the Michigan regiment. He survived the war, went into the regular army and retired from the regular army. You know, people should recognize the sacrifices that these folks made, including Edgar.

Clark: And the stories are so great. Edgar had two daughters before the war, and then came back as a one-legged man. He had two sons after the war and one of those sons, Amos, is my great-grandfather. So I obviously have a strong personal connection to Edgar Clark and the Civil War. Their commitment to the cause is very clear. They knew exactly what they were fighting for, and they were willing to sacrifice everything — their lives, their liberty, their fortunes — for the cause of the Union that at that time had only been in existence for about 87 years. I know that Edgar was willing to accept anything for the cause.

Chapter Seventeen

Kentucky's many fascinating stories

The most interesting state during the Civil War — Kentucky.

It was full of contradictions: A slave state in the Union, neutral during the Civil War, with slavery connections to its mother state, Virginia, but strong economic ties to the North across the Ohio River.

Abraham Lincoln and Jefferson Davis were born about 80 miles from each other in Kentucky. While Lincoln's father moved north to the free states of Indiana and Illinois to escape the unfair competition of slavery, Davis moved to Mississippi where his brother staked him to a slave-based fortune.

President Abraham Lincoln said he could not afford to lose that state to the Confederacy, figuring the other Union slave states of Missouri, Delaware and Maryland would follow suit, and the Union would be lost.

Kentucky is split into different cultural and economic pieces. Eastern Kentucky, with its mountains and no cotton plantations, had little connection to slavery. The mountainous areas of Appalachia — Kentucky, West Virginia, Tennessee, North Carolina and Alabama — were hotbeds of Union support. Northern Kentucky, with its trade with Ohio, provided strong economic reasons for neutrality. However, tobacco farmers in the Lexington area used slaves.

Kentucky had relatively few slaves compared to states in the Deep South. By the time of the Civil War, enslaved people represented about 20 percent of the Kentucky population. Given its proximity to free Ohio, Kentucky was a key site on the Underground Railroad. While living in Cincinnati, Harriet Beecher Stowe came into contact with escaped enslaved people, which helped to inspire her to write "Uncle Tom's Cabin."

Stowe, the wife of a preacher, wrote that slavery simply was evil, it considered people as property and gave them no legal rights. In contrast, Kentucky native Jefferson Davis wrote that "our cause was just and holy." Obviously, there was no compromise between these two views, though leaders in the U.S. and Kentucky tried.

Kentucky had several anti-slavery movements before the Civil War but none of them bore fruit due to the huge financial stakes of maintaining the status quo. This is described in "Slavery in Kentucky, 1792-1865" by Ivan Eugene McDougle. He wrote that Kentucky was not adapted to plantation life. Yet serious abolitionist movements resulted in backlashes that protected the slave system. In 1849, Henry Clay presented his gradual emancipation plan that relied on sending slaves to Africa. But within a few days of the publication of his plan, the House of Representatives in Kentucky voted 93 to 0 to condemn it, opposing emancipation "in any shape or form whatever."

Lincoln wasn't popular in his birth state. When he ran for president in 1860, he got next to nothing from Kentucky. Lincoln received less than 1 percent of the vote in a four-way race

— 0.93 percent. Lincoln was swamped by a Kentuckian, John Breckinridge, who received 36 percent of the vote in Kentucky. John Bell of Tennessee got a plurality of the Kentucky vote with 45 percent. Stephen Douglas received 17.5 percent.

During the Civil War, the Confederacy made several attempts to invade Kentucky but failed on every try and never received an expected outpouring of support. As for the Union military that came to Kentucky, only one of nine regiments complied with Kentucky's Fugitive Slave Law, wrote John Cohassey in "The 22nd Michigan Infantry and the Road to Chickamauga." Runaway enslaved people were flocking to federal lines. Union soldiers put them to work and paid them. For instance, Col. Moses Wisner, a former Michigan governor in charge of the 22nd Michigan Infantry Regiment, was ordered to provide a list of all escaped enslaved people in the camp. He protested: "I came here to fight for my country and can never degrade myself to the level of slave catcher or to inform against fugitives from slavery." In another instance, Col. Charles Doolittle of the 18th Michigan Infantry was put on trial for refusing to give up a runaway. Charges were dropped.

Though Kentucky remained neutral, it contributed over 20,000 African Americans to the Union cause. Early in the war, two federal laws stated that "contrabands" — escaped slaves described as if they were property — could be accepted into the Union Army and thus earn their freedom. Then the Emancipation Proclamation stated that escaped slaves could join the Union Army and be free. The addition of 200,000 African Americans became crucial late in the war when there were draft riots throughout the North, when soldiers were declining to reenlist, when 90,000 Northern males escaped to Canada and when Northern newspapers were filled with names of killed soldiers.

Camp Nelson in Nicholasville just south of Lexington was a major training center for African American soldiers. It was so big that the wives and children of enslaved men flocked there. At one point, more people were living at Camp Nelson than either Lexington or Louisville.

Kentucky slave owners weren't thrilled with losing their enslaved people to the Union Army. According to Thomas D. Mays in the book "Black Soldiers in Blue," White people "reacted violently to the arming of their former slaves." But opposition eased when White people realized that Black men would count toward a quota for the draft and that they can stop a bullet just as effectively as White men.

Henry Clay: Contradictions

Abraham Lincoln's political views were influenced by Henry Clay. He was most effective in developing compromises over slavery. Those compromises were doomed to fail because there is no compromise with freedom.

Clay, like Thomas Jefferson, was a native Virginian who lived with contradictions regarding slavery. Both men were on record as decrying the institution, yet both became major slaveholders, influenced by the wealth that followed from enslaving people. Jefferson in 1820 at the age of 77 wrote: "Slavery is a hideous evil, a foul blot on our country. It makes a mockery of our sacred creed, embodied in the Declaration of Independence." Jefferson also stated that he initially expected slavery to "wither away." After the Missouri Compromise separated slave and non-slave states, he feared that slavery would tear apart the country, and "burst on us like a tornado." He welcomed death before the nation committed suicide.

Clay moved from Virginia to Kentucky seeking to advance his career. In Lexington, he saw a pen with a dozen slaves, awaiting auction like cattle. "The spectacle disgusted me," Clay wrote. Nearby, a male enslaved person was getting a public whipping while a crowd watched. "His screams made my skin crawl," Clay wrote.

As a young member of the Lexington bar, Clay plunged into the abolition movement. But that didn't last. Clay soon learned that to compete at the highest level in Lexington, he had to participate in the slavery system. Though he "abhorred" the system, he found that slavery was a "necessary evil." In short, money talks.

Clay's proposals for emancipation always included the migration of freed enslaved people to Africa, which never produced much enthusiasm from African Americans. As freed man Thomas Smallwood wrote: "Do they think to drive us from our country and homes, having enriched it with our blood and tears, and keep back millions of our dear brethren, sunk in the most barbarous wretchedness, to dig up gold and silver for their children? Tell us no more about colonization, for America is as much our country as it is yours. Treat us like men, and there is no danger but we will all live and peace and happiness together." (Quoted in Scott Shane's book, "Flee North.")

Clay owned more than 100 enslaved people. Eric Brooks, curator of Ashland, The Henry Clay Estate, said in an interview with the author that Clay freed just seven of his enslaved people.

In any case, Clay is known as the "Great Compromiser" because he was intimately involved in the Missouri Compromise of 1820 and the Compromises of 1850. Though the compromises were doomed, they gave the Union enough time to build the strength to win the Civil War, which required that the Union conquer a huge land mass. Imagine if the Civil War had broken out in 1850 with Millard Fillmore as president!

Mary Todd Lincoln: Turbocharger

Abraham Lincoln's wife, Mary Todd Lincoln, knew Henry Clay. Perhaps that is one reason she saw a connection with Abe.

Mary Todd Lincoln is one of the most fascinating figures in Civil War history. The wife of Abraham Lincoln was born and raised in Lexington, but like others from her hometown, she found more opportunities in Springfield, Ill. Mary Todd also had a strained relationship with her stepmother. Lincoln scholar Michael Burlingame of the University of Illinois — Springfield wrote a compelling book, "An American Marriage: The Untold Story of Abraham Lincoln and Mary Todd." He also explored the Lincolns' marriage in an earlier book, "The Inner World of Abraham Lincoln."

Burlingame used his decades of research into Lincoln to document many of the flaws of Lincoln's wife, including her tantrums toward her husband. Even a supportive biographer, Ruth Painter Randall, listed 17 negative traits of Mary Todd Lincoln: "willful, impulsive, imprudent, superficial, vain, childish, stingy, jealous, emotionally unstable, tactless, gossipy, malicious, materialistic, sharp-tongued, acquisitive and indiscreet." As an apparent sufferer of bipolar illness, her manic periods were characterized by shopping binges. For instance, she once bought 300 pairs of gloves.

Nevertheless, Burlingame wrote that "Lincoln may never have become president if his wife had not turbocharged the restless engine of his ambition." If true, and I am convinced it is, we can forgive Mary Todd Lincoln her many faults. In the late 1840s, she predicted that Abraham would become president or else she would not have married him, "for you can see he is not pretty." She convinced him not to take a position in the new state of Oregon, she convinced him not to accept a vice presidential nomination in 1860 and she always believed that her husband would be president.

When Lincoln questioned his fitness for president, his wife laughed at him and said, "You've got no equal in the United States."

When Lincoln ran for president in 1860, he was a compromise candidate with a skimpy resume: a former state legislator, a one-term congressman and a twice-failed U.S. Senate candidate. When he took the presidency after beating three other major candidates, he had the lowest popular vote percentage in history — just 39.9 percent.

Yet historians today generally consider Lincoln the greatest president for the way he handled the incredible difficulties of the Civil War. The nation needed a great president during the Civil War. An average president would not do, and especially not a failure like Andrew Johnson or James Buchanan, the presidents who bracketed Lincoln's presidency.

Burlingame, interviewed for the podcast by the author, said that Mary Todd Lincoln clearly gave the president practice in dealing with difficult people. She publicly humiliated him, physically abused him, disgraced him by her unethical conduct and made his domestic life "a burning, scorching hell," in the words of Lincoln's law partner, William Herndon.

She was treated badly by the Eastern press who saw the Lincolns as hicks despite her elite education. Her abrasive personality did her no favors, especially since she did not promote her good deeds. Presidential Historian Richard Norton Smith, quoted in the book "First Ladies" by Susan Swain, noted that the president's wife often visited soldiers in hospitals, wrote letters for them and brought them fruit and other gifts. Smith noted that Mary Todd Lincoln was "a surprisingly contemporary figure." She was a feminist long before women had gained the right to vote.

In fairness, Burlingame said that Lincoln probably wasn't the easiest husband to live with, awkward around women, prone to bouts of melancholy, often away from home in Illinois and probably not the most attentive husband given the huge task of saving the nation. Lincoln's law partner, William Herndon, said that Lincoln should not have married anyone. If Lincoln had remained a bachelor or married a less ambitious wife, I am convinced he would not have been elected president.

The tragic aspect of Mary Todd Lincoln's life was that she made so many enemies, including the wife of Gen. U.S. Grant. Julia Dent Grant had a previous run-in with Mary Todd Lincoln. On April 14, 1865, the Grants were not present at Ford's Theatre, meaning that Grant's military aides were not there when John Wilkes Booth attacked.

Lincoln's wife had a sad widowhood. She had seen three of her four children die, witnessed her husband murdered in front of her and was committed to an insane asylum by her only remaining son, Robert. Whatever her flaws, and Burlingame itemizes many of them, the nation owes Mary Todd Lincoln a thank-you for helping her husband save the Union and destroy slavery. She recognized his genius when nobody else did.

After the war, Kentucky embraced the Jim Crow South. The joke was that Kentucky seceded after the war. That has a grain of truth, since Kentucky was the only state not to immediately ratify any of the 13th, 14th or 15th Amendments to the Constitution that destroyed slavery, promised citizenship for any native-born Americans and enshrined voting rights. Kentucky ratified those amendments a century later in 1976, the Bicentennial year.

Chapter Eighteen

Lost Cause: History matters

"History is literally present in all that we do." — James Baldwin.

"Those who cannot remember the past are condemned to repeat it." — Spanish philosopher George Santayana.

"To a large extent, we are a compilation of memories. Memory is the most powerful thing in human existence." — Howard Suber, distinguished film professor from UCLA.

What if our nation's collective memory is faulty, based on a myth like a bad dream? The Lost Cause rewrote the true history of the Civil War.

The Lost Cause myth turned defeat into victory, evil into goodness, brutality into romance and villains into heroes. It was taught to children by beloved teachers. It was taught in history classes with religious-like persistence and used as a cloak to cover up the many injustices that followed the end of Reconstruction. It played upon the desire of Americans to reunite after the Civil War.

Robert E. Lee is often credited with the origin of the theory with his statement to the troops after surrendering at Appomattox in 1865. Lee said: "After four years of arduous service, marked by unsurpassed courage and fortitude, the Army of Northern Virginia has been compelled to yield to overwhelming numbers and resources." While Lee's statement was true at that moment, it was not an accurate representation of the entire war. The statement was expanded in 1866 with a book from journalist Edward Pollard titled "The Lost Cause: A New Southern History of the War of the Confederates."

I asked several historians for their comments on the Lost Cause for the podcast that accompanies this book.

Ronald Jackson II, assistant professor of history, Jacksonville University: "The Lost Cause is an attempt to frame what the Civil War was about. Right after Reconstruction ended, there was a big push to redeem the South, to reclaim it, and part of that reclamation project involved creating a mythology about the war and a celebration of the service of some of the Confederate leaders and soldiers. One of the things they tried to minimize was how slavery was an integral part of it. That is something that has carried on for generations, that when people try to remove Confederate statues and memorials they cling to states' rights, and connect their push to the Founding Fathers. They overlooked what was written when these Southern states declared independence. When you go to the actual documents, as I do in my class, there are ways you can check. Through all of the documents, there is a mention of slavery."

Justin Rogers, assistant professor of History and Africana Studies at the University of North Florida, said the Lost Cause mythology was characterized by "partial truth, outright lies and self-delusions." He is most familiar with Mississippi's Articles of Secession. "It basically said that slavery is the height of civilization and we are willing to secede from the Union to defend it or else 'we must submit to degradation and the loss of property worth $4 billion.' It was very clear to people at the beginning of the war that the cause was slavery and the expansion of slavery."

Author Edward Bonekemper III called the Lost Cause "a tangle of falsehoods." He is author of "The Myth of the Lost Cause: Why the South Fought the Civil War and Why the North Won." He stated that the Lost Cause movement may have been the "most successful propaganda campaign in American history." I would add that it was the most *consequential* propaganda campaign in American history. By changing the way Americans remember the Civil War, it paved the way for the loss of civil rights for African Americans, the failure to prosecute over 4,000 cases of terror lynchings, the denial of mortgages, widespread segregation and eliminating the vote for African Americans.

Sadly, it worked. Today, several Southern states like Florida still recognize as official holidays Confederate Memorial Day and the birthdays of Robert E. Lee and Jefferson Davis. Who lost the war, again? There is nothing wrong with remembering the dead but not as official holidays — as if the Confederacy still existed. Michael Burlingame, author of about 20 Civil War books and professor of history at the University of Illinois—Springfield, commented to this author: "It's hard to imagine that having any resonance in the modern world because the Confederacy is widely regarded quite reasonably as dedicated to the principle that Blacks were an inferior race, and should be kept an inferior race and that slavery should be protected and preserved and expanded. So that is a little shocking."

The Lost Cause is the story of passionate advocacy by Southerners and pitiful acceptance by many Northerners to rewrite the history of America's most important historic event, the

Civil War. Through slanted academic studies and powerful popular media like "Gone With the Wind," the Lost Cause myth became conventional wisdom in both North and South. One of the most effective advocates of the Lost Cause was a Columbia University professor, Archibald Dunning.

I grew up in Michigan. I recall the State Capitol in Lansing in the 1960s filled with Civil War memorabilia for the 100th anniversary of the Civil War. Yet, my wife and I have lived 75 percent of our lives in Jacksonville, the most Southern big city in Florida. This is the city that spawned Lynryd Skynrd, the band that wrote "Sweet Home Alabama," their answer to Neil Young's "Southern Man." Southerners were taught the Lost Cause fiction by teachers they loved and respected.

Eva Sheppard Wolf is history professor at San Francisco State University and author of a book on slavery in colonial Virginia: She said i an interview with the author that it hurts to lose something important, to say what you were fighting for was wrong rather than confront the truth. "There was a concerted effort to remake what the Civil War was about, and to fashion a memory of it. ... It's a painful history."

Here are a few examples of the Lost Cause from the Tony Horwitz book, "Confederates in the Attic: Dispatches from the Unfinished Civil War." He found a catechism that was produced for Children of the Confederacy, an offshoot of the Daughters of the Confederacy.

Q. "What causes led to the War Between the States from 1861 to 1865?"

A. "The disregard of those in power for the rights of the Southern states."

The catechism failed to mention that Southern leaders them-selves made it clear in their Articles of Secession that the South was fighting for rights that were directly connected to the enslavement of 4 million people forever as property, as well as the right to hunt down escaped enslaved people in the North without opposition. Here is the second sentence of Georgia's Articles of Secession: "For the last 10 years we have numerous and serious causes of complaint against our non-slaveholding confederate states with reference to the subject of African slavery." Early in the Texas Articles of Secession, it was mentioned that the Confederacy would be "maintaining and protecting the institution known as slavery." The evidence is clear as day. There is no debate. Southerners were proud of their peculiar institution. It was enshrined in the Confederate Constitution.

As for the enslaved people, the catechism states: "They were faithful and devoted and were always ready to serve them." That doesn't explain why the South needed a Fugitive Slave Law to stop enslaved people from escaping. If slavery was so wonderful, why weren't Northerners flocking to the South to be enslaved? Absurd, right? Yet the absurdity persisted. If enslaved people were so well treated, why did 200,000 of them join the Union Army and Navy during the Civil War? As further proof, 6 million African Americans fled the South after Reconstruction ended and a new form of White supremacy was introduced.

Regarding the Battle of Gettysburg, the catechism states that the Confederacy lost due to being greatly outnumbered by federal supplies and forces. That is false, as well. Actually, the Army of Northern Virginia was well supplied by its invasion of Pennsylvania, while the Army of the Potomac was exhausted by a march in the heat, trying to catch them. In fact, Gettysburg was the rare major battle in the East where Gen. Robert E. Lee's forces were not outnumbered 2 to 1 or more. There were about 90,000 Union soldiers vs. about 75,000 Confederates. After the first day's battle, Lee decided to assault federal forces, which held high ground with narrower interior lines, meaning Lee was constantly at a tactical disadvantage at Gettysburg. The Union had to defend an interior line of just 3 ½ miles while Lee's Confederates were spread out over an exterior line about 6 miles. As Confederate artillery commander Gen. Porter Alexander stated after the war, Lee's decision to attack "was almost as badly chosen as it was possible to be." There is no excuse for Lee's bad decision on the third day to send troops up a mile-long incline toward Union troops — Pickett's Charge. It was like the Union defeat at Fredericksburg and the Confederate defeat at Malvern Hill. Lee knew better.

So while the Daughters of the Confederacy and other apologists were rewriting history, millions of Americans saw their civil rights being stripped. Others saw careers sacrificed for the Lost Cause. One example came in 1911, the 50th anniversary of the Civil War. Enoch Banks, a native of Georgia and chair of the History and Economics Department at the University of Florida, wrote a column for the New York Independent in which he declared the Civil War was fought over slavery, that the South was "relatively in the wrong" and the North was "relatively in the right." He called for both sides to accept that fact and get along. Banks was far from a radical. In that same piece, he supported suppressing the African American vote and proposed a new form of a plantation economy based on hired labor. But Banks' opinions offended some powerful Florida politicians and newspaper editors. In response, he was forced to resign from the university and died months later from an unspecified illness. Banks was just one of the countless victims of the patchwork of lies, excuses and rationalizations known as the Lost Cause.

The Lost Cause knew no bounds. One example came in 1909 when the Georgia Chapter of the United Daughters of the Confederacy built a monument to Capt. Henry Wirz, the commandant of Andersonville prison. Wirz was the only soldier executed for war crimes after the Civil War. Ovid Futch, in his book "History of Andersonville Prison," called the trial and hanging of Wirz a "legal lynching." It's fair to say Wirz paid the price for many others. Nevertheless, Wirz was no hero. At best, he was incompetent. In 1958, the Georgia Legislature voted against repairing the monument. Rep. Ulysses Lancaster, whose uncle served at Andersonville, described Wirz as a "malevolent sadist" and said that Confederate veterans recalled Wirz and Andersonville "with horror."

Mark Twain (Samuel Clemens) was raised in the slave state of Missouri to believe that there was nothing wrong with slavery, that God approved of it in the Bible, that it was a holy thing. Later in life, Twain said that "Our Civil War was a blot on our history but not as great a blot as the buying and selling of Negro souls."

Gen. George Thomas, a Virginian who fought for the Union, called the Lost Cause claim "a species of political cant, whereby the crime of treason might be covered by a counterfeit varnish of patriotism."

Let's examine some of the biggest myths.

Myth: Secession and slavery

Every rationalization used to justify slavery ignores the importance of liberty for human beings. The inherent evil of using people as property is understated or avoided.

Harriet Jacobs, who escaped from slavery and wrote a memoir, "Incidents in the Life of a Slave Girl," wrote that "slave owners seem to satisfy their consciences by saying that God created Blacks to be their slaves" and that inhumane slave owners were few. Even if slaves were treated well, they had no freedom to leave. While there was plenty of racism in the North, there were meaningful differences in opportunity for African Americans.

Anyone interested in Civil War history is forced to account for the inaccuracies of the Lost Cause myth. Chapter One of this book ends with the fact that Southerners themselves declared they seceded over the issue of slavery. The Articles of Secession of the Confederate States make it abundantly clear. Confederate Vice President Alexander Stephens in his Cornerstone speech of 1861 said that the "status of the Negro ... was the immediate cause" of secession.

As for the contention that the war was fought over states' rights, the Articles of Secession put that into the context of slavery — Northern states were not complying with the Fugitive Slave Act. The Constitution (Article IV, Section 2, Clause 3) does state that "a person (note the reference was not to property) held to service or labor who flees to another state is to be returned to his or her master in the state from which he escaped."

A law to that effect was enacted in 1793, and a far more extreme law was passed in 1850. Outrage in the North after 1850 was so severe that many Northern cities and states passed laws that basically nullified the federal law. Personal liberty laws were passed by the states of Michigan, Maine, New Hampshire, Vermont, Massachusetts, Connecticut, Rhode Island, New York, Pennsylvania, Illinois, Indiana, Wisconsin and Iowa.

As historian and author Eric Foner wrote, the longest paragraph in South Carolina's Articles of Secession involved Northern obstruction to returning fugitive enslaved people.

The Supreme Court's Dred Scott decision of 1857 was the last straw in the slavery debate because the court stated that African Americans could not be citizens and thus had no rights. At that point, further compromise was impossible. As Abraham Lincoln said, the nation must either be entirely slave or entirely free. The Dred Scott decision meant slavery for the entire nation. Compromise was impossible. There was too much wealth involved in slavery.

Myth: Number of enslavers

This is true but misleading. There were few enslavers but there is strong evidence Southerners did not support secession. But they had no power. If you owned more enslaved people, you gained more political power.

As author Shelby Foote said to author Tony Horwitz: "I'd be with my people, right or wrong. If I was against slavery, I'd still be with the South." Foote's great-grandfather opposed secession but fought for the South. As William Tecumseh Sherman wrote, "The South's planter class ... the ruling class" had tricked the working class into fighting a futile conflict. Even non-slave-owners had a reason to protect their place in the caste system, which put every White person above every Black person.

Historian David Williams wrote in his book "A People's History of the Civil War" that the South was facing a war on three fronts: the North, White dissenters and Black resisters.

In many cases, the wealthy planter class didn't allow the people to vote on secession. As Howell Raines wrote in his book "Silent Cavalry," the Alabama governor called a secession convention on his own. "The elected Legislature might have too many small farmers and philosophical opponents of slavery to provide enough votes for secession, whereas the big landowners could more easily dominate a small, one-issue convention." Many of the Southern justifications of the Lost Cause, in Raines' words, were "painfully prolonged rationalizations of the indefensible." The Lost Cause campaign was marked by "omissions, distortions and subterfuges," Raines wrote.

A study by David Potter concluded: "At no time during the winter of 1860-61 was secession desired by a majority of the people of the slave states."

Two-thirds of Texas voters opposed secession. Gov. Sam Houston refused to call a secession convention due to the vote, so the secessionists organized one. Also, a secession convention was narrowly defeated by the voters in North Carolina. So, the wealthy planter class ignored the vote and went ahead with secession anyway. In Georgia, while 33 percent of voters owned enslaved people, 87 percent of the secession convention's delegates were slaveholders.

In fact, the "West Point History of the Civil War" notes this startling fact: There were just 46,274 plantation owners who held 20 or more slaves out of a total Southern population of 31.5 million. Yet, this 1.5 percent of the population ruled the South and dominated the nation until the Civil War. If the South had won, it would have produced an awful result. A slave empire probably would have expanded to the Caribbean as well as Central and South America. There would have been continued violence in the United States over border issues. Millions of Americans would have lost their freedom.

Yet the Civil War did end slavery in the United States for all time. Through the pro-freedom Constitutional Amendments spawned by the war — the 13th, 14th and 15th — America enacted the new birth of freedom that Lincoln foretold. The Southern backlash produced Jim Crow laws that overruled the three Civil Rights amendments. A Second Reconstruction was needed with the Supreme Court's 1954 decision that banned segregated schools along with civil rights laws in the 1960s that guaranteed the vote and banned discrimination in housing, employment and public accommodations.

Myth: Wishful thinking

Northern states gradually dropped slavery after the founding of the nation because it never fit well with an industrial economy. So the theory goes that eventually the South would have turned away from slavery as well. Maybe, but not White superiority. Even when slavery did die, a caste system placed African Americans at the bottom of the economic and social ladder.

Look at Jim Crow. It lasted nearly 100 years, from the death of Reconstruction in the 1870s to the Civil Rights bills of the 1960s. It took federal action to force a second Reconstruction on the South. How long would it have taken for the South to grant civil rights to African Americans without being forced by the federal government? Centuries?

The racist theory of White superiority and Black inferiority has infected the nation as a whole but especially the South. For instance, lynchers were seldom prosecuted for their murders. After all, a federal law banning lynching was unable to be passed until 2022. Southern senators blocked anti-lynching bills by using the filibuster, which required 60 votes. The tyranny of the minority has been a regular feature of the slaveocracy.

Myth: Slavery as superiority

Pollard, the Lost Cause popularizer, wrote in his 1866 book, "Southern History of the War." that American slavery was "one of the mildest and most beneficent systems of servitude in the world." Harriet Beecher Stowe sought to combat that myth with her popular novel, "Uncle Tom's Cabin." That book produced a terrific backlash in the South, claiming her portrayal of the evils of slavery were lies or gross exaggerations. So Stowe felt compelled to defend herself with a second book, "Notes on Uncle Tom's Cabin." She explained that she underplayed the violence of slavery in "Uncle Tom's Cabin" for fear of turning off readers.

While living in Cincinnati, Stowe had come in contact with escaped enslaved people. In "Notes," Stowe went to great lengths to compare the American system of slavery to historical systems in Roman and Latin culture and among the ancient Jewish people. In nearly every case, the American system was more cruel because it was based on perpetual slavery and the racially based subhuman status of the African race. American slavery, a product of the British system, could not justify slavery and the proposition that "all men are equal" unless the Africans were considered inherently inferior. In ancient societies, enslaved people often were the product of war. It often was a temporary state.

In an essay, Thomas Jefferson wrote that when he wrote in the Declaration of Independence that "all men are created equal," he meant every person of every race. That is why Alexander Stephens, the vice president of the Confederacy, in his Cornerstone speech of 1861 wrote that the Founders were wrong. Stephens was defending the Confederate Constitution that enshrined slavery. Stephens wrote that slavery and subordination to the White man "is his natural and normal condition." In contrast, Lincoln did not say that the White and Black races were equal in every respect except that all human beings deserve the opportunity to receive wages for their work. That was too radical for Southerners who wanted to treat people as property.

Southerners like to contend that a slave's life was better than a poor immigrant's life working in a Northern sweatshop. That ignored one great moral fact: Freedom. A Northerner in a sweatshop could leave a job, go to a new city, earn an education and give his children a better life. Enslaved people had no liberty to do any of those things: They could not leave, they could not get a better job without permission, they could not testify in court, they were banned from getting an education and their children could be sent away from their parents.

Here again, evidence does not back the claims of slavery's apologists. Charles Dickens, during a stay in New York City in 1841, was stunned to read advertisements in newspapers for escaped enslaved people. Identifying marks were consistent with torture, such as a brand on the cheek, a missing portion of a finger or a large scar on the breast.

Tom Costa, a history professor at the University of Virginia-Wise, has spent decades researching advertisements for runaway slaves. Many of the ads refer to identifying marks on the escaped enslaved people from whippings and beatings. The Lost Cause myth suggests that slaves were kindly treated: "Slave defenders were claiming that no master would willingly inflict harm on a piece of his property. But if you look at those runaway advertisements and the scars, and the stories of whippings and shackling, that's kind of surprising," Costa said. His students are surprised at the way many slaves were treated.

As Abraham Lincoln facetiously said about the peculiar institution, slavery is the only "good" thing that people don't seek for themselves. As he said, "People of any color seldom run unless there is something to run from." In fact, in Northeast Virginia, almost half the male enslaved men of working age fled in the first two years of the Civil War, reported Andrew Delbanco in his book, "The War Before the War."

In 1855, a female enslaved woman killed her master for raping her, reported Delbanco. She had no rights when it came to claims of rape and self-defense because she was treated as property but she was treated as a person when it came to her conviction and hanging for murder.

Myth: The North's numbers

Author Shelby Foote said in the Ken Burns Civil War documentary that the Union's manpower advantage was so strong that it fought the war with one hand behind its back. At any time, Foote said, it could have brought out the other other hand. Evidence does not support that. The North had wide opposition to the war. David Williams, author of "A People's History of the Civil War," makes several important points that explode this myth. About 90,000 Northern men fled to Canada. Draft riots occurred throughout Northern cities, not just in New York City. And most soldiers declined to re-enlist. That is why President Lincoln said that the North could not have won the war without African American soldiers. By the end of the war, they were providing essential manpower.

Though the North had a 4-to-1 advantage in White men of fighting age, opposition in the North meant that advantage was never available. Both North and South had about 1 million native-born White soldiers. The North, though, had 500,000 immigrants as well as 500,000 Southerners, both Black and White. In fact, as Richard Nelson Current wrote in his book, "Lincoln's Loyalists," there were more Union soldiers from Virginia than from Minnesota. Every soldier from the South who fought for the Union represented a double loss for the rebel army.

Surely Southern leaders knew about the North's overwhelming advantages in manpower and resources when they seceded. As James McPherson asked in his book, "The Mighty Scourge," by seceding were they guilty of "criminal folly" or "colossal arrogance?" Or were they just tragically wrong about the North's will to fight? Surely they learned about the North's will after a year or two of battle.

The South's refusal to enlist enslaved people in the Confederate Army until it was too late illustrated the point that slavery was more important to the South than its independence. As Edward Bonekemper III wrote in "The Ten Biggest Civil War Blunders," slavery and White supremacy were "the primary foundations of that would-be nation."

Despite the manpower disadvantage, the South was two months away from winning its independence. By late August of 1864, about two months before the presidential election, Northerners were tired of the bloodshed. The sieges of Atlanta and Petersburg seemed endless and the casualties were mounting. President Lincoln's advisors told him he was doomed to be defeated for a second term. Lincoln, as a result, wrote a blind memo for his Cabinet in which he stated if he lost reelection he expected his Cabinet to join him in winning the war before the inauguration in March of 1865.

Confederate President Jefferson Davis disagreed with the defensive approach of Gen. Joseph Johnston at Atlanta and replaced him with the more aggressive Gen. John Bell Hood. Thus Union Gen. William T. Sherman was able to defeat the Confederates and deliver Atlanta to the Union just days after Lincoln wrote the memo. That major victory, combined with turning back Jubal Early's Northern invasion in the Shenandoah Valley, improved Northern attitudes toward the war. Lincoln won reelection in 1864.

Myth: Lee vs. Grant

Once President Lincoln won reelection, with Sherman bullying his way through the South, Lee knew that he was doomed to lose a siege at Petersburg. Yet he continued to fight. And Grant was the butcher?

Consider: Which general won two sieges, broke a third siege, won a battle up the side of a mountain, gained the surrender of three armies and then freed two of the enemy armies rather than send them to prison camps? And which one fought a brilliant campaign in the enemy's territory that is studied today in the U.S. War College? Answer: U.S. Grant.

Grant won the sieges of Fort Donelson, Vicksburg and Appomattox. He gave paroles to Confederates at the last two. His forces waged a successful attack up the side of a mountain at Missionary Ridge and Lookout Mountain at Chattanooga. In the Vicksburg Campaign, Grant won five battles against two different Confederate armies in Mississippi and won a siege despite leaving his supply lines. He broke the siege at Chattanooga.

Author Edward Bonekemper III in his book "How Robert E. Lee Lost the Civil War" documents how Lee lost more troops in battle than any Civil War general, North or South: 121,000 men killed or wounded, 27,000 more than any general. Even in one of Lee's greatest victories at Chancellorsville, he couldn't afford to lose about 11,000 soldiers to death and injury.

In short, the South could have won its independence by doing what the American colonies did to the British — hold out till the opponent gave up. Confederate Gen. James Longstreet promoted defensive tactics combined with a strategic offensive — the Fredericksburg approach — which Lee resisted at Gettysburg. If Lee had found favorable high ground in Pennsylvania and invited a Union attack, he would have had a massive advantage.

Consider: Which general lost the most important battle of the war by sending his troops to be slaughtered up a slope when he knew from previous experience it was fatal? Answer: Robert E. Lee at Gettysburg. Lee's troops lost at Malvern Hill during the Seven Days Campaign against a retreating federal force.

And Lee won at Fredericksburg when defenders easily repulsed repeated courageous attacks by federal forces. So why did Lee suddenly think his soldiers were invincible at Gettysburg? It was a fatal mistake.

Lee lost two major battles in enemy territory (Antietam and Gettysburg) in contrast to Grant's multiple victories in the South. In any case, the South could not afford to lose so many casualties even when they won battles.

In addition, Lee gave his subordinates too much leeway, which they used to their detriment at Gettysburg, along with complicated plans that could not be coordinated when faced with long exterior lines of attack.

Conclusions

The Lost Cause myth turned the cruelty of slavery into a romantic tale of chivalry and nostalgia. The myth was a diabolical defense mechanism for a defeated society, one entirely in keeping with the relentless lengths taken in the South after Reconstruction to enforce a system as close as possible to slavery through sharecropping, vote suppression, lynching, vagrancy laws, chain gangs and legalized segregation.

The story of slavery in the United States is filled with complications and contradictions. But at its most basic level, the issue is simple: Human beings lost their liberty for purely financial reasons. Racism, the theory that African Americans are inherently inferior to White people, was the excuse that was used to justify slavery. This form of slavery was perpetual. It treated Black people as either people or property, depending on the whims of the enslavers. It left African Americans — either slave or free — with "no rights which the White man was bound to respect," in the words of 1857's Supreme Court's Dred Scott decision. It took the 14th Amendment to the Constitution to overturn

Dred Scott and affirm that all people born in the United States are citizens.

The Lost Cause, as David Blight wrote in "Race and Reunion," created false history marked by "defections, evasions, careful remembering and necessary forgetting." Its impact has been felt ever since Reconstruction ended.

Blight quoted the Baltimore Afro-American Ledger in 1913 on the 50th anniversary of the Battle of Gettysburg: "Today the South is in the saddle, and with the single exception of slavery, everything it fought for during the days of the Civil War, it has gained by repression of the Negro within its borders. And the North has quietly allowed it to have its own way." At that time, President Woodrow Wilson was segregating the federal workforce while lynching and voter suppression continued without federal law enforcement. Then came redlining, in which neighborhoods North and South were segregated racially by a combination of federal action, banking policies, real estate practices and deed restrictions.

The victims of the Lost Cause mythology were the 4 million enslaved human beings and their progeny, the true reason for the Civil War. While White people, North and South, sought to put aside bitter feelings spawned from the Civil War, Blacks were left behind. The followers of the Lost Cause discriminated against African Americans in schools, in law enforcement, in the courts and in popular culture. Even today, many Americans are not inclined to believe that Black people are treated differently by the police until videos provide proof.

However, in recent years, change has happened. Historian Justin Rogers notes these startling statistics: Just five Confederate monuments were taken down between 1865 and 2014, but 166 were taken down between 2015 and 2021. Monument Avenue in Richmond, Va., which once was marked with multiple statues of Confederates, including a large image of Robert E. Lee, now has no Confederate monuments.

In my city of Jacksonville, the name of Nathan Bedford Forrest High School was changed to Westside High School after years of controversy while a memorial to the Confederacy was removed from a historic city park. The park was renamed for Jacksonville's most famous and talented native son, an African American, James Weldon Johnson. Nationally, African American museums have become tourist attractions. The National Museum of African History and Culture in Washington, D.C. is regularly sold out.

In short, it took a relentless, twisted propaganda campaign to turn the real history of the Civil War upside-down. Thankfully, with the removal of Confederate statues across the nation, it seems the Lost Cause is being widely recognized as false history.

Second Lost Cause?

Today, a new tyranny of the minority uses social media to spread misinformation, in part because people want to believe fiction like stolen national elections, just like many prefer to believe that the Civil War was not fought over slavery. What makes misinformation so effective is that it tells stories that many people want to believe. Also, many of the lies circulating through social media are more interesting than the subtle grays of the truth. In short, the correction never receives as much publicity as the rumor.

Now we are living through a new Lost Cause campaign in which anything racial that makes some White people feel uncomfortable is being suppressed, books with racial themes are being banned and social media is creating a platform for lies to spread like wildfire. Today, there are echoes of the Lost Cause mythology through diabolical efforts to reduce the vote in minority neighborhoods by restrictive registration requirements, reducing the number of polling stations and fear of voting irregularities out of proportion to reality. The aim is to produce another era of minority rule, just as the Founders did through voting restrictions. At the time of the founding of the United States, only White male property owners could vote. Typically, 15 percent to 20 percent of adults were able to vote. Non-property owners, women and enslaved people were banned from voting. It wasn't until the 1960s that all adult Americans were able to vote in a more perfect Union.

Eric Wittenberg is author of many books on the Civil War, especially on the Battle of Gettysburg: "It worries me that the neo-Confederate movement that we see going on these days is continuing to gain momentum. How often have you heard people from Texas threatening to secede? Now you hear that parts of Oregon want to secede and that Northern California wants to secede. I find it very alarming."

I spoke to tens of thousands of newspaper readers as an ombudsman for 15 years. It was incredible to hear lawyers and engineers who believed that Barack Obama was not born in the U.S., despite two birth certificates and birth announcements in two different Honolulu newspapers. By the same token, many in the South wanted to believe the Civil War was not fought over denying freedom to 4 million African Americans.

DeAnne Blanton, co-author of a book on women who fought as men in the Civil War, noticed that similar stories were ignored or suppressed after the war. "It's not surprising that there's always a backlash when traditional history meets new history, women's history and African American history," she said.

Who was Jim Crow?

Jim Crow was a character in minstrel shows, usually a White man in blackface, in which African Americans were portrayed as ridiculous entertainers, which underscored the myth that they were childlike creatures who needed the protection and ultimate rule by White people. The origin is credited to a struggling White actor, Thomas Rice, but eventually became a stock character along with Sambo and others. According to the Jim Crow Museum at Ferris State University in Big Rapids, Mich. (jimcrowmuseum.ferris.edu), "White audiences were receptive to the portrayals of Black people as singing, dancing, grinning fools." This type of character was popular in both North and South. In fact, to illustrate support for African Americans fighting for the Union, a popular song during the Civil War was titled "Sambo's Right to be Kilt."

Chapter Nineteen

Final thoughts

Edgar W. Clark's letters illustrate how he, his family and others survived the terrible hardships of the Civil War.

He experienced just about everything the Civil War had to offer — loneliness, hunger, cold, illness and injury — just not death. He was willing to risk his life for the love of his country.

Of the five Civil War battles with the most casualties, Edgar fought in four of them: Gettysburg, Spotsylvania, the Wilderness and Chancellorsville. He was not at Chickamauga. (Source: Statista).

For much of the Civil War, the common Union soldier persisted in the face of the incompetence of the generals. President Lincoln wrote this: "Oh, it is terrible, terrible, this weakness, this indifference of our Potomac generals, with such armies of good and brave men."

"What saved the nation," said U.S. Grant after the war, "was the coming forward of the young men of the nation. They came from their homes and fields, as they did in the time of the Revolution, giving everything to the country. To their devotion, we owe the salvation of the Union."

That same concern for the citizen soldier occurred during World War II when Gen. George Marshall, chief of staff of the U.S. Army, asked director Frank Capra to make motivational films under the title "Why We Fight." In his autobiography, Capra quoted Marshall as saying: "The Germans and Japanese are counting very heavily on these kids running like hell when the first shot is fired. I don't think so. I don't think free people will run when fired at. But can they take homesickness? Can they take discipline? The dirty, lousy discipline of the desert, the jungles? Can they stand doing nothing for months upon months? That takes more discipline than the actual shooting."

Edgar passed that test. He experienced just about every emotion possible during nearly three years of service, including 40 days of combat in the Civil War.

He experienced the loneliness of leaving his young wife and two daughters, ages 1 and 3. He experienced his mother-in-law's accusation that he had abandoned them. He experienced a renewed appreciation for his wife, which inspired him to veer from his matter-of-fact writing style to flights of romantic poetry.

He experienced the pride of protecting the country he loved from a rebellion that tried to tear it apart. He expressed this patriotism in personal terms, stating his dislike of men who would not volunteer to fight for their country. He experienced the hatred of Copperheads in the North who were trying to undercut the effort to keep the country united.

He experienced support for the concept of total war — whatever it would take to put down the rebellion, even if it meant burning Confederate businesses and taking food items and rails from Virginians.

He experienced the long-term weakness caused by diarrhea and, while in a Union hospital, watched strong young men like him perish. He experienced hunger on a limited soldier's diet and longed for boxes of food from his wife.

He experienced the terror of being surrounded by bullets and being pummeled by exploding artillery shells.

He experienced optimism about the leadership of Gen. U.S. Grant while fighting continuously during the summer of 1864.

He experienced pride in the variety of men who were fighting with him, including the Black soldiers who joined the 3rd Michigan Infantry. He supported the Emancipation Proclamation and freedom for African Americans.

He experienced the disgust at poor generalship that led to Union soldiers firing on each other at night at Chancellorsville and a delayed assault that resulted in his wound at Petersburg. He experienced the trauma of losing a leg and the pain of gangrene treatments that burned the skin.

He experienced a positive outlook that he could be useful after the war with the use of a cork leg. And he experienced relief when his wife repeated her love for him.

Finally, he experienced the continued joys of fatherhood, siring two sons after the war.

Thousands of soldiers wrote letters during the war or memoirs after the war. Few of them could claim to have been involved in the middle of so many important battles. Clearly, Edgar W. Clark's letters are special to me as one of his descendants. But I think they also can be useful to Americans today who are curious about what it was like to be a soldier in America's most important historical event.

Edgar would have wanted complete honesty from me, which meant that I described why the Civil War was about slavery and not the fiction of some Lost Cause. It's why I described why slavery was a pox on the entire nation, including the North. The North was not innocent. It looked the other way while slave-trading ships used the port of New York City and slave traders were treated gently by the criminal justice system. The border states of Ohio, Indiana and Illinois passed Black Codes that made it clear that formerly enslaved people were not welcome there.

The sheer evil of the American brand of slavery was described brilliantly by Harriet Beecher Stowe in her "Notes on Uncle Tom's Cabin." Abraham Lincoln was prophetic when he stated that the nation could not remain half-slave and half-free. War or appeasement to slavery became inevitable. Finally, in 1857, the Supreme Court made compromise impossible with its Dred Scott decision that stated Black people had no rights. That, officially, was the last straw. It meant that Lincoln was right in stating the nation must be entirely free or entirely slave-based. A series of desperate compromises finally came to an end with the war in 1861.

Few Americans at the time realized just how awful the war would be, but it did result in the death of slavery and a new birth of freedom. The slavery issue was settled in blood, from hundreds of thousands of Americans who fought for the cause of the Union and for freedom.

About 2 million Union supporters like Edgar W. Clark fought to unite the nation so that 4 million of their countrymen could be free. It's one of the greatest stories ever told and it's why the Civil War remains so compelling.

The focus by historians on generals has distracted future generations from the tremendous sacrifices made by individual soldiers, wives and families. This was especially true in the North where soldiers persisted through poor generalship in the East.

Austin Blair, Civil War governor of Michigan, spoke of men like Edgar when monuments to Michigan soldiers were dedicated at the Gettysburg National Cemetery in 1889: "Our men engaged here were not mere soldiers, they were fellow citizens engaged in a mighty struggle, and with a definite purpose of view. They were volunteers who had enlisted in this great war with an intelligent sense of patriotic duty."

Edgar W. Clark's letters personify the statement of novelist and Civil War veteran John W. DeForest: "The man who does not dread to die or be mutilated is a lunatic. The man who, dreading these things, still faces them for the sake of duty and honor is a hero."

The letters of Edgar W. Clark to his wife Catherine confirm that statement.

Chapter Twenty

Bibliography

- Edgar W. Clark's Civil War Letters (1862-1865).

- National Archives: Documents addressing the service history of Edgar W. Clark. He joined the 3rd Michigan Infantry Regiment in the Army of the Potomac in August 1862 and was discharged from the 5th Michigan Infantry Regiment in February 1865.

- Alexander, E. Porter: "Fighting for the Confederacy: The Personal Recollections of General Edward Porter Alexander."

- Allman, T.D.: "Finding Florida: The True History of the Sunshine State."

- Asbury, Herbert: "The Gangs of New York."

- Ayers, Edward L.: "The Civil War and Emancipation in the Heart of America."

- Bailey, Fred Arthur: "Free Speech at the University of Florida: The Enoch Marvin Banks Case," Florida

Historical Quarterly, July 1992.

- Michael Barton and Larry M. Logue: "The Civil War Soldier: A Historical Reader."

- Bernstein, Iver: "The New York City Draft Riots: Their Significance for American Society and Politics in the Age of the Civil War."

- Ira Berlin and Leslie S. Rowland: "Families & Freedom: A Documentary History of African American Kinship in the Civil War Era."

- Billings, John: "Hardtack and Coffee: The Unwritten Story of Army Life."

- Blaisdell, Robert: "The Civil War: A Book of Quotations."

- Blanton, DeAnne and Lauren Cook: "They Fought Like Demons: Women Soldiers in the American Civil War"; and Zoom interview with Blanton.

- Blight, David W., Sterling Professor of History, of African American Studies and of American Studies, and Director of the Gilder Lehrman Center for the Study of Slavery, Resistance and Abolition at Yale University; Open Yale Courses, 27-episode podcast, HIST 119: The Civil War and Reconstruction Era."

- Blight, David W., editor: "Passages of Freedom: The Underground Railroad in History and Memory;" and author of "Race and Reunion: The Civil War in American Memory."

- Bonekemper, Edward H. III: "The Myth of the Lost Cause: Why the South Fought the Civil War; "The Ten Biggest Civil War Blunders"; "Why the North Won"; and "How Robert E. Lee Lost the Civil War."

- Boritt, Gabor S.: "Why the Confederacy Lost" and "Lincoln's Generals."

- Brands, H.W.: "The Man Who Saved the Union: Ulysses Grant in War and Peace."

- Brown, Ira C.: "Civil War has commenced," Bentley Historical Library, University of Michigan.

- Brown, Kent Masterson: "Retreat from Gettysburg."

- Burlingame, Michael: "Abraham Lincoln: A Life;" "The Inner World of Abraham Lincoln"; "An American Marriage: The Untold Story of Abraham Lincoln and Mary Todd"; and Zoom interview.

- Cairnes, John E.: "The Slave Power: Its Character, Career and Probable Designs."

- Capra, Frank: "The Name Above the Title."

- Catton, Bruce: "Glory Road."

- Chernow, Ron: "Grant."

- Churchill, Winston: "A History of the English Speaking Peoples."

- Clay, Henry: Essay on slavery, included in "The Approaching Fury: Voices of the Storm, 1820-1861" by

Stephen B. Oates.

- Clinton, Catherine: "Noble Women as Well" in the collection "Ken Burns' The Civil War: Historians Respond."

- Coggins, Jack: "Arms and Equipment of the Civil War."

- Cohassey, John: "The 22nd Michigan Infantry and the Road to Chickamauga."

- Collins, Chuck: "Born on Third Base: A One Percenter Makes the Case for Tackling Inequality, Bringing Wealth Home" and "Committing to the Common Good."

- Cornish, Dudley Taylor: "The Sable Arm: Black Troops in the Union Army, 1861-1865."

- Costa, Tom: History Professor at the University of Virginia-Wise; Zoom interview.

- Current, Richard Nelson: "Lincoln's Loyalists: Union Soldiers from the Confederacy."

- William Darity Jr. and A. Kirsten Mullen: "From Here to Equality: Reparations for Black Americans in the Twenty-First Century."

- William Darity, Thomas Craemers, Daina Ramey Berry, and Dania V Francis: "Black Reparations in the United States, 2024: An Introduction" in the Russell Sage Journal of the Social Sciences.

- Daniel T. Davis, Chris Mackowski, Kristopher D. White: "Don't Give an Inch: The Second Day at Gettysburg, July 2, 1863, From Little Round Top to Cemetery Ridge."

- Davis, Burke: "The Civil War: Strange & Fascinating Facts."

- Davis, William C.: "The Lost Cause: Myths and Realities of the Confederacy."

- Delbanco, Andrew: "The War Before the War: Fugitive Slaves and the Struggle for America's Soul from the Revolution to the Civil War."

- Dempsey, Jack: "Michigan and the Civil War: A Great and Bloody Sacrifice."

- DeTrobriand, Regis: "Four Years with the Army of the Potomac."

- Dew, Charles W.: "Apostles of Disunion: Southern Secession Commissioners and the Causes of the Civil War."

- Dickey, Christopher: "Our Man in Charleston: Britain's Secret Agent in the Civil War South."

- Donald, David Herbert: "Lincoln" and "Why the North Won the Civil War."

- Donaldson, Francis Adams: "Narrative of Gettysburg, July 2-3, 1863."

- Douglass, Frederick: "Our Work is Not Done," speech

Dec. 4, 1863, Philadelphia.

- Emerson, Jason: "Mary Lincoln for the Ages."

- Faust, Drew Gilpin: "This Republic of Suffering."

- Foner, Eric: "The Fiery Trial: Abraham Lincoln and American Slavery;" "Forever Free: The Story of Emancipation and Reconstruction;" and "Gateway to Freedom: The Hidden Story of the Underground Railroad."

- Flood, Charles Bracelen: "1864: Lincoln at the Gates of History."

- Futch, Ovid: "History of Andersonville Prison."

- Gallagher, Gary: "The Union War," Introduction to "The Annals of the Civil War."

- Gary W. Gallagher and Alan T. Nolan: "The Myth of the Lost Cause and Civil War History."

- Garrison, Webb: "Brady's Civil War: A collection of memorable Civil War images photographed by Mathew Brady and his assistants;" also "2,000 Questions and Answers About the Civil War: Unusual and Unique Facts About the War Between the States"; and "Civil War Stories: Strange Tales, Oddities, Events and Coincidences."

- Gates, Henry Louis Jr.: "Stony the Road: Reconstruction, White Supremacy and the Rise of Jim Crow."

- Gillispie, James B.: "Andersonvilles of the North: The

Myths and Realities of Northern Treatment of Civil War Confederate Prisoners."

- Grant, U.S.: "The Memoirs of General Ulysses S. Grant."

- Griffith, Paddy: "Battle Tactics of the Civil War."

- Guelzo, Allen: "Gettysburg: The Last Invasion" and "Robert E. Lee: A Life."

- Hacker, J. David: "A Census-Based Count of the Civil War Dead," Civil War History magazine.

- Harman, Troy D.: "Lee's Real Plan at Gettysburg" and "Did Meade Begin a Counteroffensive after Pickett's Charge?"

- Harris, John: "The Last Slave Ships: New York and the End of the Middle Passage."

- Hasegawa, Guy: "Mending Broken Soldiers: The Union and Confederate Programs to Supply Artificial Limbs."

- Hess, Earl J.: "The Union Soldier in Battle: Enduring the Ordeal of Combat."

- Hessler, James A.: "Sickles at Gettysburg: The Controversial Civil War General Who Committed Murder, Abandoned Little Round Top and Declared Himself the Hero of Gettysburg;" and Zoom interview.

- James A. Hessler and Britt C. Isenberg: "Gettysburg's

Peach Orchard: Longstreet, Sickles and the Bloody Fight for the Commanding Ground Along the Emmitsburg Road."

- Howard, Bill, "The Riots of New York," Times-Union (Albany, N.Y.), July 13, 2013.

- Howe, Thomas J.: "The Petersburg Campaign: Wasted Valor June 15-18, 1864."

- Hunt, Jeffrey: "Meade and Lee after Gettysburg: The Forgotten Final Stage of the Gettysburg Campaign, From Falling Waters to Culpeper Courthouse July 14-31."

- Hunt, Jeffrey William: "Meade and Lee After Gettysburg: The Forgotten Final Stage of the Gettysburg Campaign From Falling Waters to Culpepper Courthouse July 14-31, 1863."

- Hyde, Bill: "The Union Generals Speak: The Meade Hearings on the Battle of Gettysburg."

- Jacobs, Harriet: "Incidents in the Life of a Slave Girl."

- Jackson, Ronald II: Assistant Professor of History, Jacksonville University, in-person interview.

- Ruby West Jackson and Walter T. McDonald: "Finding Freedom: The Untold Story of Joshua Glover, Runaway Slave."

- Jefferson, Thomas: Essay on slavery, 1820, included in "The Approaching Fury: Voices of the Storm, 1820-1861" by Stephen B. Oates.

- Joint Select Committee on the Conduct of the War: "Fort Pillow Massacre."

- Jorgensen, Jay: "Gettysburg's Bloody Wheatfield."

- Kadzis, Peter: "Blood: Stories of Life and Death from the Civil War."

- Keckley, Elizabeth: "Behind the Scenes in The Lincoln White House."

- Lardas, Mark: "Roughshod Through Dixie: Grierson's Raid 1863."

- Lee, Robert E.: "The Wartime Papers of Robert E. Lee."

- Leonard, Elizabeth D.: "Don the Breeches and Slay Them with a Will!: A Host of Women Soldiers," as part of the book "The Civil War Soldier: A Historical Reader."

- Levine, Bruce: "The Fall of the House of Dixie: The Civil War and the Social Revolution that Transformed the South."

- McCullough, David: "The Pioneers: The Heroic Story of the Settlers Who Brought the American Ideal West" and "The American Spirit: Who We Are and What We Stand For."

- McDougle, Ivan Eugene: "Slavery in Kentucky, 1792-1865."

- McGaugh, Scott: "Surgeon in Blue."

- McMillan, Tracie: "The White Bonus: Five Families and the Cash Value of Racism in America."

- McPherson, James M.: "Battle Cry of Freedom;" "The War that Forged a Nation: Why the Civil War Still Matters;" "Tried by War: Abraham Lincoln as Commander in Chief"; "The Negro in the Civil War: How American Blacks Felt and Acted During the War for the Union;" "For Cause and Comrades: Why Men Fought in the Civil War": "The Mighty Scourge: Perspectives on the Civil War"; and "Abraham Lincoln and the Second American Revolution."

- James M. McPherson and William J. Cooper, Jr.: "Writing the Civil War: The Quest to Understand."

- Meacham, Jon: "And There Was Light: Abraham Lincoln and the American Struggle."

- Miller, Donald L.: "Vicksburg: Grant's Campaign that Broke the Confederacy."

- Motts, Wayne: President emeritus of the National Civil War Museum, "Wolverines at Gettysburg," Winter Lecture at Gettysburg National Military Park.

- Nevins, Allan: "The War for the Union."

- Michael F. Nugent, J. David Petruzzi and Eric Wittenberg: "One Continuous Fight: The Retreat from Gettysburg and the Pursuit of Lee's Army of Northern Virginia, July 4-14, 1863" and Zoom interview with Wittenberg.

- National Park Service: Pamphlets, web sites and plaques from Fredericksburg, Chancellorsville, Gettysburg, Petersburg and Andersonville.

- Oakes, James: "Crooked Path to Abolition: Abraham Lincoln and the Antislavery Constitution."

- Oates, Stephen B.: "The Approaching Fury: Voices of the Storm, 1820-1861."

- Pfanz, Harry: "Gettysburg: The Second Day."

- Pinchon, Edgcumb: "Dan Sickles: Hero of Gettysburg and 'Yankee King of Spain.'"

- Potter, David M.: "The Impending Crisis: 1848-1861."

- Price, William H.: "Civil War Handbook."

- Raines, Howell: "Silent Cavalry: How Union Soldiers from Alabama Helped Sherman Burn Atlanta and Then Got Written Out of History."

- Ransom, John: "John Ransom's Civil War Diary."

- Richardson, Heather Cox: "How the South Won the Civil War: Oligarchy, Democracy and "The Continuing Fight for the Soul of America."

- Roberts, Cokie: "Capital Dames."

- Robinson, Randall: "The Debt."

- Rogers, Justin: Assistant Professor of History and

Africana Studies, University of North Florida, in-person interview.

- Emil and Ruth Rosenblatt: "Hard Marching Every Day: The Civil War Letters of Private Wilbur Fisk, 1861-1865."

- Ross, Marissa: "A Soldier's Secret: The Incredible True Story of Sarah Edmonds, a Civil War Hero."

- Richard Rothstein and Leah Rothstein: "Just Action: How to Challenge Segregation Enacted Under the Color of Law;" and Richard Rothstein interview with the author.

- Rubinstein, David M.: "The American Experiment: Dialogues on a Dream."

- Rusling, Gen. James: "Things and Men I Saw in Civil War Days."

- Rutkow, Ira, "Bleeding Blue and Gray: Civil War Surgery and the Evolution of American Medicine."

- Thomas J. Ryan and Richard R. Schaus: "Lee is Trapped and Must be Taken: Eleven Fateful Days After Gettysburg, July 4-14, 1863."

- Sandburg, Carl: "Abraham Lincoln: The War Years" and "Storm Over the Land: A Profile of the Civil War.'

- Sauers, Richard: "A Caspian Sea of Ink: The Meade-Sickles Controversy."

- Sears, Stephen: "Chancellorsville."

- Seidule, Ty: "Robert E. Lee and Me: A Southerner's Reckoning of the Myth of the Lost Cause" and the "Was the Civil War About Slavery?" podcast on Prager U.

- Brooks D. Simpson, Stephen W. Sears and Aaron Sheehan-Dean: "The Civil War: The First Year Told By Those Who Lived it" and "The Civil War: The Third Year Told by Those Who Lived it."

- Shaara, Jeff: "Civil War Battlefields: Discovering America's Hallowed Ground."

- Shane, Scott: "Flee North: A Forgotten Hero and the Fight for Freedom in Slavery's Borderland."

- Sherman, William: "The Memoirs of General William Sherman."

- Smith, John David: "Black Soldiers in Blue: African American Troops in the Civil War Era."

- Smithsonian: "The Civil War Visual History."

- Soper, Steve: "The Glorious Old 3rd: Biographical Sketches of the men who served in the 3rd Michigan Infantry Veteran Volunteers 1861-1864."

- Spratt, L.W.: "The Philosophy of Secession," The Charleston Mercury, Feb. 13, 1861.

- Stampp, Kenneth M.: "Causes of the Civil War" and "The Imperiled Union: Essays on the Background of the Civil War."

- Stilwell, Leander: "The Story of a Common Soldier."

- Stine, J.H.: "History of the Army of the Potomac."

- Stowe, Harriet Beecher: "A Key to Uncle Tom's Cabin."

- Surby, Richard W.: "Grierson's Grand Raid in the Civil War."

- Stevens, George, Jr.: "The Great Moviemakers: Hollywood's Golden Age at the American Film Institute."

- Trudeau, Noah Andre: "Like Men of War: Black Troops in the Civil War 1862-1865." Also, "The Last Citadel: Petersburg, Virginia June 1864-April 1865."

- Tsiu, Bonnie: "She Went to the Field: Women Soldiers of the Civil War."

- Tucker, Glenn: "High Tide at Gettysburg: The Campaign in Pennsylvania."

- Mark Twain and David Rachels: "Mark Twain's Civil War."

- United States Military Academy: "The West Point History of the Civil War."

- VanAcker, Matthew, "Lansing and the Civil War;" and Zoom interview.

- Varhola, Michael: "Everyday Life During the Civil War."

- Varon, Elizabeth: "Armies of Deliverance: A New History of the Civil War."

- Waldman, Michael: "The Second Amendment: A Biography."

- Warren, Robert Penn: "The Legacy of the Civil War."

- Waugh, John: "Reelecting Lincoln: The Battle for the 1864 Presidency."

- Wert, Jeffry: "General James Longstreet: The Confederacy's Most Controversial Soldier."

- White, Jonathan W.: "Emancipation: The Union Army and the Reelection of Abraham Lincoln."

- Wilentz, Sean: "No Property in Man: Slavery and Antislavery in the Nation's Founding."

- Wiley, Bell Irwin: "The Life of Johnny Reb" (1943) and "The Life of Billy Yank" (1952). "Southern Negroes: 1861 to 1865.

- Wilkeson, Frank: "Recollections of a Private Soldier in the Army of the Potomac"

- Williams, David: " A People's History of The Civil War: Struggles for the Meaning of Freedom."

- Wolf, Eva Sheppard: "Race and Liberty in the New Nation: Emancipation in Virginia from the Revolution to Nat Turner's Rebellion;" and "Almost Free: A Story About Family and Race in Antebellum Virginia"; and Zoom interview.

Chapter Twenty-One

About the author

Michael P. Clark is the oldest son in an Irish-American family. He is the great-great-grandson of Edgar W. Clark, whose letters to his wife, Catherine, form the foundation of this book.

Like Edgar W. Clark, Michael was born and raised in Lansing, Mich. He has two brothers (Peter and Thomas) and two sisters (Candace and Elizabeth). His father, Stanley Clark Jr., built a successful insurance business. His mother, Suzanne Graham Clark, was a homemaker and a popular artist later in life.

Michael attended Catholic schools from first through 12th grade, then was graduated in 1971 from Michigan State University with a bachelor's degree in journalism. A few months later, he married his college sweetheart, Molly DuCharme.

He spent two years reporting for the Illinois State Journal in Springfield. He and Molly moved to Jacksonville in 1973.

For 15 years, he was the ombudsman for The Florida Times-Union, including a stint as president of the Organization of News Ombudsmen. For his last 15 years in journalism, he was Editorial Page Editor for the newspaper and also edited a quarterly magazine on downtown Jacksonville. He and his staff won city, state, regional and national journalism awards for opinion writing. He retired in December of 2020.

He and Molly have two children, Claire and Bridget, who live in Lexington, Ky. Claire and her husband, Simon Padmanabhan, have twins, Shannon and Jonathan Padmanabhan. Mike and Molly live in Nocatee, a suburb of Jacksonville.